D0107782

Dear Reader,

Old Man Winter is a psychological thriller that will keep you up at night and have you guessing what's going to happen next.

With the rugged North Philadelphia area as the backdrop, you get to walk in the footsteps of Philadelphia Police Detectives Frank Bruno and Penelope Bryce as they try to track down a man they believe is responsible for the disappearance of nine elderly people across eight cities and seven states.

This story incorporates both real-life and fictional situations and people whose stories must be told. While the ending to some real-life characters and situations has been fictionalized for dramatic effect, those portrayed in the book are important, and I am proud to shine a light on their relevance and story.

I hope you fall in love with these characters and are thrilled at all of the twists and turns that this fast-paced drama that will keep you turning the pages and questioning everything.

Happy Reading,

Praise for Old Man Winter - Heavenly Gates

Everything I look for in a great read

First book from this Author but not my last. The characters and the "truth" the writer brings to this story is amazing, the characters and locations and history are well intertwined. This is more than a book it's an experience.

Rhonda Conway

Another Brilliant Novel by Michael Cook

I read both of the Black Earth books and found them to be among the best books I've read. When Mr. Cook came out with his third novel I expected a similar story, but NO, he went in a completely new direction and once again hit it out of the park!

This novel is a crime/mystery story with many turns. The character development is outstanding and by the end you just want more. I believe the lead female character was based loosely on a real-life female detective in the Philadelphia PD.

I highly recommend this new book from Mr. Cook and look forward to what he brings us next. I promise you will love this story and find it hard to put down.

Bob Nielsen

Truly talented

After reading other books from this author, I can honestly say that this was not what I expected at all! A really good psychological thriller with an interesting twist at the end. Again, Michael Cook delivers a great book well worth the read. Highly recommended! I will be watching for more from Michael.

Collette O.

Great mystery Thriller

Michael Cook has written a great mystery thriller in Old Man Winter. It keeps you guessing throughout with plenty of twists, turns, and nuances that should keep any mystery fan happy.

Vern Preston

This is one of the best books I've ever read

You get hooked on the story very quickly. I am not going to tell anything about the story in the book because I want you to read it yourself. It is a long book, but you don't want to miss a page. Please give it a try. Michael Cook is an amazing writer, and you will really like this book of his.

Phyllis H. Pajka

Last hundred pages need to be set to music! Awesome stuff!!!

Mike writes with incredibly rich imagery and detail. If you close your eyes, the book turns into a movie. I read many books, but this is what makes Michael Cook's writings different. The storyline is unique, and the story unfolds "jussstttt in time" to keep you from going crazy. Not gonna say why but the ending literally made me gasp. I just didn't see it coming and I loved that...we all try to guess our way to the ending of books, but you won't do it on this one so don't try. My advice to the author...stick with Psychological Crime Drama books. I'll read every damn one of em and watch the series on Netflix! Nice job!!!

William Marr

Supernatural Thriller that keeps you guessing to the end!

It was interesting to see what it was like in the 70's for women in a male-dominated field. The prejudice that women faced then and having to prove themselves over and over still exists somewhat today, though it is better than it was. Younger people reading this book may be shocked at how bad it was. That was just one element of a delicious mystery that Michael Cook has cooked up (oh yeah, pun intended), with multiple surprises that are revealed at the end. And has you shaking your head in disbelief as you uncover each tasty morsel. With the 70's as a backdrop for the main part of the story as being part of a larger story that spans over 100 years, it ties together into a thrilling mystery that you just don't want to put down.

Rose

Holy Heavenly Gates!

Outstanding fast paced book with great characters and a lovely little twist.

Kath

Acknowledgments:

Thank you for letting me share this work of fiction that ties in some actual historical events and places. The story of Old Man Winter came to me in a dream, but making that dream come true took many individuals that are all very important to me.

I'd like to thank my wife and children: Kristin, Aubrey Carin, Lola Kristine, Maggie Mae, and Carrick Michael, for helping me to breathe life into the characters that you're about to meet. I'd also like to thank my beta-readers and editors, Maribeth Pickens, Vern Preston, Karen Cook, and Lane Edwards. All of these wonderful friends and family members were all so supportive in my journey, and without them, this book doesn't get written.

To my best friend and business partner, Piyush Bhula, thanks for always being there at every turn. And finally, to Jeremy Ledbetter, for always being there and for his wonderful cover design work.

Fine Print:

www.OldManWinterNovel.com

"Walls covered with tear-filled cracks
What stories could they tell?
The pain that lies within this room
Could make sick a man who's well"

Michael Cook is a published poet, author, and accomplished business professional and entrepreneur. Michael is also the owner of the #7 Escape Room experience in the World, Odyssey Escape Game, located in Alpharetta, GA, and Schaumburg, IL.

A resident of Suwanee, GA. Michael is a father of four children, a husband, a brother, and a friend.

Old Man Winter

Heavenly Gates ©

He comes for you in the Winter

A novel by Michael Cook
© 2021

Prologue – A Penny for your Thoughts

Final ramblings of retired Philadelphia Police Detective Frank Bruno – Christmas Eve, 2016.

"It still stands, you know? *FalconClaw.* Some still call it *Heavenly Gates* or the *Haunted Mansion.* I guess it just depends on who you're talking to. For me, well, I just call it, Hell. It just stands there on the side of that hill overlooking Bedford Street, like it always has. Almost seems like it's looking down over all of us in judgment. Judging everything around it for getting younger, newer, more modern. It just stands there in judgment, as if bitter. Bitter that time forgot about it. Forgot about the memories there. I suppose some good, some bad."

"For me, however, the memories are all bad. The evil that lives there, well, it's just evil, that's all. That place is responsible for taking at least three lives: Samuel Crenshaw back in 1920, Victor Rogers in '69, and my friend, Penny Bryce, in 1974. If you ask me, that woman was a saint."

"I remember those three souls like it was yesterday. The others, however, at least seven that I'm aware of, probably more, I've forgotten their names. Heck, I forget lots of things these days. But I won't ever forget the evil that once lived at FalconClaw, though; it's probably still there. That evil set out on a path of darkness, and it didn't stop until it took my friend."

"You know, it's said that every cop who stays on the force long enough will go to their grave with an unsolved case that haunts them until the end. Well, here I am, in Nazareth Catholic Hospital, lying in my death bed thinking about them. I should be thinking of my Jeanie, my children, grandchildren, and the wonderful memories of my life, all of it. But instead, I lay here thinking about him and her: the devil and the saint. And those damn numbers, 8-8-8, they're all I think about, all I dream about. I can't get them out of my head."

"FalconClaw's been around since before the Civil War. Over the years, it's served as a private home, a retirement community, twice, hospice care for the old and dying, a military academy, and a psychiatric hospital. During our investigation, Penny, and me, even discovered that the CIA used FalconClaw for mind-control experimentation back in the fifties. The last time I was there, though, it was a retirement home called *Heavenly Gates.* Nothing heavenly about that place. I never admitted it to anyone, but that place always gave me the willies, you know, the creeps. Didn't like going there, didn't like it at all. They changed the name back to FalconClaw in the late 70s after it re-opened. That name made it even creepier, scarier. I never understood it, though. A falcon is a ravenous bird, and birds don't have claws. They have talons. Guess it doesn't matter much; claws and talons, they both leave scars."

"It finally closed down for good in '98. The city tried to save it a couple of times, but it was just too old, too evil. No matter what they call it, it'll never erase the memory of what happened there."

"The locals pass by it every day; they don't even give it a thought, I guess. It's just a big old eyesore, a black splotch on the map of Old Germantown; people try hard to ignore it. They just pretend it isn't there. For me, though, I can't seem to look away. I try, though. I just can't get it out of my mind. It's been forty-two years since that night. I used to drive by it twice a day, to and from work. Sometimes I'd go the long way around just so I wouldn't have to see it, so I wouldn't have to remember. I just want to burn it all down; the place, and the memories."

"I think back to that night in '74 and the mystery that unfolded on Christmas Eve. To this day, it's never been solved. My friend and fellow Philadelphia Police Detective, Penelope Bryce, went missing that night, and with her went missing the devil himself: Garrison Winter, Garrison O'Donnell, Gordan Daniels, Gerald O' Day, whatever his real name was. That son of a bitch took my friend!"

"The fall and winter of 1974 were the best of times and the worst of times. Penny finally got promoted to the rank of detective after her four-year legal battle with the city, and then Satan had to walk into both of our lives and bring it all down."

"I'm not as upset with the cancer as I am with the knowledge that I'll die, never knowing what happened to Penny. Her poor kids, her husband Joe, they deserved to have that woman in their lives far longer than they did. Trust me, I know what they had to live through. A loss like that changes you."

"As for me, I always thought a bullet would take me down. In this case, the silent enemy got me, prostate cancer. I don't think it's the old age or the cancer that'll finally take me, though. I think Old Man Winter will come calling again. Just who was the mystery man that appeared in all of our lives back in '74 and then, just as quickly, disappeared again, taking Penny with him?"

"It's the damndest thing, not knowing, worse than death itself. I lay here in my hospital bed, actually welcoming death. If there's a Heaven, I've probably done just enough to get in. If I do, maybe somebody up there will be nice enough to tell me what actually happened back then. What really happened to my friend, Penelope Bryce?"

Chapter 1 – Heavenly Gates

Location: Philadelphia, Pennsylvania – Heavenly Gates Retirement Home – December 7, 1920 – Early Morning.

Garrison O'Donnell stood in the recreation room of the Heavenly Gates retirement home. The time was 7:14 am. After emigrating from Dublin, Ireland, O'Donnell had been employed with Heavenly Gates as a custodian since 1912. O'Donnell was an eighty-three-year-old man but wasn't a retirement community resident but rather an employee. He was beloved by both residents and co-workers alike. Though he was much older than the rest of the staff, he was a junior compared to the retirees living there, who averaged 91 years of age. Garrison had a special relationship with one of the residents, Samuel Crenshaw, Heavenly Gates' first resident. Crenshaw was 94 years old but usually had a skip in his step and a youthful smile. Perhaps that's why Garrison took to him ever since his first day on the job.

To both staff and residents, Garrison O'Donnell was known as Old Man Winter. How he got the nickname, folks weren't sure. Perhaps it was because it was his favorite time of year, or maybe because he would always volunteer to shovel the snow come wintertime. No one on the staff raised their hand when asked to shovel the long winding sidewalk that led away from the main entrance of Heavenly Gates. The sidewalk winded its way some one hundred and twenty feet down a slight hill to the wrought iron gates near Bedford Street, located in the East Germantown section of North Philadelphia.

Heavenly Gates was a majestic mansion originally named FalconClaw by its owner. It was constructed in the early 1860s. It had 72 rooms and sat on 14 acres. It served as the primary residence for its owner until 1900, when he donated it to the City of Philadelphia for the sole purpose of elderly care.

By the turn of the century, people living to old age increased dramatically. Life expectancy had increased by ten years in the

1800s, and those still alive at the age of sixty-five could expect to live until their mid-eighties. As medicine advanced, fewer children died from Tuberculosis, Bacillary Dysentery, Typhoid fever, Diphtheria, or Scarlet fever. As life expectancy grew, cities around the U.S. had a problem; what to do with the aging population? Historic mansions owned by the wealthiest Americans were being donated by their owners, who no longer needed large residences as they grew older. Many of these mansions across North America were converted to hospitals, mental health institutions, monasteries, or private schools.

Only the wealthiest families could afford such lavish care for their aging loved ones, and Heavenly Gates was no exception. By 1920, the retirement home had a full-time resident population of thirty-four and a staff of sixty. The staff included: a medical doctor, a psychiatrist, nurses, custodians, cooks, maids, handymen, and farmhands.

Samuel Crenshaw and Garrison O'Donnell grew close in their eight years together. The two would play endless hours of chess and backgammon and were known to take daily walks around the sprawling grounds. Old Man Winter lived on the grounds in staff housing, consisting of only a few private quarters and bunkhouses for the lower-level staff. In total, more than thirty of the sixty-person staff lived on the grounds of the Heavenly Gates retirement home.

"Good morning, old friend," Garrison greeted his friend, Samuel.

"Who are you calling old?" growled Crenshaw.

Garrison chuckled while Samuel was in his usual morning funk, barking at orderlies and nurses alike until he'd been given his morning orange juice and toast.

"Where's everyone at?" grumbled the older Crenshaw.

Garrison turned from the massive solarium windows that looked over a three-acre courtyard, smiled at Sam, and said, "You ask that same question every single day. You know very well it's only you and me this early in the morning."

"Yeah, well, where's my breakfast?"

"I suspect the cooks are in the kitchen getting breakfast ready for everyone. It's only a quarter after seven, and breakfast isn't until eight. But then again, you already know that," Garrison joked, dismissing his older friend.

"What's all that white stuff on the ground out there? It wasn't there yesterday!" Sam looked perplexed as he joined Garrison in looking out the window.

"I suspect that's snow," he paused, "and a good bit of it," offered Garrison. At least a foot had fallen overnight.

"Well, who put it there?"

"I'd surmise that it fell from the sky overnight," Garrison shook his head and smiled.

"Well, I'd surmise that you have no actual proof of that," Sam poked back.

As the men turned from the window to take a seat, Garrison noticed that Sam had forgotten to put on his house slippers again. He'd been forgetting things more and more lately.

"Sam, where are your slippers?"

"Rubbish! I don't wear those things. They're for the old Ninnies that walk around here thinking that they own the place." Sam waved off the concern of his friend.

"Sam, you know very well that girls are smarter than boys and that the ladies of the house rule for a reason. They know what they're talking about," Garrison reasoned with his friend, who was growing increasingly agitated and losing more and more of his memory in recent months. "It seems one of them gals upstairs has her eyes keenly set on you."

"Blah-blah-blah! Gladys Ringwald is not my type. Now c'mon, let's play!" Sam crept slowly toward the backgammon table located in the formal dining room just off the solarium.

"I suppose one final game is warranted," said Garrison.

"I get the brown checkers today," said Sam, who seemed to be emerging from his morning haze.

"Like every other morning," Garrison smiled and nodded in agreement.

As the two men set up their checkers, Garrison asked his old friend, "Sam, you've lived a long life, a good life. Would you change anything about it?"

"What are you asking me? You trying to sound philosophical or something?" Sam snickered, not wanting to answer a question that he perceived as silly.

"Just a question, Sam. That's all," he paused. "Well, would you?"

"You know the answer to that question already," Sam was reluctant to answer his friend's query.

"My guess is that it has something to do with Rebekah?" Garrison posed his answer as a question.

"She should have outlived me!" Sam had bitter sorrow in his voice. "I guess that's what I get for living too long!"

"Sam, you're a great man. Your life is paralleled by few. If the only regret you have is outliving your wife, well then, I guess you did okay."

"There're many more things I would change. I wish I did more for people when I was younger. So self-consumed with wealth and material things," Sam looked agitated, shaking his head. "I was selfish. I could have done more."

"Sam, you've lived a stellar life. You've helped build half of this country and given away nearly every penny that you've ever earned. You served your country even though Abraham Lincoln exempted you from military service. Your three children are all highly respected civil servants....and," Garrison was cut off.

"And, what?!" barked Sam.

"And you provided a home to all of these people in their dying years and a worthy job to all of the staff members, including me." Sincerity dripped from Garrison's words. "I know the truth about this place, Sam."

"What are you talking about?" Sam ground his teeth.

"I know that Heavenly Gates was once called FalconClaw. I know that you owned it and lived here with your Rebekah and your boys."

Sam's face went white. "You don't know what you're talking about! Now roll the damn dice!" Crenshaw growled.

Garrison rolled the dice and moved his checkers. "I know that you donated this place to the city of Philadelphia back in aught-one, after living alone here without your Rebekah. I know that you did it under an assumed name."

Sam looked momentarily stunned and didn't immediately respond to Garrison.

"Sam, I'm your friend. I know more about you than any living person. I know about your entire life to this point. And..."

"And what?" Samuel Crenshaw almost trembled as he spoke.

"And I know that you're dying." O'Donnell was solemn.

"Well, if that ain't the worst-kept secret around here. We're all dying, you fool. And you are too. From the day we start living, we start dying. Some just longer than others." It was now Sam that was attempting to be philosophical.

"What I am trying to say is that I have more to do before I die, but you, my friend, well, it just might be time," said Garrison O'Donnell.

Sam squeezed the dice in his hand with a raised upper lip and snarled, "I'll go when I'm damn ready to!"

"Look outside, Sam; everything is dead. That's what winter is. It's the end. The end of a life cycle. Spring signals birth and rebirth, summer represents youth, the fall represents adulthood and the decline of our youth, while winter represents death and dying."

"Alright, Professor, now I know why they call you Old Man Winter, too damn fond of the cold."

"Sam, this is the winter of your life."

"You know, that's not the most profound thing you've ever said to me," snickered Sam.

"No, what was?" inquired a curious Garrison.

"That time when you told me when to take the tomatoes down off the vine. That was far more profound than the gibberish you just belched."

"Well, I do admit, I wasn't exactly meant for this world that you live in."

"You keep sayin' nonsense. Just roll the dice!" quipped Sam.

"Those die there; they represent life. From the moment you let them go, they know exactly what number they're going to land on. People think it's just dumb luck, but it's not," explained Garrison. "There's no such thing. There is purpose in everything. Meaning in everything. People just don't know. Not yet anyway."

"Next, you're gonna tell me that that's why they call them *die*?" Sam fussed at his friend. "Cuz we're all dying, right?"

Garrison O'Donnell smiled and was gentle as he placed a die into his old friend's hand and said, "Go ahead, roll it." Then, he stood from his chair.

"Alright, fine, I will." Sam rolled the die, and a single dot lie face-up on the board. "There, I got a one."

Garrison looked Sam in the eye and then rolled the other die on his side of the board. When the die came to a rest, a single dot lay face-up. Garrison smiled and walked back over to the window in the solarium.

"I knew what you were going to roll, Sam. I knew what I was going to roll, too, even before I let it go." As he looked out into the falling snow, hands in pockets, he sighed and then turned back to Sam. O'Donnell was neither surprised nor startled to see Sam standing close to his side.

"I'm ready for that walk now," said Sam.

"What walk?" smiled Winter, happy that his friend was beginning to understand him.

"The one you were just about to ask me to go on."

Garrison placed his hand on Sam's shoulder, smiled, and said, "A walk it is then."

"Let me get my shoes, jacket, and my cane," said Sam.

As he turned and headed for the coatroom, located near the mansion's front door, Garrison touched his arm. "It's okay, old friend. You won't be needing a jacket or shoes where you're going."

Sam smiled at his friend, and the two walked through the dining area and into the foyer. No words were spoken until they'd made it to the massive double steel doors at the front entrance of Heavenly Gates.

Now standing in the doorway, the two men looked out and admired the pristine white snow as the wind howled. Sam said, "You know, it's not as cold as I thought it would be."

"No, it isn't," Garrison agreed.

Just minutes later, the cooks and orderlies prepared the dining room for the breakfast reception that lasted from 8 to 10 am daily, when one of them felt a cold draft coming from the foyer. Walking into the long hall, the man noticed the two front doors were standing wide open. "Oh my goodness, it's frightfully cold out there!" he said. The orderly hurried as he closed the doors, wondering how they came to be open. It was the only sign that Sam, Garrison, or anyone else had even been downstairs that morning. In the dining room sat a backgammon game with no winner. A single dot lay face up on each die.

It was now after nine o'clock, and several people were wondering where Sam was.

"Carol, have you seen Mr. Crenshaw?" asked Gladys Ringwald.

"No, I'm afraid I haven't," responded Carol Wickens.

Gladys walked around the large dining area, asking those in the room if they'd seen Samuel. Everyone seemed disinterested and told her that they had not.

"Mr. Johnson, have you seen Mr. Crenshaw this morning?"

"Why no, I haven't, Ms. Gladys," said Carl Johnson, an orderly and kitchen hand. "I set his toast and orange juice over by his chair around eight, but it seems that it hasn't been touched. The two looked over toward his empty chair near the backgammon table."

Gladys Ringwald was in a slight panic, now expecting the worst. She knew that it wasn't like Sam to be late. He was always the first down to breakfast. Minutes later, she found herself on the third floor of the mansion. She stood at the end of the thirty-foot-long hallway that had six bedrooms, three on each side. Sam's was the last one on the left. With trepidation in each step, she nervously made her way down the red-carpeted hallway adorned with paisley patterned wallpaper. Now outside of Sam's bedroom, she tapped on the partially open door.

Fearing what she might find inside, her lips quivered, "Sam, are you in there?"

Knocking with more purpose, the thud of her white knuckles hitting the door in fear caused it to open a little more. Now veering into the modest room, dread befell her face when she saw it was empty. She was not surprised to see that the room was in pristine condition as everyone knew Sam to be very neat and orderly. The curtains were tied back, and his bed was made to perfection, hospital corners with the blanket so tight you could bounce loose change off of it.

Not wanting to jump to any conclusions, Gladys reasoned that Sam must be somewhere else in the fifty-three-thousand square foot mansion with five levels.

Now racing from the room, she bumped into another resident of the third floor, Clara Thornberg.

"Clara, have you seen Mr. Crenshaw? I can't seem to locate him this morning, and I'm worried."

"Earlier, I think I saw him and Old Man Winter from my window. It seemed odd, though," said Clara. "They were walking down the hill towards the woods. The snow, it seemed so deep, I couldn't even see his boots. I thought I was seeing things, so I didn't make a fuss or anything."

With a confused look, Ringwald said, "What do you mean? It's freezing outside! He would have never gone for a walk in those conditions!" Gladys was overwrought with concern. "Why didn't you tell someone?"

"He and Winter always go for walks. That's nothing new," said a now defensive Thornberg. "Odd? Yes. Out of the ordinary? No."

"But. But it's so cold out," stuttered Ringwald.

"Find Mr. O'Donnell, and you'll find Mr. Crenshaw," Thornberg encouraged her friend.

Several minutes later, a frantic Gladys Ringwald found herself in the coatroom where she'd noticed Sam's jacket still hanging on its hanger and his winter boots, just below. She'd inspected the jacket to see if it was wet from being outside and determined it was not. Racing back to the common area, she ran into Garrison O'Donnell, who was just leaving the breakfast area.

"Oh, Mr. O'Donnell, there you are!" sighed an out-of-breath Ringwald. "I've been looking for you."

The old woman appeared to be desperate in O'Donnell's opinion. "Mrs. Ringwald, what is it? Is everything alright?"

"I've been looking all over for Mr. Crenshaw. Might you know where he is? I'm quite worried about him."

Garrison O'Donnell looked at Gladys and reassured her that he was certain that Sam was alright. "I haven't seen him yet this morning, but it appears he's been downstairs from his room as his toast and juice are sitting untouched near his chair."

"So you haven't seen him either?!" Gladys was confused as her friend told her she'd seen Sam with him outside earlier that morning. Now worried that he wandered off and might have fallen or had been hurt, she said. "Something's wrong! Something terrible has happened!"

"Mrs. Ringwald," Garrison attempted to calm the panicked woman standing before him. "I will help you look for him."

Gladys rushed by Garrison and ran to the office of Mr. Bradley Carlsbad. It was a Tuesday and the administrative staff arrived by nine o'clock, and it was just after. For the past ten years, Carlsbad had been the Administrator of Heavenly Gates retirement home and was considered highly competent and well-liked by staff and residents.

Barging through his door without knocking, Ringwald shouted, "Mr. Carlsbad! Samuel Crenshaw is missing!"

"What do you mean missing?" Carlsbad was alarmed by the intrusion and the claim as he finished hanging his overcoat and removing his shoe rubbers.

"I've looked everywhere, but he's not here!"

Now seated behind his desk, Carlsbad said, "Mrs. Ringwald, I'm sure there's a simple explanation. I'm quite certain that Mr. Crenshaw is not 'missing,' as you say."

"But I've looked everywhere, spoken to everyone, no one has seen him, except for...."

"Except for whom, Mrs. Ringwald?"

"Clara Thornberg told me that she saw him outside, walking in the snow with Mr. O'Donnell."

The statement concerned Carlsbad because of the harsh conditions and Crenshaw's age. "Outside?! When?!" Carlsbad leapt from his chair.

"Follow me, Mrs. Ringwald." Carlsbad led her down the hall to address those in the expansive dining area where breakfast was still being served. Along the way, Carlsbad stopped his assistant, Clarice Jenkins, walking toward them in the hallway. He instructed her to summon all of the staff members to the Dining Room at once.

Seeing the urgency in his eyes, she nodded without words and ran off in haste.

Moments later, Carlsbad addressed the group of roughly twenty residents and four kitchen staff. "Ladies and gentlemen, I need your attention!" Carlsbad spoke over the subdued chatter. "It appears we are unable to locate Samuel Crenshaw. Has anyone seen him at any time this morning?"

Those around the room looked at each other before shaking their heads. At that moment, additional staff and other residents made their way into the room, and the volume of chatter began to grow.

"Folks, please, if I can again have your attention. Is Mrs. Thornberg in attendance?" asked Carlsbad.

Again, those present looked at each other and around the room but were unable to locate Thornberg. Only minutes later, Clarice Jenkins walked into the room with Clara Thornberg.

"Oh, there you are," voiced Carlsbad in Clara's direction. "Mrs. Thornberg, we are all quite concerned with the whereabouts of Samuel Crenshaw. Mrs. Ringwald tells me that you witnessed him walking outside of the building some two hours ago. Is this true?" asked a concerned Carlsbad.

"Why, yes, I did," said Thornberg. "I saw him walking in the snow away from the main house on the southwest side of the estate toward the woods. He was with Mr. O'Donnell."

At that moment, Garrison O'Donnell walked around the corner and seemed surprised by the large contingent of staff and residents staring at him in silence.

"Why, what's all this?" said the eighty-three-year-old custodian as the room remained silent with his appearance.

"Mr. O'Donnell," said Carlsbad, "have you been in the presence of Samuel Crenshaw this morning? And have you been outside at any point today, sir?"

"Why no, sir, Mr. Carlsbad. It's frightful outside," Garrison looked both confused and uncertain with the goings-on. "Why would anyone venture outside on such a morning?"

Carlsbad looked relieved, believing that if O'Donnell hadn't been outside, it was likely that Clara Thornberg was simply mistaken.

"Thank you, Mr. O'Donnell." Carlsbad raised his hand to again calm the rising chatter. "Ladies and gentlemen, please. If I may have just another moment of your time. We must all do our part to search the building and ensure that Mr. Crenshaw is in good health. Now, please, excuse yourselves and help us put an end to the mystery of Mr. Crenshaw's whereabouts."

With most of the room now empty, Thornberg approached Carlsbad. Standing nearby were several orderlies, along with Clarice Jenkins, Gladys Ringwald, and Garrison O'Donnell.

"Mr. Carlsbad, I can assure you that I saw Mr. Crenshaw in the company of Mr. O'Donnell here," Thornberg launched an accusatorial stare at Old Man Winter.

"Mrs. Thornberg, Mr. Carlsbad, Ma'am," O'Donnell nodded to a pale-faced Gladys Ringwald. "I can assure you that I did not leave this facility on this day, nor have I seen my friend, Samuel Crenshaw, at any time this morning. I have no reason to lie."

"Mr. O'Donnell, I saw you with him from my window early this morning!" Thornberg was defiant.

"Mr. Carlsbad, sir. Mrs. Thornberg's quarters are on the third floor, and the windows are nearly iced over." O'Donnell attempted to defend himself when Thornberg, sharp with her words, cut him off.

"I can see the footprints from my window!" shouted Clara Thornberg. "Two sets!" she displayed two fingers on her wayward hand.

"With her words came a fear-stricken look from everyone."

In a subdued panic, Carlsbad instructed the orderlies to dawn their boots and coats and for Clarice Jenkins to notify the proper authorities. "At once!" he shouted.

Chapter 2 – Bryce v. Philadelphia

Location – Philadelphia, Pennsylvania. Frank's Spaghetti House, Corner of Glendale, and Castor Avenue – Thursday night, August 29, 1974.

"Hey, Penny! Congratulations! Get over here and give Big Frankie a hug!" yelled Frank Ricci as he walked from behind the bar.

Frank was the long-time owner of the corner spaghetti house that Penny Bryce had frequented since she was a little girl. Ricci knew everybody from the Rhawnhurst neighborhood in North Philly, and everybody knew him.

"Awe, thanks for closing down the place for us, Frank. You're a good man." Penny hugged Big Frank, and as usual, he held on a little too tight and a little too long.

"Listen, you put up a good fight, and you won! You beat those bureaucrat bastards, Penny." Frank continued to clutch Penny's shoulders while wearing a proud smile as if she was his daughter.

Penny's friends and family members passed by the two en route to the dining area in the back of the tiny restaurant where red and white checkered tablecloths adorned the tables. Each person who passed Penny and Ricci paid their respects to the man affectionately known as *Big Frank*. Ricci was a large man, standing six foot two inches tall while weighing more than 275 lbs., earning his nickname.

"Yuz did it," said Frank in his heavy Italian accent. "Yuz did it for all the little girls in Philly. My Angie would have been proud. God rest her soul." Big Frank crossed himself, motioning his right hand to his head, then his heart, then left, then right chest.

In a show of respect, Penny crossed herself too. "God rest her soul, Frank. She was a good woman."

Ricci's dear departed wife, Angela, died of cancer in the spring of '72 at the age of sixty-seven, not living long enough to see the end of Penny's lawsuit. Penny and her family had been very close to Angela Ricci over the years. Like her husband Frank, she knew all the kids in the neighborhood and watched them grow into adults. She was like a second mom to them.

"Okay, okay, enough already." Frank escorted Penny back to where her friends and family were getting seated. "Listen up, everybody! Yuz, eat free tonight! And the booze is on me, too. It's a big day for Penny and all the girls of North Philly." Frank was loud and proud of Penny as his hands flailed wildly in the air. "But hey! You make sure you tip my girls good tonight."

Cheers from the raucous crowd of twenty-plus were loud and appreciative as the word "Saluti" chorused from the rear of the spaghetti house.

"Awe, Frank, you don't have to do that," Penny was overwhelmed with Big Frank's generosity.

"It don't mean nothin', but you, you mean everything tonight, Penny. This is your night! Oh, if Angie could see you now." Both Frank and Penny crossed themselves again.

"Thanks, Frank!" Penny gave Ricci a side hug as her husband looked on. She buried her left ear into Frank's right shoulder, blushing as she closed her eyes while showing her gratitude.

Before heading back to the bar, Big Frank raised Penny's arm in the air and shouted to the group, "Philadelphia's own, DETECTIVE, Penny Bryce!" The group cheered.

In 1970, Penelope Denise Bryce filed suit against the City of Philadelphia, alleging that the Philadelphia Police Department discriminated against women in hiring and promotion practices.

Since 1960, Penny Bryce had been a full-time, uniformed police officer for the city, following in the footsteps of her father, grandfather, and two brothers. First in 1965, then '66 and '67, Penny had taken the test to become a detective. After outperforming her male counterparts in test scores, Bryce failed to get promoted, scoring in the ninety-fifth percentile on three separate occasions over three years. In February of 1968, she'd filed a formal complaint with the police department and city council. On August 19, the all-male council of ten voted 9-1 that women were not prepared, neither mentally nor physically, to be a police detective in Philadelphia, citing that, "Women didn't have the hormones needed to do a 'man's job." It was suggested that estrogen made women weaker and too emotional to present good judgment in stressful situations.

After two additional council meetings, one in each of the following two summers, a motion was made and unanimously passed that the council would not take up the motion again. Undeterred, Penelope Bryce hired a big shot lawyer from across the river in Camden, New Jersey, who'd had his eye on the complaints filed by Bryce and subsequent press coverage. Gaylord Conrad, ESQ., had represented many high-profile politicians, shipping tycoons, and celebrities. He'd even taken on the Federal Government. He'd won more than ninety-five percent of his cases over his thirty-year career.

Being the father of five grown women, Conrad took a special interest in the complaints filed by Bryce. In January of 1970, representing Penny Bryce, he filed a class-action lawsuit in federal court against the City of Philadelphia. The complaint alleged gender-based discrimination against more than ninety-six women. The lawsuit sought a uniformed officer hiring ratio of thirty percent women to men each year, along with promotions and back-pay in the amount of one million dollars to be awarded to all the women named in the suit.

During the four-plus years that the case dragged on, Penny was demoted to the position of Juvenile Aid. At the time of the original court filing, less than one hundred women worked in the department, with only thirty uniformed officers working the streets. Of those women, nearly all fell under scrutiny and were subjected to further discrimination and workplace harassment. Many of them came to resent the very woman who was fighting for their equal rights as women.

During the early days of the proceedings, both the Police Commissioner, Joseph O'Neill, and Philadelphia Mayor, Frank Rizzo, weighed in publicly. O'Neill was quoted as saying, "Women have an extra layer of fat on their bodies, which makes them slower and more vulnerable when being attacked by an assailant." Rizzo argued that Bryce was 'incompetent' and publicly called for her firing.

Adding that, "God, in all of his wisdom, made women different than men for a reason."

In court, it was argued by experts for the city that, "Tragically, women, once a month experience an ailment that renders them incapable of rationality, making their professional duties virtually impossible to carry out."

After four years, millions of dollars in court costs, and bad publicity for the *City of Brotherly Love*, the City of Philadelphia and the federal government agreed to settle the case. More than $700,000 was awarded to ninety-six women, and Penny Bryce was finally named Detective.

Later that evening, after the celebration at Frank's Spaghetti House, Penny Bryce was getting ready for bed, where she'd join her husband, Joe.

From the bathroom, Penny yelled, "So, I canceled my appointment with Dr. Goldberg."

"For when? Tomorrow?" Joe responded.

"No," Penny peeked her head out the bathroom door, "forever," she smiled.

"You can't stop seeing him just because you won the case," cautioned Joe. "You went through hell, and it's gonna get worse."

"Penny, have you considered what life is going to be like at work now that the case is settled?" asked her husband of seventeen years.

"Joe, if it gets out that a Philly Police Detective is seeing a psychiatrist, then they'll have another reason to want me gone. Whatever credibility I have will go out the window. It's tough enough being a female cop in this city. Imagine being one that needs to see a shrink."

"That's horseshit!" said Joe. "That guy helped you through your darkest days."

"Joe, I'll be fine. I mean, think about it, if I can't handle politicians, then how can I handle the scum walking the streets?"

"Penny, you're making my point. I think you should keep seeing him."

Penny turned off the bedroom light in the tiny upstairs of their duplex at 2125 Fuller Street and crawled into bed. "Joe, I don't need help anymore, and besides, those bastards can't fire me now. At least not for a while anyway," she exhaled, modest in her new self-perceived invincibility.

"Penny, I'm serious. It was bad before, but it's bound to get worse. Those pricks are going to make life hell for you," Joseph looked at her, his face drenched with concern.

"Joe, I can handle it. I'm going to be forty in December, and I'm a Police Detective for the City of Philadelphia. I've been working those streets for almost fourteen years. I think I'm tough enough to handle it."

"Yeah, but you're a woman. Don't forget that," Joe winked and smiled and reached for the light.

"Ha-ha, wise-guy! No sugar for you tonight."

The next morning Penny got off the bus that stopped in front of the 39th Police District, located on the corner of Hunting Park Avenue and Schuyler Street, the place where she'd worked for the past seven years before getting demoted. As she approached the arched doorway, Philly's Bravest from Ladder 18 and the Engine 59 firehouse were outside, and they cheered her on. The firehouse was situated in the same building as the police district, located just to the left as you approached the police station. The two were separated by an arched tunnel that led to a fenced-in police parking lot that backed up to Yelland Street. Statues of a fireman flanked the tunnel to the left and a police officer to the right.

The men were mostly sincere and congratulatory of her victory against the city and that she was now a detective. Her victory fed into the ongoing grudge between Philadelphia's 'Bravest' and 'Finest.' A few reporters were also there, as they had been time and time again, to ask her for comments on the trial and her subsequent victory, but she declined to answer any questions. She didn't want to show up her rivals that stood just inside the arched doorway she was about to enter.

As Penny walked through the door, the reception was cold. Most of the uniformed officers avoided making eye contact with her. Even the one female officer that worked there chose not to acknowledge her. Penny had made life hard on the women of the force by bringing increased ridicule and insult into their male-dominated workplace. Those who did make eye contact launched a look of disdain in her direction. She did get some subdued congratulatory nods but nothing overt, not a handshake, an 'Attagirl,' or even a smile. The only ally she had in the entire building was a seasoned detective named Frank Bruno. Frank and Penny were regular lunch buddies and frequented Tony's Pizzeria across the street from the firehouse on many occasions. Frank didn't take shit from anyone and could care less if he was judged for liking Penny.

Frank Bruno had become famous amongst his peers in law enforcement circles the previous year when he'd coined the phrase *Cold Case* during an FBI seminar on the new science of psychological and criminal personality profiling.

Penny grabbed a cardboard box off her old desk in the police officer hall and made her way to the Detective Room on the building's second floor. There, she was unceremoniously sworn in by Chief of Detectives for the 39th District, Ron McClain, and given her detective badge. The swearing-in ceremony was witnessed only by a radio dispatcher downstairs named Pam. The woman loudly chewed her gum and flapped her lips during the brief ceremony, causing Penny to roll her eyes, exhaling with contempt several times.

Penny was a tough cop but had feelings too, she'd hoped there was more fanfare during the presentation, but there was none. She thought to herself, *"Fuck it!"* and disregarded the advice she'd given herself earlier and went outside to let the one remaining reporter take her picture. Subsequently, the picture was sold to the Associated Press and made newspapers in Philly, Camden, Cherry Hill, Voorhees, Harrisburg, and Scranton. The smile she wore was bogus, but she hammed it up in an effort to stick it to the male establishment. Seeing the headlines the next day, Ron McClain was pissed at what he thought was an attention grab.

Friday, September 6, 1974 - After several days of being ignored by the other four detectives in the Detective Room, and Chief Detective McClain, Frank Bruno was finally back from his two-week vacation, and Penny was happy to see a friendly face.

"Hey, Penny! Congrats! Finally made it up to the second floor! Come over here and give old Frankie a hug."

"Thanks, Frank. You're the first person to acknowledge that I got promoted." Penny hugged the only friend she'd had in the entire Philadelphia P.D.

"Fuck these guys around here," said Frank. "You're a good cop, and you deserve it! You're twice the cop that they are." Frank sat down at his desk, which butted up against Penny's, and got ready for his day.

"Frank, listen, outside of swearing me in and giving me my badge, McClain hasn't said a word to me all week. He sent Coons and Riggins out on a job that I could've handled. He then sent Tubbs and Taylor on another job that a rookie cop could handle on their first day."

"Well, if it makes you feel any better, that's the way he works when it comes to new guys," Frank caught himself. "Sorry, new detectives."

"Awe, don't worry about it Frankie, I'm one of the guys now." She looked away and muttered, "I hope so anyway. At least they put my desk next to yours."

"Listen, if he doesn't give you something by the end of next week, I'll go to bat for you."

"Thanks, Frank. You've always been a stand-up guy."

"Hey, outside of my Jeanie, you're my best girl!"

"How is Jeanie, anyway? She hasn't been around much," asked Penny.

"She's better now," Frank shuffled papers on his desk. Looking up at Penny, he said, "The girls, not so much."

"What do you mean 'better now?' Was she sick?" Penny looked concerned.

"Yeah, something like that, but she's better now."

The following Friday finally came, and no cases were handed to Penny.

"Frank, he wouldn't even give me a missing dog case or send me to investigate who spray-painted a dick on the jungle gym in Huntington Park. I thought for sure the prick would give me that one."

Penny was sad but not surprised. She headed out for the weekend, and only Frank and Ron McClain remained in the Detective Room. Frank gave her a nod and a wink as if to say, *'I got your back,'* just as he'd promised.

A little later, and before leaving, Frank stuck his head into McClain's office and noticed his boss was on the phone. Ron held up his finger in a wait-a-minute gesture while he finished his call.

Frank had always admired the tiny office of his boss as it was adorned with Philadelphia Eagles' memorabilia. Ron's favorite player was #17. He even had an autographed helmet that Harold Carmichael had signed the year before. His office was filthy, but the helmet was shiny as it sat with pride on the shelf above his desk.

The Eagles kicked off their season that Sunday on the road at St. Louis, and McClain was in a good mood. The Eagles weren't very good, coming off of seven straight losing seasons, but Frank's boss was optimistic with the addition of all-pro linebacker Bill Bergey, who came over in a trade with the Cincinnati Bengals earlier that year.

In addition to the Eagles' memorabilia, at least three crucifixes were in the room that Frank could see. Frank knew McClain to be very religious.

"What is it, Frank?"

"Chief, you got a minute?"

"Yeah, sure, whatta ya need?"

"Ron, it's about Penny...."

McClain's good mood evaporated in an instant. "Alright, Frank, stop right there!" McClain shot from his desk and launched into his best detective. "That broad ain't ever getting a case thrown at her by me! She can ask for a transfer if she wants, but she ain't getting shit from me! She dragged this city through the dirt. Her and her big shot lawyer! Philly's the laughing-stock of the country for having a broad where a detective badge."

"Ron, cut her some slack. She's a good cop. Just give her something little to work on, anything," said Frank. "You could've sent her out to check on old lady Stanton's dog. She calls twice a month about that damn poodle."

"Nothing, I said nothing, Frank!" McClain was red-faced. "I'll be damned if a detective wearing a set of tits is going to represent my district out there in North Philly. No fucking way! It's not gonna happen!"

"Okay, how about this? I let her tag along with me." Frank pleaded his case as McClain shook his head. "Ron, there's six of us now. Coons and Riggins; Tubbs and Taylor, they're all partnered up now. It only makes sense. Hell, I thought that's why you put our desks together."

"Fine! You wanna take that dyke with you, fine, but she ain't getting no cases on her own. Not from me!"

"That's a deal, Chief!" Frank was happy with the compromise.

"Oh, and Chief, she's not lesbian. You met her husband and kids at the Christmas party last year." Frank defended his new partner.

"Whatever! Any woman hell-bent on doing a man's job's got issues."

"She's a good cop, Chief. That woman's going to make you look good someday."

"I want her gone. I can't fire her, but I can damn sure make her life miserable!" said McClain. "How's Jeanie, by the way?"

"She's resting comfortably. Thanks for asking," said Frank as he walked out of McClain's tiny office.

A few seconds passed, and Frank stuck his head back in McClain's door and remarked, "Like I said, she's a good cop." Walking away, he yelled, "You'll see, Chief!"

"My ass, I will!" yelled Chief McClain as Frank disappeared into the stairwell. "My ass, I will," whispered McClain under his breath.

Chief of Detectives Ron McClain was a thirty-year-man and headed up the Detective Room in the 39th District for the previous twelve years. As a uniformed cop, he'd been shot twice in 1954 when responding to a bank robbery downtown. Then, in 1957, McClain was one of twenty detectives to work the 'Boy in the Box' case, where a 4-6-year-old boy was found dead, his naked body wrapped in a blanket and stuffed in a box just off of Susquehanna Road in Fox Chase, northwest of Rhawnhurst. The case gained national attention in the media because the boy hadn't been identified, and the case had remained cold since 1957. The case had always haunted McClain.

McClain and several of the other detectives working the case had theorized that the boy belonged to the step-daughter of a man who ran a local foster home less than two miles from where the body was found. They believed the man disposed of the body to protect the young, unwed mother, who they believed murdered the boy or caused his accidental death. An autopsy revealed that the boy was severely malnourished and had suffered multiple fractures in his short life. Several scars were also found, including a large L-shaped one under the boy's chin.

When visiting the foster home, McClain found a bassinet similar to one that the local J.C. Penny's sold. It was a bassinet box of the exact model that the boy was found in. McClain also found similar blankets as the one found wrapped around the boy, hanging on a clothesline in the rear of the foster home. Despite the circumstantial evidence, the case was filed away and remained unsolved.

His colleagues had said that McClain, a father of five boys, was never the same after working the crime scene and still believes that the stepdaughter murdered her son.

McClain wasn't fond of Penny Bryce because Ron McClain wasn't fond of women.

Chapter 3 – Cold Case

After three weeks of ride-alongs with Frank, Penny was getting itchy. She was bonding with her new partner but wanted to solve a crime greater than a petty theft at the Ben Franklin's Nickel & Dime store.

"So, where's the Buick, anyway?" Penny teased her partner.

"It's getting new struts!" Frank thought Penny was busting his balls about his pride and joy that'd seen better days.

"Damn, I like this one better." Penny chuckled.

"Yeah-yeah, whatever!"

"So, Frank, when's the last time you actually handled a murder?" Penny asked Frank as they drove back to the station in a department-issued '73 Plymouth Fury. The two had just finished interviewing some local youths about graffiti found on the pillars of the historic Germantown High School on High Street in North Philly.

"April. Don't you remember that floater in Queen Lane Reservoir over on Roosevelt and Fox?"

"Oh, yeah. I didn't know that was your case. Whatever became of it?"

"Suicide, but not until after he killed his boss. The guy delivered Chinese food for *Wok & Roll,* that place over in Belmont Village, on the other side of the Schuylkill River. Apparently, he'd hated his boss so much that he buried a meat cleaver in the guy's forehead, shot him, and then went home."

"Geez-Louise!" Penny winced. "Whattaya think set him off, bad egg rolls?" she joked. "Isn't that out of our jurisdiction, though?"

"Yeah, ours ends at the river. I had to work with the boys over at the 19th. Sorry, I meant the 'detectives.'

"Frank, stop. I'm one of the boys now." Penny looked out her window and nodded her head in self-recognition.

"Well, you ain't no boy, that's for sure."

Penny turned to Frank and tilted her head. "You flirtin', Frank?"

"Nah, just some guys think you're a....," Frank caught himself. "Ah, nothin, just forget it."

"A what?" Penny's face turned serious. "Go ahead, say it, Frank! You think I haven't heard it all?"

Frank hesitated for a moment. "No, it's just that some of the boys, no one in particular, think you might like girls."

"You caught me! Dammit!" Penny threw up her hands and tried to look serious.

Frank took his eyes off the road for a second to focus on his rookie partner. He had a 'No shit?' look on his face but didn't say anything.

"I thought by being a cop, and then a detective was the perfect cover for being queer?" Penny kept a straight face. "You male detectives are really smart."

"You fucking with me right now, Penny?"

"Of course, I'm fucking with you, Detective Einstein!" Penny busted out a 'You're a dumbass' look.

Frank nodded in recognition that Penny got him good.

"I'm not a lesbian, Frank. And if I was, so what?" Penny shook her head and rolled her eyes. "You men always tie ability to gender. Times are changing, Frankie Boy. You better get with it."

"I'm not the one that thought it. Like I said, you're all woman, Penny."

"So," Penny smiled in Frank's direction, "You are flirting with me, then?"

"No, Ma'am. You're just one of the guys. You said it yourself." Frank got her back for the 'Einstein' remark. "Besides, I love my Jeanie. I could never be with another woman."

Penny looked back out of her window, "So, whatever became of him?"

"Him? Frank looked puzzled. Who?"

"The floater, dumbass? How did he end up in the reservoir?"

"Oh, him. He lived in a duplex on Bowman. That guy stared at that lake from his bedroom window for twelve years. The same night he killed his boss, he went home, ate dinner, took a shower, then got his Sunday church clothes on."

"And?" Penny hung on Frank's next words.

"And then the son of a bitch waded out into that reservoir at three o'clock in the morning and shot himself in the head," explained Frank. "The gun sank to the bottom of the lake."

"How'd they know it was suicide if they didn't have a gun?"

"That's just it. It would've been quite the mystery, but the gunshot woke up everybody in a two-block radius. Plus, nobody forces their victim out into the middle of a lake and shoots them dead," reasoned Frank. "So, we dragged the reservoir, and two days later, we had the weapon. Turns out it belonged to his boss. We found the cleaver in his clothes hamper in the bathroom, which still had blood on it."

"What were their names?" Penny was curious.

"Who?" asked Frank.

"The victim and the perp. What were their names?"

Frank shook his head. "Penny, it doesn't matter what their names were. They're dead."

"It matters to me." Penny seemed surprised by Frank's indifference.

"Penny, you're gonna find out in this racket that you have to forget the names....but," Frank paused.

"Why?" Penny looked confused.

"Because you'll remember. You'll remember how many," Frank lamented. "But...," he hesitated again.

"But what?" Penny prodded her partner, who for a moment looked forsaken.

"You'll never forget..." he paused, staring into a void, eyes focused on nothing.

"Forget what?" Penny was beginning to get impatient.

"Their faces. That's what." Frank looked like he wanted to change the subject. "You'll never forget their faces, Penny."

A few minutes later, after Frank emerged from his fog, Penny was excited. "I can't wait for my first murder case." She looked anxious, stopping short of rubbing her hands together and licking her lips.

"Penny. First of all, you're wishing somebody dead," offered Frank. "Second of all, there's nothing fun about a murder case. Faces, don't forget what I said about the faces."

"I'm not wishing death on anyone, Frank. I just want to solve something big." Penny didn't feel like a detective yet.

"Penny, ninety-nine percent of all the cases that get dropped on your desk won't involve a homicide. You watch too much *Columbo*. Make sure you manage your own expectations," Frank offered up some life advice. "That's the secret to life, Penny. The successful management of people's expectations."

Frank took a left onto Hillside, and as the wheel spun back straight, he looked at Penny and said, "Starting with your own, young lady."

Penny smirked, "Okay, Professor. Oh, and I ain't no spring chicken, nothing young about me. How old are you, anyway?"

"Just turned 48."

"And you've been a detective for how long?" asked Penny with an attitude.

"Eighteen years." Frank flashed a look that said to his partner that he couldn't believe it'd been that long.

"See! Now that's bullshit!" Penny looked pissed.

"What's bullshit?" asked Frank, looking a little defensive. "I put in my time!"

"You're only like eight years older than me but have eighteen years in plain clothes. That's some male-dominated profession bullshit right there," Penny fumed.

"Yeah, well, you're one of the guys now." Frank offered more life advice, "Look forward. Never back."

After several minutes, the radio in the car crackled and caused Penny to break the silence.

"I'm gonna talk to him myself," revealed Penny.

"Him? Who?" Frank had no idea who Penny was talking about.

"McClain. That's who. I'm gonna demand more responsibility."

"Penny, don't do it," warned Frank. "If you piss him off, he won't let you ride along with me anymore."

Penny laughed, "That wouldn't be the worst thing that ever happened to me. Your farts smell like old hotdogs."

"Okay wise guy, I mean girl, lady, whatever. You'll miss me when I'm gone," Frank poked back.

"That might be a chance I'll have to take," Penny was feeling fearless. "He can't keep holding me back, and I ain't asking for a transfer. No way!"

Frank was pragmatic. "Alright, but wait until I'm outta the office. I don't want him to think that I put you up to this. And it'll look like I'm fighting your battles if we both go at him."

"What's the worst thing that can happen?" asked Penny.

"He'll have you typing case reports for the five of us in the Detective Room until you quit or request that transfer."

"Well, I ain't quittin, and I ain't asking for a transfer. They'll send me down to the Southside, and that commute will take forever. Nope, I'm stickin it out."

"Nothing I can do if you fuck this up," Frank shook his head. "I already went to bat for you once."

An hour later, now back at the office, Penny shot Frank and the others a smile and then headed for Ron McClain's office. Frank motioned 'no,' and mouthed the words, "Wait 'til I'm gone." Penny smiled and went in anyway.

Frank shook his head, looked at the others, and said, "Watch this, boys. I give that conversation...."

Before Frank finished his sentence, the five detectives heard an avalanche of expletives coming from their boss's office but not a peep from Penny.

After several minutes of shouting, Penny walked out of McClain's office glassy-eyed. She looked like Muhammad Ali getting up off the canvas in the fifteenth round in Madison Square Garden, after Philly's own, Smokin' Joe Frazier sent him there with a wicked left hook. In that bout, though, Ali held his own. It didn't sound to anyone within earshot like Penny even landed a punch.

Penny looked deflated as she stood at her desk, saying nothing to Frank or the others. Out of concern, Frank rose to see if she was okay. She immediately waved him off, grabbed her purse, then walked out the door. Frank ran downstairs to catch her before she got on the bus. The street noise was loud, so he touched her shoulder to get her attention. When Penny turned, Frank noticed that she was crying.

"What did he say, Penny?"

"You mean you didn't hear?" Penny was purposeful in her sarcasm, wiping tears from her eyes.

"I heard plenty, but what happens now?"

"Fuck this job! Fuck that asshole!" Penny was livid. "Nobody needs to hear what I just heard."

"Penny, you don't quit! You hear me?" Frank pointed his finger in Penny's face. "You're my partner, and partners don't quit on each other. I need you."

The bus pulled to the curb, and without saying a word, Penny turned away from Frank, grabbed the handrail, and stepped up onto the bus. As the bus drove away, Penny stuck her head out the window and yelled, "Fuck that asshole! I ain't quittin'!"

Frank smiled in relief and said out loud, "That's my girl!" He gave her a wave and then went back inside.

Minutes later, he walked into the detective room where his boss was briefing the others. When McClain saw Frank approaching, he turned, held up his hand, and stuck his finger in Frank's face. "Don't even say it! That bitch ain't worth getting yourself in trouble, Frank."

When Frank tried to speak, McClain raised his hand again and said, "Don't do it!"

Frank bit his tongue and waited until his boss disappeared into his office, slamming the door behind him.

"So, what'd he say?"

Jack Riggins spoke up, "Desk duty for eight weeks."

"Yeah, and she has to do all of our paperwork. Can't leave each day until all the files are in his box," added Doug Coons, Riggins' partner.

That following Monday, Penny was in the office before anybody else, filing reports and looking through old case files. Three Mondays later, she was still getting there early. She hadn't said a word to anyone during that time, not even Frank.

Frank had had enough and got up to go to lunch. When he did, he intentionally pushed in his chair hard enough so that it would push his desk into Penny's. "Get up!" he said, "We're going to Tony's for a pepperoni pie. That's an order!"

"You ain't my boss!" Penny snapped back.

"So, she speaks?" Frank grinned. "It's about time!"

Penny rose from her seat, shouldered her purse strap, and said, "You're buying."

As the two passed the *Unsolved Crimes* closet on the way out, they heard something fall. Penny stopped, looked at Frank, and then pushed opened the door. The door was obstructed by two large file boxes that had fallen from the top shelf. Penny pushed through the hundreds of papers that now littered the floor and said, "Of course that son of a bitch is gonna make me clean this up."

Ten hours later, Penny was still organizing files. In addition to the files that hit the floor, Penny took the liberty to sort through and reorganize other cold cases as well. It was now 2 am, and the phones rang out in the Detective Room. It was Joe calling.

"I don't know, Honey. Soon, maybe," she said to her worried husband, who'd wondered when she'd be home.

The next day, when Frank arrived, Penny wasn't there. It was the first time in weeks he'd beat her into the office. Her desk was immaculate, as was the office. When Frank turned to hit the head, he noticed that the sign above the Unsolved Crimes closet had been replaced. The new sign said *Cold Cases*. Frank smiled.

Penny walked in an hour later, set her bag on her desk, looked at her partner, and said, "Frank, what do you know about *Heavenly Gates*, 1969?"

"Penny, you went through those old cases in there, didn't you?" Frank lifted his chin, motioning to the newly named Cold Case closet.

"I can't get into trouble. McClain instructed me to clean it all up."

With suspicion, Penny looked around the room. Tubbs and Taylor were just settling in, and the others, including McClain, weren't in yet. "What time's the boss getting in?" Penny whispered to Frank so the others couldn't hear her.

"He's not." Frank paused, "He's on vacation. Two weeks. Lucky you, finally caught a break."

"No shit? Two weeks?" Penny looked thrilled.

"I read about the 'Boy in the Box' case. I don't hate McClain anymore. I get it though, he's damaged goods after that one. He thinks a woman did it, the mother. I understand now why he might hate a woman in his ranks."

"Yeah, that was a tough one for McClain, ...for the whole city."

"There's something else, though..." she paused. "Frank, there's something I need to tell you, but not here."

"Penny, what's going on? What are you up to?" Frank saw something in Penny's eyes. It was something that would change everything for both of them.

From that moment on, time would be measured by what came before that day and what came after. Their two destinies were now connected forever, and forever would be too long for one and far too short for the other.

"FalconClaw," she said.

Chapter 4 – FalconClaw

The next day, Wednesday, October 30, Frank, and Penny met before going into the office. The two sat in the back booth of the Arlington Diner in West Kensington, on the corner of Huntingdon and American.

"Two coffees, black," Frank motioned to the skinny blonde waitress, moments after the two sat down.

It was raining outside, and the warm temperature and gray skies seemed to match Frank's mood.

"Ok, Penny, here we are, a secret rendezvous so that you can tell me exactly what?"

"Not tell you, but ask you," whispered Penny.

"What the fuck are you whispering for?" Frank wanted the mystery of why the two were meeting solved. "Spit it out, for Christ's sake."

"What do you know about the missing person's report for Victor Rogers from '69?" Penny pulled a file from her leather bag and laid it on the table.

"The guy from 'Heavenly Gates' thing? That's what all this is about?"

"Yes, what do you know about it?"

Frank spun the file around to face him, opened it up, and perused its contents, acting only mildly interested.

"It wasn't my case," said Frank. "Langhorne and Gaffney worked it. I transferred over to the 39th about six months after the disappearance. They shelved that case just a few months after they opened it." Frank was going off of memory.

"Why?! Why did they close it so quickly?" Penny tapped on the case file laying between her and Frank. "He was a missing person!" Penny displayed a subdued look of anger to go along with her obvious empathy.

"He was old," responded Frank.

"Da' fuck does that mean?" Penny's eyes narrowed in disdain.

"I don't know, you got the file. Didn't you read it?" Frank was at a loss. "It was five years ago, and it wasn't my case."

"I read every word of it, and he's still missing! It says he was ninety-five years old. Why aren't we out there looking for him?"

"There, you answered your own question!" Frank closed the file and slid it back across the table to his naïve partner.

"What are you talking about?" Penny looked offended.

"Penny, he was ninety-five years old; that was almost five years ago. He's dead, Penny!" Frank was still confused about what the secret meeting was about. He was sure it wasn't about Victor Rogers.

"He's dead. Murdered, fell in a ditch, old-age. Either way, he's dead. That's why nobody's looking for him. They're nowhere near enough detectives in Philly, or any city for that matter, to keep looking for every single person that goes missing, especially when you know they're dead."

Penny was appalled. "Maybe he is, maybe he isn't, but the 'how' and the 'why' deserved to be answered. No?"

"Penny, you heard about the girl that went missing up the river in Burlington back in June?" Frank's eyes narrowed with the question.

"Yeah, still missing, that's a tragedy. Breaks my heart." Penny looked out the window, thinking for a moment about her two teenage boys back at home.

"She's fourteen, Penny! Margaret Ellen Fox is fourteen years old. She's a five-foot, two-inch, sweet little girl, and she disappeared right up the river in Jersey four months ago. Oh, and she's white." Frank was now displaying empathy as he, too, had two kids at home.

"I saw her picture posted on a telephone pole on the way here. She's sweet and cute, too, with red hair and freckles. All she was doing was trying to lock down a babysitting job, and poof, she's gone."

Penny focused once again on the case in front of them. "Okay, what does one have to do with the other?" Penny was confused by Frank's mentioning of the missing girl.

"This ain't the 'Boy in the Box,' this ain't Margaret Fox, Penny! People don't care about a dying ninety-five-year-old man that wandered off from an old folks home and disappeared. That was in the news for one day!" Frank clapped his hand down on the table. "Now, if a little white girl comes up missing, that's news! You don't get to abduct little girls without everybody and their brother out looking for them," Frank was adamant. "You're an old guy, and nobody gives a shit. Papers stop writing about it; police stop investigating it. It sucks, it ain't right, I don't agree with it, but that's the world we live in. Wrap your head around that, Detective."

"That's some bullshit, right there!" A look of realization paralyzed Penny's face. She now understood how it all worked. Old people don't matter as much as the young do. She reasoned, like everybody else, that old people had their day, lived a long life, and can no longer contribute to society. *"Who gives a shit about them?"* she thought. "It's all bullshit, all politics."

Frank looked pissed. He thought Penny was so hungry to solve a case that she grabbed the first one she picked up off the floor in a heap in the Unsolved Crimes closet the night before. "Now, are we done here?!" Frank was firm, looking Penny straight in the eye.

Frank looked over his left shoulder, motioned for the check to the girl behind the counter, and then looked back at Penny.

"Frank, there's something else." Penny took on a very serious look.

"Penny, that's enough! You want to work a case so bad that you're digging up old guys. We're done here!" Frank motioned again to the waitress.

Penny took a deep breath and revealed something that Frank or the others in the 39th didn't know. "Frank, he's not the only person to go missing from the Heavenly Gates retirement home."

At that moment, the waitress walked over and laid the check on the table. Frank looked up at her and said, "We'll need some more coffee over here."

"Alright, Penny, solve the mystery of why we're both here, right now."

Penny took a deep breath and began her story.

"Frank, my maiden name is Crenshaw. I was born in December 1934, a bad time for babies, what with the Great Depression and the Lindberg baby being kidnapped two years earlier. Anyway, by the time I was old enough to ask questions about my family history, the story was old news."

"What was old news?" asked Frank, wondering where Penny was going.

"Stay with me, Partner," Penny lifted her hand, telling Frank to be patient. "By the 1940s, no one really talked about it anymore, but it turns out that in 1920 my great-grandfather went missing from...."

Penny couldn't finish her sentence before Frank said, "No shit? Heavenly Gates?"

Penny nodded. "Frank, my great-grandfather's name was Samuel Crenshaw. He was a railroad magnate back in the mid-1800s. He even served in the Lincoln administration. He was super-rich, and get this, he actually owned Heavenly Gates before donating it to the City of Philadelphia in 1901. It used to be called FalconClaw."

"Your family-owned that monstrosity on the hill? You come from money? What in the hell are you doing making eight grand a year and living in North Philly?" Frank was shocked and dismayed. "And what in the hell does FalconClaw mean?"

"Not sure. Construction started in 1860 and finished in 1863. My great-grandfather lived there alone for several years after his wife died, and three sons grew up and moved away. After that, he donated it to the city and, as it turns out, kept living there after it was converted into a retirement home. The old man never left," revealed Penny. "Until somebody took him, that is."

"I can't believe your family owned that eyesore. That was some unimaginable wealth right there."

"Frank, stay focused. Joe and I are broke. The settlement from the lawsuit saved us from losing our house, but no one in my family has owned that place since 1901, and no one in my family has money; we're all working stiffs. Besides, that ain't the point." Penny tried to reel Frank in and have him focus on the real story.

"Sorry, I thought you were royalty or something," Frank smirked.

"Frank, listen, I read the entire file last night, and the story matches my great-grandfather's almost word for word."

"Okay, break it down for me, high-level stuff first," said Frank.

"Alright, my great-grandfather was ninety-four years old and went missing on December 7, Victor Rogers was ninety-five and went missing on December 23."

"I'll be damned!" Frank shook his head.

"That's not the half of it." Penny took a deep breath and then exhaled. "Listen to the next part. Both Rogers and my great-grandfather were last seen with an employee of Heavenly Gates, a custodian."

"This is all quite a coincidence," thought Frank out loud, racking his brain.

"It's too coincidental if you ask me." Penny wasn't finished with the case comparisons yet. "Frank, the last person to see each man alive was a male employee, eighty-three years of age...."

Franked mouthed the words, "eighty-three," while shaking his head.

"They disappeared in the early morning hours, in the snow, never to be seen again."

"Jesus Christ! What are the odds of that?" Frank said, "It's not possible they're connected though. They're forty-nine years apart. The odds of that happening is ZERO."

"Yeah, one would think." Penny didn't know what to make of it all, but her gut was talking to her. "Listen, Frank, I'm gonna need to talk to both Langhorne and Gaffney," she added.

Frank shook his head, "I'm afraid you're out of luck, Detective Bryce."

"Why's that?" Penny was caught off guard.

"Charles Gaffney died of a heart attack two years ago, and Spencer Langhorne had a stroke last fall. Care to guess which old folks home he's living at today?"

"Heavenly Gates?" Penny's eyes went wide. "This case just keeps getting stranger and stranger."

"Did you just say, case?" Frank looked astonished. "Penny, this isn't a case. There's nothing to investigate. Coincidences forty-nine years apart don't constitute opening up an investigation. Besides, McClain won't have any of it. If you want to investigate this, it will be on your own time. And if you've got that kinda time, I'd suggest you help those parents up in Burlington look for their daughter."

"There's more here than meets the eye." Penny shook her head, sure that they were somehow connected. "There must be!" she mumbled under her breath.

"Listen, I've been in plain clothes for a long time. In my professional opinion," Frank paused and shook his head, "there's no way they're connected."

"Well, I look forward to talking to Langhorne, And while I'm there, I plan on having a sit down with that custodian," Penny opened the file on the table, "Says here his name is Garrison Winter."

"Penny, this isn't the best way to win over McClain. You're just giving him another reason to doubt you. Chiefs of Detectives are like Grand Juries; they decide if the case should move forward based on merit and evidence. Hell, if I was McClain, I would think you're crazy for thinking the disappearances are somehow connected. Coincidence? Yes. Connected? No."

"Well, I've got two weeks before he gets back. Can you buy me some time tomorrow? I'll need half a day."

"Fine, only because I like you, though. But for the record, you're wrong about this one. Don't let the fact that a distant family member being involved cloud your judgment." Frank was starting to think that maybe Penny might lack some basic instincts of a good detective. "You need to look at this one professionally, not personally," he added.

"Thanks, Frank, you won't regret taking a chance on me. Something's amiss here, and I'm going to find out what it is. There's a connection. I know it!"

"Penny, this isn't a case, and it never will be. I'm humoring you because McClain's out of town, and you're my friend," said Frank. "You're green, and this will be a good lesson for you. Oh, and for the record, I know nothing about you going up there tomorrow. Your neck will be on the line, not mine."

Frank was always pragmatic. If his gut told him a lead shouldn't be followed, he didn't follow it. Instead, he'd have his junior partner chase the rabbit down the hole, in this case, Penny.

What Frank didn't tell Penny was that his gut was starting to talk to him. Something wasn't right. He felt it in his bones. Penny may have been influenced by the fact that it was family, but it wasn't personal for Frank, and his professional opinion was beginning to change.

Chapter 5 – Garrison Winter

On October 30, 1974, Detective Penny Bryce got out of a cab at 888 Bedford Street in the Germantown neighborhood of North Philadelphia. Standing in front of the wrought iron gates, she peered through them and laid her eyes on the hulking mansion on the hill. Penny felt strange when looking at it. She felt as if it was looking back at her. Looking down on her, in judgment, almost. As if she somehow wasn't supposed to be there, like she somehow didn't belong.

Standing directly in front of the driveway gate, Penny tugged and saw that it was locked and that it looked to have a motorized mechanism that somehow opened it remotely. *"Pretty sophisticated for such an old property,"* she thought. She was impressed, not sure of what, though. Was it the actual technology or the fact that her great-grandfather built the place?

Penny and Joseph Bryce barely made ends meet and lived in row-housing that started popping up at the turn of the century, primarily to house the expanding working population. North Philly, in particular, was known as a working man's town and one of the most important manufacturing centers in the world. The increased population, flowing in from all over Europe in the early 1900s, brought both unimaginable wealth and poor immigrants looking for work in Philadelphia's now booming city. But today, Penny and everything around her was anything but booming or wealthy. And Penny certainly considered herself working class.

As she again looked through the gates at the mansion on the hill, she was left with the thought that the one-time home of her great-grandfather, Samuel Crenshaw, was now nothing but a mere remnant of the Gilded Age. A time that saw rapid economic growth in the northeastern and western cities of the United States, and Samuel Crenshaw was a large part of that growth. As industry exploded in the North Philly area, railways were constructed to move the flow of products out of Philly to the rest of the rapidly growing U.S. population, and Crenshaw's railroad company built hundreds of miles of railway tracks crisscrossing in every direction in Philadelphia alone.

Samuel Crenshaw was a wealthy young man by the mid-1800s, wealth passed on for generations, as Crenshaw was a descendant of the original Crashaw family from Lancashire, in Northwest England.

Crenshaw's enormous wealth, however, came from his own hard work. Samuel Crenshaw owned a small railroad company that grew into one of the largest in the United States by 1860. His railroad would help transport Union troops during the civil war, giving the Union a distinct advantage over the less developed Confederate South. Abraham Lincoln added the then thirty-four-year-old Crenshaw to his cabinet, where he'd served as Transportation Secretary for a brief time in 1861 and 1862, thus exempting Crenshaw from wartime duty in the Union Army.

Penny looked left, then right, and saw two pedestrian gates flanking the main driveway gate. The driveway split into a fork just as it entered the property with traffic designed to flow right up the hill, cross in front of the home, and then circle back down the hill, enabling vehicles to enter and leave the property without ever having to turn around. The driveway also included a service drive that split at the top of the hill and went right, just before the main drive passed in front of the mansion, eventually winding around the northeast side of the property to the rear or west side of the estate.

Inside, or just south of the main gate, was a gatehouse, vacant today, but one that used to house servants and staff of the estate. The tiny house also served to welcome incoming guests, allowing them access through the gate and onto the main house at the top of the hill. Then, as they left the property, the gatekeeper would allow them to egress the gate upon departure.

Penny chose the left gate and, to her surprise, found that it was unlocked. She then noticed a small callbox attached to the gate that appeared to be out of order. Penny opened the receiver box anyway in an attempt to announce her unscheduled visit. When opening the creaky door, she saw that the phone receiver that once inhabited the call box was ripped out, likely years before, and replaced with leaves and cobwebs. Penny was almost offended, reminding herself that this was once her family's home. "Damn, kids!" she said aloud as she pushed the heavy, rust-covered gate open. The sight and sound of rust crackling and falling from the hinges told Penny that people no longer entered the estate through the pedestrian gates. Not in years, she'd suspected.

Letting herself through the gate, she rubbed the dirt from her left hand and wiped it on her gray overcoat. Once doing so, she'd immediately regretted it as it left a gray smudge on the left lapel of her favorite jacket, the one her husband, Joe, called, her 'Detective Jacket.'

She looked left inside the compound and saw no signs of activity in the Gate House but walked over and knocked on its door anyway. No one answered. She instead decided that she would walk up the sidewalk that led to the main house.

As Penny traversed the hill, she discovered that it was far steeper than it appeared from street level. Breathing heavily now, she realized that her forties were going to be far tougher on her body than her thirties were.

Standing in front of the steps leading to the main entrance, catching her breath, Penny was in awe. Anyone living in North Philadelphia had passed by Heavenly Gates at least once and saw it as an eyesore to the landscape, but for a fleeting moment, Penny was transported back to the *FalconClaw* of the 1800s.

In Penny's estimation, the flanking marble columns, two on each side, each stood some twenty feet tall and framed the massive double doors. An entrance built to welcome home a king, she thought. The German-crafted wood, glass, and steel doors sat just beneath a majestic arched window that would allow the morning sunlight in. Penny said, "Huh," as she turned to look over her left shoulder, squinting at the morning sun. She shrugged in acknowledgment of why the front of the house was situated to face slightly southeast. "Of course," she thought aloud, they needed the sun for lighting the inside of the house during the day. Penny found herself impressed by the 1860s German planners, or was it her great-grandfather's idea to position the house that way? She was starting to feel smart and proud of her heritage for the first time in her life.

Hesitating for a moment, Penny took a deep breath and mustered the courage to climb the six steps to ring the doorbell. After what seemed like several minutes, waiting for an answer, Penny had a fleeting thought that the place was empty, maybe even abandoned.

Before turning to walk down the steps to investigate the mansion's northeast side, Penny heard a crack of thunder as a strong wind gust blew up the hill behind her, causing her jacket's tail to hastily dance. Spooked for a moment, Penny reconsidered her reasons for being there and thought perhaps it might be best to leave. Just then, the left side of the double doors opened. When it did, an eerie sound rattled her psyche. There, standing before her, was a slight woman who'd stepped forward to greet her.

"Yes, hello," said a fifty-something-year-old woman, looking surprised by Penny's arrival. "Deliveries are to be taken to the rear of the house." The woman then peeked out, pinching her collar to protect her exposed neck from the morning chill and sudden gustiness of the wind. Leaves blew across the front lawn behind Penny making the sound of an angry ocean. The woman looked to both her left, then right, looking for the vehicle that the stranger pulled up in.

Penny looked down over her left shoulder as if acknowledging the woman's strange curiosity and then clutched her brand new detective badge and its black leather wallet with her left hand, ready to snatch it from the deep pocket of her gray, dirt-smudged jacket.

The woman looked back at Penny and said, "How did you get through the gate? Where is your vehicle?"

Penny said, "I walked through it."

"That gate remains locked at all times. You need to be buzzed in," said the woman, now standing broadly in the open door, as if to shield Penny from the secrets hiding inside.

"The pedestrian gate is unlocked. I promise you I did not jump the fence." Penny assured the woman.

"How can I help you?" The woman seemed a bit inconvenienced by Penny's presence.

The moment had finally arrived, the one Penny had waited for, for fourteen long years. Penny was about to pull her badge from her pocket and say the words that every young cop dreams of saying one day. She then matter-of-factly pulled her badge, flipped it open with one hand, and shoved it in the woman's face.

"Ma'am, I'm Detective Penelope Bryce with the Philadelphia Police Department, and I'm going to need to come inside."

"Oh, I see." With purpose, the woman wore a look that told Penny she was neither impressed by her shiny new badge nor her dirt-smudged jacket.

Penny looked down at the smudge and returned her badge to its home in the bottom of her now defaced favorite jacket.

"Well then, Officer, please do come in."

"Um, it's Detective, Ma'am," said Penny as she stepped through the door while trying to brush away the smudge on her jacket.

"Yes, of course, whatever you policemen, excuse me, policewomen, call yourselves these days." Standing just inside of the entrance's lavish foyer, the woman said, "So, why would the police send a detective to investigate vandalism? I wasn't aware of any drop in violent crimes in this city."

"Vandalism? Ma'am?" Penny was confused.

"Is this not about the graffiti and broken solarium windows on the building's southside?"

"No, Ma'am. This is about the 1969 disappearance of Victor Rogers."

The woman was caught off guard by Penny's statement, turning slightly, indicating to Penny that she was uncomfortable with the revelation and now seemed more timid and less forceful.

"Oh, I see," the woman now extended her hand to formally introduce herself. "My name is Bernice Gruber. I am the personal assistant to Dean Travers. Mr. Travers is the Executive Director of Heavenly Gates, as I'm sure you're aware."

"Thank you, Mrs. Gruber...."

"It's Miss Gruber," said the woman, offended by her guest. "Never married, thank you."

"My apologies, Miss Gruber," Penny tipped her head. "While I would very much like to speak to Mr. Travers...."

"He's not married either," offered Gruber.

Penny thought the woman's utterance was strange and out of place. "Yes, why, thank you for sharing that bit of information with me," Penny flashed an insincere smile. "What I was about to say was, I'm looking to speak to a Mr. Garrison Winter. Might he be working today?"

Gruber's eyes went narrow. "Now you listen, that old man has been through enough. Mr. Winter was questioned extensively and has nothing more to say to the police. He had nothing to do with the disappearance of Mr. Rogers. They were very close friends."

"Miss Gruber, I never said I believed that Mr. Winter had anything to do with the disappearance of Mr. Rogers," Penny paused. "You did, though." It was at that moment that Penny Bryce started to feel like a real detective.

"Oh, don't you dare twist my words, Detective." Gruber was defensive and her words coarse. "I know how you people treated that sweet old man back in early '70. We won't stand for it this time."

"No, I'm sure you won't, Miss Gruber. Now, if you'll please take me to Mr. Winter."

Detective Penny Bryce followed Gruber down a grand foyer that was as tall as it was long. Pillars ran down each side of the hallway, and the arched ceilings were crown-molded with hand-painted murals and frescos. The Victorian-styled colors and decorations were as abundant as they were bright. And the paisley-patterned wallpaper and marble statues contrasted the classic dark wood floor.

As the two made a left at the end of the twenty-five-foot-long hallway, they turned into the dining room, which had wallpaper with green silk woven into the lining. The room was forty-six feet wide and sixty feet long and had twenty-foot pillars, in clusters of four, running down the west side of the room, with a massive balcony overhanging the room's east side. The dining area had also served as the Grand Ballroom, with three massive chandeliers running down the center of the room. The arched crown molding made visitors and guests alike feel as if they were in an other-worldly place.

"This way, Detective," Gruber motioned. "Mr. Winter can almost always be found in the solarium this time of the morning. He's likely enjoying his toast and orange juice by now."

"Isn't he a custodian?" Penny was confused. "It sounds like you're describing a resident."

"Oh no," Gruber shunned the thought. "Mr. Winter is retired now. He's been a resident since the Spring of 1970."

"Just after the disappearance," mumbled Penny under her breath.

"I beg your pardon, Detective. Were you saying something?"

"Just admiring the décor. That's all." Penny shook off the question. "It's really beautiful in here."

"Yes, it is. You must feel quite out of place in a home like this," uttered Gruber.

"Excuse me?" Penny wasn't sure if Gruber was being condescending or not.

"Oh, no. I mean no offense." Gruber was mildly embarrassed. "It's just that there are very few homes in North America with such exquisite décor and lavish amenities. At the time of its construction, this home was a hundred years ahead of its time."

"Mrs. Gruber, I'm wondering if you know who the original owner was?"

"As I mentioned upon your arrival, it's Mizzz, not Mrs.," Gruber was again offended. She presumed that the detective misspoke on purpose. "And yes, I do know who the original owner was. Prior to being donated to the City of Philadelphia, it was the private home of a Stephen Crenshaw. I believe he was some sort of exporter of goods."

Penny sighed in judgment of the misinformed woman. "I'm surprised a woman of your considerable education and social standing would simply guess at the answer as opposed to just admitting you weren't sure." Penny enjoyed having the upper hand. It was something she rarely had at home and never had at work.

"I beg your pardon?" Gruber was appalled. "I can assure you...."

Penny launched back in, cutting off the pretentious woman. "MIZZ Gruber, before you butcher the facts again, please let me tell you who the real owner was. In 1860, Mr. Samuel Crenshaw of the Crashaw family of Lancashire, England, built and lived in the house with his wife Rebekah and their three sons until 1901. He wasn't in the business of exporting anything. Rather, he owned a railroad company." Penny found it hard not to tell Gruber that she was the great-granddaughter of Samuel Crenshaw.

Gruber stood aghast, rendered speechless.

"Perhaps if you're going to work here, you should be in possession of the facts as opposed to just pretending that you are." Penny again nodded her head, feigning respect for the arrogant woman standing before her.

Gruber and Penny continued into the solarium without further conversation. There, he found Mr. Garrison Winter sitting in his favorite chair, enjoying a backgammon game, and enjoying his morning orange juice.

"Here we are," Gruber tried to be cordial but found it hard. "Mr. Winter, you have a guest. I'll leave the two of you alone, then." Before turning to leave, she launched a wicked stare at Penny. She wanted nothing more to do with Detective Penny Bryce.

Winter rose to meet his visitor. He stood, looked her up and down, and was gregarious, "Good morning, Detective. What brings you here today?" Winter wore a smile that indicated to Penny that he rarely got visitors and was more than happy with her unannounced arrival.

Penny cocked her head while closing one eye and raising one hand to her chin. "Hmm. I don't believe Mrs. Gruber introduced me by name or profession, Mr. Winter. How did you know I was a detective?"

"I noticed that you called her Mrs. as opposed to Miss," the old man smiled. "I'm sure she introduced herself as Miss, and I'm equally sure that you didn't overlook that fact, being a detective and all."

"You're very perceptive, Mr. Winter."

"Why did you do that?"

"Because I don't like her very much. She comes off as uppity, and I don't like pretentious people, Mr. Winter."

"Please, call me Garrison, Detective. And yes, Miss Gruber can have that effect on people. She does mean well, though."

"Please have a seat." Winter motioned to the large sitting chair opposite his on the other side of the backgammon board. "Shall we play?"

Penny was gracious, "No, thank you, I don't know how to play that game. I'm not even sure I remember what it's called."

"Oh no!" Winter's face went from a look of eager anticipation to one of a downtrodden vagrant. "It's been so long since someone took up a game of backgammon with me...."

Penny snapped her fingers. "Yes, of course, backgammon."

"Yes, as I was saying. It's been years since any of the residents played with me. I have to sit here and play the game alone, and well, that's not very entertaining."

"So, again, Mr. Winter, how did you know I was a detective?"

"Again, please call me Garrison. Ah yes! As for your question. A couple of things gave it away, Detective. First, you don't live here, and I have no friends or family that visit. Second, the last people that visited me were two detectives back in 1970, and you're dressed very much like them. Except their jackets were old, and their slacks weren't pressed."

"Very good, Mr. Winter." Penny pursed her lips and nodded in acknowledgment of his keen observations.

"So, not only are you a detective, but you're a new detective. First day, I'm guessing?" Winter tilted his head and raised his brows. "What with the hard crease in those slacks and the fancy new detective jacket," Winter smiled. "I can't figure the dirt on the lapel, though. I'm sure it had to happen somewhere between here and home. Am I right?"

Before speaking, Penny's first impression of the old man was that he seemed charming, sweet, sincere, and far from a killer. But she also would not let a possible killer fool her like he likely had Victor Rogers.

"Mr. Wint..." Penny was cut off.

"Ah!" The old man held up his finger.

"Very well, Mr. Winter. So, Garrison," she paused, smiled, and nodded, seeking his approval.

Winter nodded back and smiled in approval.

"You said that it'd been a while since anyone would play backgammon with you. Is that correct?"

"Yes, several years, in fact."

"Who was that person who last played with you?"

Winter smiled. "Detective, you asked that question as if you already knew the answer."

"That would be tricky of me, wouldn't it, Garrison?" said Penny. "The fact is, though, I don't know the answer. I was just curious."

"Well, if you must know, it was my dear friend, Victor."

"Do you mean the late Victor Rogers?"

"Oh, dear." Winter's face went white. "Are you here to tell me that you found him?"

"No, I'm not Mr. Winter."

"You referred to him as the 'late' Victor Rogers," said Winter. "That sounded like the worst possible outcome. Why did you do that? Was that intentional, Detective?"

"Maybe, maybe not," Penny acted coy. "Call it a rookie mistake."

"Hmm, I see," said Garrison. "Perhaps your game is Chess, then, Detective?" Winter's smile ran away from his face.

"And why is that?" asked Penny.

"Because you've been playing it since you walked into the room."

Penny shook her head. "Nope, can't say I know the game very well. Always had trouble remembering which pieces go sideways and which pieces go diagonal. I only know that the King can move in any direction and only one space at a time." Penny was beginning to enjoy her conversation with the old man and even more playing the part of a real detective.

"Very good, Detective. You're well on your way to learning the game, it would seem. Now, enough with the shenanigans. Please tell me how I can help you?"

"I was wondering if you know the whereabouts of Victor Rogers?"

"I wish I could answer that question, Detective. But as you can see, he's not here, and I haven't left this place in years."

"That's not an answer, now is it, Mr. Winter? You either know where he is, or you don't."

"I can't really say." Winter was evasive.

"Can't or won't?" asked Penny.

"Can't, I'm afraid." Winter buttoned his lips.

Penny smiled. "On a hunch, was it Mr. Rogers who was the last to play backgammon with you just before he disappeared?"

"Yes, he was, I'm afraid. He came up missing just hours later." Winter released a wistful sigh. "I do miss him dearly. This place just isn't the same without him around, but I'm sure that wherever he is, he's enjoying himself immensely."

"What makes you say that?" Penny thought it was an interesting presumption by Winter.

"Just a feeling, that's all."

"Mr. Winter, did you have anything to do with the disappearance of your friend, Victor?"

"Detective, I answered all of these questions in the past. Perhaps you can read over the file of the late Detectives that interviewed me back in 1970."

Penny's eyes went tight, and her head cocked to the left. "Mr. Winter, you just said 'late detectives,' as in plural. It's my understanding that of the two Detectives that interviewed you back in late '69 and '70, that only one of them has passed on. Why would you suggest both are dead?"

"Oh, I'm sorry, Detective, but haven't you heard?"

"Heard what?" Penny looked both curious and concerned.

"Spencer Langhorne passed away just yesterday."

"What?! When?!" Penny was shocked. She had hoped to meet with him after speaking to Winter.

"Yes, it was yesterday morning, I'm afraid. So sad." Winter pursed his lips and shook his head. "He and I had become such good friends." He paused, "Well, I'm sure he's in a better place now."

Penny was again shocked. It was just yesterday that Frank told her that Langhorne lived at Heavenly Gates.

"Hmm," said Penny, trying to look less bothered than she actually was. "Thank you for your time, Mr. Winter. I hope you don't mind if I stop by again to speak with you."

Winter beamed. "Oh, I would enjoy that very much, Detective! And please, do bring your partner next time, won't you?"

Penny did a double-take. "My partner?"

"Yes, you detectives often travel in twos. Do you not?"

"Ah, yes, we do." Penny thought it was eerie that Winter seemed to know more about her than he was letting on. It was as if someone tipped him off to her visit.

"Detective, you know, I never did get your name."

"It's Detective Bryce. Have a good day, Mr. Winter." Penny nodded to the old man and then began to walk away.

"It was nice meeting you, Penelope!"

Just as Penny turned to leave, she was stopped dead in her tracks by the old man's comment. "Mr. Winter. I never told you my first name."

"Oh, didn't you?" Winter looked puzzled. "Perhaps Miss Gruber relayed that information to me." the old man shrugged.

"No, she didn't." Penny was confused and was now somewhat terrified by the man standing before her.

"Interesting, it may be that you look like a Penelope." Winter looked off and smiled. "Ah yes, I always loved that name. It reminds me of a lollipop. I bet your father called you Penny for short."

Penny didn't know what to make of Winter's comments. Turning again to leave, she abruptly stopped and turned and said, "Mr. Winter, how did you know that Detective Charles Gaffney passed away?" Penny did her best *Columbo turn*, trying to play 'gotcha' with the old man like Peter Falk did in the television detective show. She'd reasoned aloud that it couldn't have been retired Detective Langhorne, as he could no longer speak or communicate effectively after his stroke.

Winter stood with his hands in his pockets and said, "No, he couldn't talk Detective Bryce, but he communicated with me just fine. If you must know, I learned of his passing by reading about it in the newspaper. Reading the obituaries has always been a hobby of mine. It was back in '72, I believe."

Penny thought that was odd. "That seems like an awfully strange hobby, Mr. Winter."

"Oh, not at all, Detective. I take great pleasure in learning of the good that people have done in their lives before moving on to Heaven."

"Yes, well, very good," Penny nodded. "Thank you again for your time, Mr. Winter. I'll see you very soon." Penny turned and walked away but was again stopped by the old man.

"So, I was right, wasn't I? Your family did call you Penny?" Winter yelled out.

Penny stopped, turned, smiled, and then continued walking without answering Winter's question.

As she walked away, she could hear the old man say, "Such a shiny penny, aren't you?" His words sent a shiver down her spine.

Chapter 6 – God's Glory

Later that day, on October 30, the teletype machine came to life inside the 39th District and began spitting out more work for Frank Bruno and the skeleton crew of detectives. While Penny hadn't arrived yet, and with the other four detectives out on calls, Frank was slow to respond to the incoming query, not feeling motivated to do much of anything.

Frank was wrestling with life outside of work, his personal life was in turmoil, and the cracks in his grizzled exterior were starting to show. Others had noticed a change but said nothing to the rock-solid detective who never wore his heart on his sleeve. Frank Bruno would never tell anyone at work that something outside of the office was bothering him. Let alone the fact that Jeanie left him and the girls a little more than two months earlier.

At 12:06 pm, Penny walked through the second-floor detective office door and looked like she was about to burst. She felt that what she had to share with Frank needed to be done face to face, so she didn't call him after leaving Heavenly Gates earlier that morning.

"Better late than never!" Frank was moody toward Penny for the second day in a row.

Penny ignored his attitude. "Frank, listen, we need to talk, but not here."

"Penny, everyone's out on calls. Nobody's here. It's just us."

"I've got news, and it's not good."

"Spit it out already!" Frank was in no mood for theatrics.

"Spencer Langhorne is dead!" Penny's eyes were the size of headlights and just as bright.

"You mean Charles Gaffney? I told you that yesterday."

"Frank, Spencer Langhorne is dead too!"

"When? When did he die?"

"Right around the time we were at breakfast yesterday!" Penny seemed suspicious. "Now, what are the chances of that?"

"How do you know?"

"You're not gonna believe who told me."

"Penny, just spit it out already."

Penny paused for a second, looked around the room, making sure that no one was within earshot, and said, "Garrison Winter told me."

"Winter? Well, that's a hell of a coincidence," Frank shook his head, not knowing what to make of the revelation.

"Frank, do you realize that for a veteran detective, you use the term 'coincidence' a lot?"

Frank, pragmatic as always, wanted to ensure that his 'eager to solve a murder' partner stayed grounded and didn't jump to the conclusion that everyone was a murderer.

"Penny, Langhorne just suffered a stroke last October. His time of death is peculiar but not the actual fact that he died. He was in bad shape. He couldn't even talk, last I'd heard."

"Frank, gimme a break! You know that this is all too strange to be a coincidence." Penny knew Frank better than that. She also knew that her gut was screaming foul play. "Twenty-four hours before I interview the only suspect in the case and the last living detective to investigate him, Langhorne dies? In the same house where the suspect lives?" Penny shook her head. "Come on! You're not going to tell me that this doesn't stink."

"Alright, fine! It stinks. It all stinks! But don't be chasing rabbits again! They live in holes, and you don't want the Chief to get back and see that you're mired in there with them."

"You mean 'we'!" Penny smiled.

"Here we go!" Frank rolled his eyes, leaned back in his chair, locked his fingers behind his head and exhaled, then put his feet up on his desk. He knew that Penny was right. The whole thing stunk, and Frank's gut was talking to him.

Just then, the phone started to ring. Frank motioned to Penny that he'd get it.

Frank unlocked his fingers, leaned forward, and picked up the phone. "Thirty-ninth District, Detective Bruno speaking."

"Detective Bruno, this is Detective Kenzo Kowalczyk from the Pittsburgh P.D. I was wondering if you got the teletype I sent over a little while ago?"

Frank raised his eyebrows as his feet fell to the floor. "No, but I did hear something come through earlier, though. Let me check the box. I'm gonna put you on hold for a minute."

"What's all that about?" asked Penny.

Frank shrugged and shot Penny a quizzical look as he walked across the tiny office and reached into the wooden box positioned just beneath the teletype machine.

The 39th District was the only police district in North Philly with a teletype machine. It was one of only three in the entire Philly P.D. It was cost-prohibitive for every district house to have one. It was still new, and Frank and the others were still trying to figure out how to send a telefax, though they'd received several each day.

Frank pulled the roll of perforated paper from the box, tore it from the machine's bottom, and turned back toward his desk.

"I got something here. It looks like it's from you guys. So, how can I help you, Detective?" asked Frank, who'd rather just hear it from the caller as opposed to reading the message.

"Yeah, well, Frank, listen, we're working on a missing person case from '65, and we've had a break in the investigation."

"Okay, so how does that involve the Philly P.D.?"

"Well, one of my guys used to work in your department and remembered a case from a few years ago that sounded a lot like ours."

Frank listened as he began to peruse the details on the teletype. He saw the headline, 'Retirement Home – Missing Person,' and his jaw dropped. His eyes motioned to Penny to come closer.

"Detective Kowalczyk, give me a second, I've got my partner here, and I want her to hear what you have to say, so I'm going to put you on the duo-phone." Frank looked serious, covered the phone, and whispered to Penny, "You're not gonna believe this!"

"Detective, you still there?" asked Frank.

"Yeah, Frank, I'm still here. Hey, call me Ken," came a voice from the speaker.

"Go ahead then, Ken," said Frank as Penny leaned in.

"Okay, so, back in 1965, we had an elderly woman go missing from a place called *God's Glory nursing home*. More of a retirement community for rich Jewish people. The place is just north of city center here in Pittsburgh, in a suburb called Oakmont."

Penny's eyes went wide again.

"Okay, so again, how does this involve Philly?"

"Well, our guy Pete over here used to be a uniformed officer for you guys back in the day, and he said he remembered a similar case from '69. Does any of that ring a bell to you?" asked Kowalczyk.

Frank played dumb, not wanting to over-react to the call's nature or timing, but his face couldn't hide it from Penny.

"Yeah, I think we got a case like that in our Unsolved Crimes closet."

"That's great! It's on our radar again because we recently got a call from detectives in Bloomington, Indiana, about a case of another elderly woman who went missing from a retirement home back in 1957. Thought it was all a little strange, to be honest with you. I mean, what are the chances three old people vanish into thin air across three states in twelve years?" asked Kowalczyk.

Frank wanted to make sure he was prepared for what the call might bring next, so he chose to cut it short, making sure he'd had all the facts. "Listen, Ken. Let me pull the file from storage, and I'll call you back later today."

"That'd be fine. Make sure you call back, though. This all sounds a little too connected for us over here. My direct line is area code 412, then 555-1212. I look forward to your callback, Frank."

"Will do, Ken," said Frank, staring at Penny with a look of shock on his face.

"Oh, and Frank," Kowalczyk yelled into the phone, hoping to get in one last question before Frank hung up.

"Yeah, Ken. Go ahead."

"Listen, you wouldn't be the Frank Bruno that came up with the term 'Cold Case,' would you?"

"I'm afraid that's me," Frank was humble in his response.

"Well then, you and I have met before."

"Oh really, where was that?" Frank's eyes flashed skepticism.

"It was last year, the FBI seminar in Harrisburg. Many cities have started calling their unsolved cases 'Cold Cases,' thanks to you."

"Wow! I didn't think something like that would have caught on."

"Okay, buddy, give us a call back after you look through the files over there."

"You got it, Ken. Talk to you later."

Frank hung up and said, "Can you believe the timing of all of this shit. What in the hell is happening?"

"I told you, Frank!" Penny was giddy. "This is bigger than we think."

"Okay, but before we dig out the file, you need to tell me everything about your visit with this Garrison Winter fellow."

Penny pulled the file from her bag; it was a small one, then set it on her desk.

"Okay, Frank, but first, I need to ask you something." Penny paused, "You need be honest with me, though."

"Of course, what is it?"

"Did you tip off anyone over at Heavenly Gates to the fact that I was going there today?"

Frank was astonished Penny would think that. "Of course not. Why in the hell would I do that?"

"I don't know," Penny shook her head and wore an uneasy look on her face. "It just felt like that old man was tipped off. Like he knew I was coming or something. It was strange."

"What was strange? Lay it all out for me," Frank prodded his rookie partner.

"Well, first of all, that place is creepy," Penny exhaled. "It appears that our suspect, Garrison Winter, is no longer the custodian there...."

Frank jumped in, "I thought you said you spoke to him?"

"I did, apparently now he's a resident there. It seems he's retired."

"How can a former custodian afford to stay there? That doesn't make any sense." Frank was perplexed, looking off into the distance with a confused stare. "Penny, write this down. We need to look into his finances."

Penny scrambled for a piece of paper.

"So, go on," encouraged Frank, anxious to learn more.

"Well, not only is he a resident there, but it seems that he's very well-liked."

"How so?" asked Frank.

"The woman who answered the door, a woman by the name of Gruber, came right to his defense the minute I told her why I was there."

"How's that?" Frank was curious.

"She went on and on about how Gaffney and Langhorne mistreated him back in the day."

"And what is her role there at Heavenly Gates?"

Penny referenced her notes. "Some kind of assistant to the director of the place, a guy named Dean Travers. I think the Gruber woman is interested in the guy."

Frank wore a curious smile and asked, "And why's that?"

"She went on about the fact that she's never been married and then randomly told me that he too was unmarried."

"Maybe they're sleeping together, and she was just trying to get out in front of it in case we find out later, or because a cute detective was encroaching on her territory?" Frank was thinking ahead and also busting Penny's chops.

"Ha-ha! Yeah, maybe. But she's not much to look at." Penny shook her head at the notion.

"Well, maybe he's not either," offered Frank, still smiling. "Okay, tell me about the old guy."

"Let me tell you something, that guy is smooth," Penny conceded. "He had a way with words. Charming, in a way."

"I hope he couldn't see that you were impressed with him?" Frank hoped that Penny hadn't revealed her perceptions to the potential killer.

"No, I did my best 'Frank Bruno' and played it cool."

"Good job, Detective," Frank displayed his approval. "So, what questions did you ask him, and how did he react to each?"

"Well, first of all, he tried to make friends with me. He kept asking me to call him by his first name, and get this," Penny looked around again, as if paranoid. "He guessed my name."

"What do you mean he guessed your name?" Frank was perplexed.

"I'm not bullshitting here. That old man guessed that my name was Penelope!"

"No way! Penelope isn't exactly a common name," Frank didn't buy it.

"Frank, that's why I asked you if you'd tipped them off that I was coming."

"That's odd. Maybe the old bastard is clairvoyant or something."

"What's clairvoyant mean?" Penny looked puzzled.

Frank shook his head, blowing off her question. "So, did you?"

"Did I what?"

"Call him by his first name?"

"Yes, eventually. I was trying to win him over. I wanted to make him feel comfortable."

"Did it work?" asked Frank. "Or was he bothered by your visit?"

"That's just it," said Penny as she looked around again, making sure no one could hear her. "He seemed too relaxed. Like he knew me or wanted to get to know me. That was part of the strangeness of the whole visit with him," Penny recounted the meeting from earlier that day. "He knew I was a detective, too."

"First of all, why do you keep looking around? There's no one here but us." Frank shook his head, laughing at his rookie partner. "This guy's clearly got you freaked out. So, how did he know you were a detective?" Frank was more serious now and curious too.

"Said it was the way I was dressed. He even suggested it was my first day on the job."

"Damn, he was close!" Frank's face revealed that he was impressed with the old man. "I see now why you thought I told them you were coming."

"That's just one of the reasons."

"So continue. What questions did you ask him?"

"I mentioned Victor Rogers, and he seemed curious if we had found him. Almost looking surprised by the notion that we might've," offered Penny. "He described Victor Rogers as a 'dear' friend. The

Gruber woman backed that up earlier by suggesting that the two were indeed close."

"And what else?"

"He refused to answer whether he knew the whereabouts of Rogers or not. He just referred me back to the case notes of Gaffney and Langhorne. I asked him if he wouldn't or couldn't tell me where he was, and he said he 'couldn't.' I found that to be odd."

"How so?" asked Frank.

"Well, it was as if he knew where he was but couldn't tell me."

"Well, that's interesting. Remind me to ask him that same question when we meet with him," said Frank.

"So, you're going to interview him, then?" Penny looked excited.

"Penny, we've got three elderly people missing between here and Indiana in the last seventeen years. This cold case," Frank winked, "is coming out of the closet."

"It's not much of a file, though," Penny looked at the manila folder on her desk. "More like an envelope."

Frank looked stunned, "So, that's the whole thing?"

"Yep!" Penny raised her brows and shook her head.

"Well, we've got to talk to this guy soon," said Frank.

"How soon?" asked Penny, who was itching to get back to Heavenly Gates and see how Frank Bruno interviewed a suspect.

"Tomorrow morning. We need to get this investigation going full speed before McClain gets back and shuts it all down."

Penny signaled with a nod and a smile that she was all in.

"First, we call back the Pittsburgh boys."

Minutes later, Frank called Ken Kowalczyk as Penny sat within earshot of the duo-phone. The two exchanged pleasantries for a minute before Frank gave Kowalczyk the case particulars. He informed the boys from Pittsburgh that the main suspect from '69 was an eighty-three-year-old custodian and that he was still alive and still employed by the retirement home.

"Frank, this is crazy, our case also involved a custodian, but we've lost track of him since," said Kowalczyk. "Disappeared into thin air, just like our victim, Polly Anne Steinman. Our guy's name is Duncan, Gabriel Duncan."

"Steinman?" Frank shook his head. "That name doesn't ring any bells. What's the middle name of your suspect, by the way? We'll run a check on our end before we talk again," said Frank.

"Olen."

"Olen, huh? Spell that for me, Ken."

"O-L-E-N."

"Got it! Okay, we'll run a check. I'll have my buddies in Camden and Scranton run a check too. If your suspect came east, we might get a hit on his name."

"That'd be great. Thanks, Frank!"

"Listen, Ken. We're gonna interview this guy tomorrow, and depending on what he has to say, we should all meet up to discuss each other's case."

"Where're you thinkin?" asked Ken. "Cuz we damn sure ain't driving all the way to Philadelphia," he chuckled.

"How about we meet in Harrisburg?" said Frank.

"That's a hike for us, Frank. How about Johnstown or Altoona?" suggested Kowalczyk.

"That's a hike for us too," said Frank.

Kowalczyk hesitated before saying, "Whatta you say we all meet up in Lewistown? That's about halfway for both of us. I was born there."

"No shit!" Frank's excitement could be heard through the phone. "I'm from Port Royal, originally."

"That's south, right? Near Mifflintown?" Kowalczyk was stunned.

"Yeah, it's right there!"

"What are the chances?" blurted Kowalczyk. "Small world, Brother!"

"That is kinda crazy!" Frank was just as surprised. "We used to go to the McCoy House Museum for school field trips when we were in grade school."

"Us too!" Ken laughed.

"Okay, I'll talk to my Chief and work out the particulars. How's your calendar looking in November?" asked Kowalczyk.

"Listen, it's got to be by the end of next week, no later than the seventh or eighth. My Chief gets back the following Monday, and he won't approve the expense. I'd rather beg for forgiveness later than ask for permission now if you know what I mean?" Frank knew McClain would never approve of the day trip.

"Never heard that one before, 'beg for forgiveness later, ask permission now,' but yeah, same here," said Ken. "Our petty cash is all but gone. But when our boss hears that we've got three cold cases going on, he just might warm up to the idea." Kowalczyk laughed at his play on words.

"Ha! I see what you did there!" Frank chuckled. "Our Chief's a hard ass. We'll see what we come up with next week." Frank wasn't too optimistic.

"Frank, let's shoot for Wednesday the sixth."

"November 6, that sounds good. I'll call you tomorrow to confirm after we talk to our guy over here in Philly."

"Will do, Frank! I look forward to meeting you again," laughed Ken.

After the call, Frank and Penny combed through what little information they had and formulated questions to ask Garrison Winter the next day. They planned to show up unannounced again, as they didn't want their suspect to prepare for their visit. Frank always liked to catch his suspects off guard so their answers would be more natural and their lies more evident.

The next morning was Halloween, and Frank got to Heavenly Gates before Penny and decided to wait outside the gate until she arrived. The two agreed to meet at 10 am, and it was now 10:06. After several more minutes and no Penny, Frank got curious and pushed his way through the iron gate to kill time. Once inside, he walked the twenty feet or so over to what appeared to be a welcome center or gatekeeper's house. Frank determined that some staff likely lived there back in the day as it was far too big to serve simply as a gatehouse. The Tudor-styled house's exterior was stone and brick with a small porch with wooden pillars holding it up. Above it, a small window centered on a gable-styled roof with chimneys flanking the tiny house's center. The slanted rooftops indicated to Frank that the second-floor rooms would be small with slanted ceilings.

As Frank sniffed around, trying to look through dirty windows, he heard the wrought iron gate behind him being pushed open and turned to see his partner.

"I see you found the gatehouse," said Penny, breathing heavily after pushing through the hefty gate. This time though, she was sure not to wipe her dirty hands on her new jacket.

"It's kind of quaint," responded Frank. "It makes you wonder what it was like when all of this was shiny new. Without all this traffic flying by. I kinda like it." Frank felt nostalgic about the place.

"Yeah?! Well, wait until you see the inside!" Penny shivered. "This whole place freaks me out," she rebutted. "Can you imagine what this place must be like at night?"

"Yes, I can. I drive by it every night on the way home. Again, I think it's kind of neat. With that said, however, if we determine that a mass murderer lives here, then I reserve the right to modify that statement."

"It's creepy in there, Frank!" said an apprehensive Penny. "The only reason I had the nerve to go inside is that my family once owned it."

"Did it feel like home when you went in?" Frank joked.

"No, it didn't," said Penny. "I can only imagine how many people have died in there with it being an old folks home for so many years." Penny was already out of breath as she and Frank began the climb up the sizable sidewalk running up the front lawn from the gatehouse to the house's main entrance.

"You okay there, Penny? Breathing a little heavy, aren't you?" Frank smiled, making fun of his partner.

"I'm not the spring chicken that I used to be, I'm afraid," Penny sighed.

"It is a little bit of a climb, though," Frank conceded.

"Listen, Frank. I don't want the guys back at the office, especially McClain, to know my family is tied to this place. I don't want the Chief to have one single reason to pull me off of this case."

"Your secret is safe with me," said Frank, pretending to button his lips and throw away the key while breathing a little heavy himself.

At the top of the hill, the two stood just feet away from the steps leading to the massive double doors. Penny looked at Frank and said, "You ready, Frankie Boy?" She smiled and added, "You look a little winded there, Partner."

"Ha-ha, wise guy," Frank took a deep breath and exhaled. "That was steeper than it looked."

"And long too. From the road, the size of the house dwarfs the hill in front of it."

"This place is huge once you're right up on it," thought Frank out loud as he looked up and surveyed the levels of the house.

The two proceeded to the door and rang the bell. Two minutes later, Frank looked at his watch and said, "Is there another way in?"

Penny replied, "It's a big house, give them another minute to get all the way up to the front door. It took a minute yesterday too."

Just then, the door handle released, and the huge, hand-crafted door opened halfway. In the doorway stood an irritated Bernice Gruber.

"Oh, it's you again," she said. "And I see that you've brought a friend back with you. Great!" Gruber looked Frank up and down, rolled her eyes, and stepped back into the foyer, then pulled the door open wide. The two detectives thought she seemed reluctant to welcome them back into the mansion.

As Frank stepped in, he said, "You must be Mizz Gruber. It's a pleasure to meet you." Frank poured on the charm and accentuated the title, Miss.

"My name is Frank Bruno, and I'm with the Philadelphia Police Department. My partner here," Frank motioned to Penny, "told me that you were kind enough to allow her access to this incredible home. Thank you again for welcoming us back." Frank held on to Gruber's hand an extra couple of seconds.

"Oh, not at all," smiled Gruber, tilting her head slightly while looking down to see her tiny hand buried into Frank's oversized Italian hand.

"Mizz Gruber, did you get word that we would be stopping by today to pay a visit? I called last evening and got someone who said they would relay the message to you and Director Travers. I hope the person I spoke to relayed that message to you. The last thing I would want to do is show up unannounced." Frank lied effortlessly as Penny rolled her eyes.

"Yes, it would be rude to show up unannounced. Very impolite." Gruber turned and glared at Penny. Looking back at Frank, she said, "Oh, I'm sure it was likely an intern who took the call," blushed Gruber. "You know, young girls," Gruber shook her head, "they're so unreliable."

"I agree, never send a girl to do a woman's job. That's what I always say." Frank laid it on thick.

"I couldn't agree more, Mr. Bruno. I'm sure your wife appreciates being married to such a wise man," Gruber was submissive, tilting her head again.

"Oh no, I'm sorry to say that I am not married. Never had the time, but I'm not as young as I used to be, and my mother keeps telling me that I need to find a good woman." Frank was as smooth as silk.

Penny just sat back and watched Frank do his thing. She couldn't help but be impressed.

"Oh my, not sure how no one's scooped you up yet?" Bernice Gruber was now openly flirting, unable to help herself. She looked Frank up and down again, this time looking more impressed.

"I could say the same about you, Bernice." Frank caught himself. "Oh, I'm sorry, may I call you Bernice?"

"Only if I can call you Frank or Detective Frank?"

"I would like that very much, Bernice."

Gruber blushed.

Penny finally chimed in, looking like she was ready to heave. "Detective Frank," she said with a sardonic smile. "I do believe we've got a busy day today. Mizz Gruber, might we see Mr. Garrison Winter please?"

Bernice Gruber rolled her eyes in disgust.

"I'm sorry, Bernice, my partner, can sometimes be a little impatient. But might we see Mr. Winter now?"

Penny mouthed the words, "My partner...blah-blah-blah."

"Of course, Frank. Please, follow me," said Gruber.

"Oh, and Bernice, might we borrow a few minutes of Director Travers' time after we're done speaking with Mr. Winter?"

"I'm sure I can make that happen for you, Frank."

Penny was getting close to slugging Bernice Gruber if she didn't stop batting her eyelids.

Moments later, Gruber stopped just short of the solarium entrance and motioned for the two detectives to walk in and see Garrison Winter, who was sitting at the backgammon table massaging the dice in his hands.

"Nice to meet you, Detective Frank!"

"Likewise, Bernice. I look forward to our next encounter." Frank shook Gruber's hand and made sure that his hand once again enveloped hers.

Frank motioned for Penny to lead the way.

Penny stepped forward, and the two walked up just behind and over the left shoulder of Winter. Garrison Winter heard the two approaching, turned, and smiled.

As he stood, he looked at Penny and Frank and said, "What in all of God's Glory brings the two of you here today?" His smile terrified the two detectives.

Before responding, Frank looked at Penny to find her already staring back at him. Their mouths draped open, both shocked with the 'God's Glory' comment uttered by Old Man Winter.

Frank knew that he and Penny were about to square off in a good versus evil showdown. He only hoped that the evil standing before him and Penny wasn't the Devil himself. For whatever reason, Frank thought of Jeanie in that moment. Was he about to confront the very evil that his lack of faith in God had welcomed?

Chapter 7 – Diagnosis

Spring of 1974 – Atlantic City, New Jersey.

"Honey, you okay?"

"Yeah, Frankie, I'm fine. Just a little tired from walking." Jeanie felt worse than she let on to Frank and the girls. For the last year, she had felt run down and always seem to be tired. Frank had barely noticed due to his long workdays and busy schedule. Many days he left before she awoke and got home after everyone was already in bed.

Frank, Jeanie, Jessica, and Madeline were on vacation during the Easter break. It was tax day, but Frank didn't let the family's financial woes get in the way of celebrating the holiday with his wife and kids. Maddie had just turned seven the week before, and Jessica was nine and a half. Jeanie stayed under the umbrella while Frank splashed water on the kids. The Atlantic ocean was pretty cold that day, so Frank and the kids only waded into waist-high water.

As a wave came in, the three were lifted by it, and when their feet settled back down into the sand beneath the water, Maddie screamed that something bit her.

"Daddy, a shark bit my foot!" Maddie sobbed.

Jessica heard 'shark,' along with some other nearby swimmers, and made her way back to the safety of Mom's towel.

Frank rushed to rescue his youngest of two girls and swiftly pulled her from the water. "Shhhh! Maddie, don't yell shark. You're gonna scare the other people in the water, Honey."

"But Daddy! It bit my foot!" Maddie continued to cry, more frightened than she was hurt.

Frank raised Maddie's feet above the water level to do a cursory inventory of her ten toes and said, "Look, Maddie, they're all still there. All ten of those little boogers. That big bad shark didn't even get a pinky toe!" Frank smiled, trying to calm his baby girl.

After Frank and Maddie got back to the towels, Jeanie said, "Oh no, what happened, Maddie Girl?"

Maddie cried, "Mommy, a shark bit my whole foot off!"

"She's okay," said Frank. "She stepped on a broken shell, that's all."

"Daddy, it was a shark!" Maddie punched her father's arm. "Don't lie to Mommy!"

Jeanie inspected Maddie's foot and said, "She does have a little cut. We should get back to the motel and clean it up."

"Sure, Jeanie, whatever you want." Frank could tell Jeanie was looking for an excuse to leave. He knew she never liked going to the beach. But he'd also noticed that she'd seemed worn out by the short walk from the motel to the boardwalk.

Jeanie was happy to get off the dirty beach, which was littered with thousands of broken shells. Atlantic City was never her favorite place to take the kids. She thought that it was dirty, crowded, and smelled like dead fish. She just wanted to be home.

Once back at the motel, the kids watched the *Little Rascals* on T.V. while Frank and Jeanie rinsed off together in the shower.

"Honey, what's going on? You're not yourself lately." Frank was concerned for the well-being of his 'best girl.'

The shower water helped to conceal Jeanie's tears. "I don't know what's wrong, Frankie. I think I'm sick. I'm scared." Jeanie clung to her husband.

"Are you pregnant?" Frank thought that having another child would be hard on the family's finances but celebrated the thought of having another girl for a brief moment.

"No, Frankie, that's not it. Look at me. I'm losing weight, not gaining." She was frustrated with her husband and the fact that he'd been oblivious to her deteriorating health. "Something's wrong, and I think I need to see a doctor."

"Sure, Jeanie! Whatever you need." Frank's face was riddled with concern.

Jeanie tried her best not to break down. She didn't want to upset her Frankie. She loved the man, and her tears were part pain, part fear. She couldn't bear the thought of leaving the girls and her Frankie alone in the world, but she knew in her heart that she was sick and wasn't going to get better.

A day later, Frank got Judy, Jeanie's sister, to watch the girls, and took Jeanie to the doctor. After only five minutes in the care of Dr. Francis Ford, Frank was approached by Ford in the waiting room.

"Frank, Jeanie's pretty upset back there, and she's afraid to give me honest answers. I'm going to ask you some questions, and I need you to be honest with me." Ford pulled Frank to the side, away from the others in the waiting room.

"Of course, Doc," Frank nodded with a concerned but hopeful look in his eyes. "Is she pregnant, Doc?"

"No, Frank, Jeanie's not pregnant." The look in Dr. Ford's eyes told Frank that it was something far more serious.

"Frank, has Jeanie experienced any of the following: Back pain? Tired all the time? Upset stomach? Has she been disinterested in eating? Excessive bleeding during her menstrual cycles?"

Frank nodded yes to each of Ford's questions. Frank began to tremble. "Doc, what is it? Give it to me straight. Is Jeanie going to be okay?"

Frank was now beginning to understand that the family life he'd had before Atlantic City was about to change in the worst possible way.

"Frank, I don't want to alarm you or Jeanie, but I think you need to take her to the hospital to get some tests run." Ford paused, "I mean, you need to take her right this second." Ford looked Frank directly in the eyes and was dead serious.

"Doc, what in the hell's going on?" Frank looked haggard at that moment.

"Frank, you and Jeanie are Catholic, right?"

"Yeah, Doc. I, I, I don't go to church much anymore because of work," Frank stuttered his excuse. "But, yes, I'm a catholic." Frank paused, fear now engulfing his eyes. "Doc Francis, what's going on? Is Jeanie going to be alright?"

"Frank, listen, I need you to start praying, Son. I'll meet you at Nazareth Catholic Hospital in one hour. You don't wait for me, though. You get there now. I'll meet up with you there in a little while. I'll call ahead. They'll be expecting you." Ford clutched Frank's left shoulder.

"Sure, Doc!" Frank's heart was racing. "Doc, she's gonna be alright, right?"

"Frankie, tonight before you go to sleep, you hit your knees. And tomorrow, when you wake up, you do it again," said Francis Ford, the doctor who'd delivered both of their baby girls and the same doctor who treated Jeanie for infertility issues just twelve years prior. "Pray, Frank. Pray, Son. And I will too."

Frank and Jeanie met in the summer of 1960. Frank was moonlighting, doing night-time security at a local bar where Jeanie was waitressing. It was love at first sight for both. Frank was thirty-four, and Jeanie was just twenty-four. Frank had just gotten a big pay-raise, and his life, both professionally and personally, was about to change.

Frank had never been married and had no children but was ready for both. Frank was a late bloomer and never had a serious relationship before meeting Jeanie. When he proposed to her just two months after they'd met, everyone thought he was moving way too fast, even Jeanie.

Jeanie's life wasn't easy. At the age of twelve years old, she'd lost her father to lung cancer. He was only forty-five. Then, at the age of eighteen, she lost her mother, who was just forty-two, to breast cancer. Jeanie was an only child trying to make it in the unforgiving North Philly area, where there was no real middle-class. Either you flourished, or you struggled, and no one Jeanie had ever known did well in life. She was a product of her neighborhood and rarely ventured out of it. Frank was her chance at a normal life. Healthcare benefits, a decent apartment, and a man who'd adored her.

Both wanted to have children immediately, but their desire was stymied by Jeanie's infertility issues, the same issues that had plagued her mother. Jeanie and Frank tried every possible method, including a new drug that was still in clinical trials called Clomid. The medical science of treating infertility issues didn't make any real breakthroughs until the mid-1970s, and in the early sixties, there were only fringe research groups and loose-knit societies studying the science.

Clomid, a drug that stimulates ovulation, was hard to come by, so Jeanie and Frank traveled up to Paramus, New Jersey. There, a doctor named Francis Ford was one of the few in the Northeastern United States to prescribe the drug to his patients. Jeanie was the first woman he'd treated that became pregnant after using the drug. Ford eventually relocated his practice to the Philadelphia area just two years later.

At the hospital, Frank and Jeanie were impatient as they waited in the Emergency Room seating area. The area was small and cramped, filled with sick or injured people and their family members. Jeanie occupied the last chair, so Frank had to squat in front of her, holding her hands as they rested uncomfortably on her lap. The sound of a baby screaming added to Jeanie's heartache. The two were a wreck, with Frank hiding his fear from Jeanie as best he could. He feared the worst and knew very well that Jeanie had lost both of her parents to cancer. Frank had always been her rock, and she counted on him, but he was close to losing it as Jeanie's hands trembled violently in his.

"It's okay, Jeanie." Frank consoled his wife. "Doc Francis will be here soon. They're just gonna take some tests."

"Frankie, I'm scared. I never had to die before," Jeanie sobbed.

"Jeanie, you ain't dying. I won't let that happen." Frank was starting to come apart. "I need you. The kids need you. Our life is great. Ain't nothin' going to happen to you. I promise."

"Janine Bruno!" the ER Nurse yelled over the noise across the packed ER waiting area.

"C'mon, Jeanie. That's us, Honey," said Frank. "They're going to make you all better." Frank held Jeanie's hand as they walked to the door where the nurse stood with a clipboard in her hand.

"I'm sorry, sir, but you can't come back here."

"But I'm her husband."

"That's fine, but only patients are allowed beyond this point." The nurse positioned herself between Frank and Jeanie, who was now crying uncontrollably.

"Frankie! Don't let them take me, Frankie!" she cried.

"Nurse, I'm a detective with the Philadelphia Police Department!" Frank stepped forward a half step, flashed his badge, and gave her a look that told her to get out of his way.

After a moment, the nurse finally relented and escorted Frank and Jeanie to an area with several beds, separated only by white curtains.

An hour after blood was drawn and x-rays were taken, Dr. Ford finally arrived. He pulled back the curtain and startled Frank and Jeanie, causing their swollen cheeks to wince and their tear-ravaged eyes to go wide. The two knew that when that curtain was pulled back, that they would get terrible news. In those moments that they were alone, they'd wished the curtains would never be pulled back. They'd gladly stay there forever, as long as they didn't have to get the news they'd both feared was coming. To their relief, it was Dr. Ford.

With the news Ford was about to share with them, their relief would turn to terror.

"Hello, Jeanie, Frank," Ford was somber. "I have some news, and I'm afraid that it isn't good." Ford's eyes went to the clipboard in his hand.

Jeanie sobbed heavily while Frank embraced her.

"Frank, may I speak to you first, in private, for just a moment?"

Frank looked at Jeanie, and she shook her head, no. "Dr. Ford, I'm not leaving her side. Whatever's on that clipboard, you're gonna have to tell it to both of us."

Jeanie nodded in agreement.

Ford paused before delivering a diagnosis that no family would ever want to hear. "I'm afraid to say that it's cancer," he said with great consternation.

"Is it treatable?" Frank was anxious, while Jeanie already knew in her heart that it wasn't.

"First of all, it's breast cancer...." Ford was cut off by Frank.

"Is it treatable?!" demanded Frank.

"Frank, Jeanie," Ford slowly removed his reading glasses, took a deep breath, and exhaled with great trepidation. "I'm afraid the cancer has metastasized...." Ford was again cut off by Frank.

"What does that mean?" Frank looked at Jeanie, then Ford, and back to Jeanie again. Jeanie wailed, knowing that it was the end for her and her beautiful life with Frank and the girls.

"Frank, the cancer is advanced, stage four. And I'm afraid that it has spread."

"Stage four? What does that mean?" Frank looked lost as he turned to Jeanie.

"Frank," Ford again paused, "the cancer has spread to Jeanie's liver, lungs, lymph nodes, and it's now in her brain stem."

Jeanie looked at Frank as if to say that she was sorry. At that moment, she felt guilty for loving, marrying, and having children with Frank. All that, just to hurt him and leave him and the girls alone in the world without her. Her heart was broken, not for herself, but for Frank and her Jessica and Maddie.

"I'm so sorry, Frankie," Jeanie's face was overwrought with guilt as she cried.

"No, Jeanie, No!" Frank lost it. "This isn't your fault!"

There was a long moment of crying between Frank and Jeanie while Ford stood by and watched. The very doctor who'd help them start the family they'd always wanted now delivered the news that would spell the end to the family they'd become.

"Frank, may I speak with you alone? Please," implored Doctor Ford, pulling back the curtain and motioning for him to come with him.

Frank looked at Jeanie to gain her approval. Through her tears, she nodded to her husband that it was okay.

Now standing in a small room just feet away from a dying Jeanie, Ford said, "Frank, I am so sorry. I have watched your family grow, and to have this happen is the most tragic outcome there is."

"Doc, please tell me that she'll live. Please!" Frank cried.

"Frank, Jeanie will not survive this, I'm afraid."

Frank Bruno fell to his knees in agony and wailed. Somehow aware that Jeanie might hear him crying, he muffled his heartbreak as best he could.

As he rose to his feet, face drenched with tears, mucus running from his nose, he cried, "How long?"

"Frank, with aggressive treatment maybe six to twelve months. But..." Ford paused.

"But what?" Frank hung on the doctor's words.

"Frank, I want you to take Jeanie home, and I want you to give her the option of not treating her cancer."

"What?!" Frank was both astonished and confused. "What are you saying...?"

"Frank, the treatment that Jeanie will receive will be so aggressive and painful, in addition to lengthy, that she'll be in the hospital more than she's at home," Ford explained.

"I don't understand," Frank was lost. Wiping his nose and tears onto his already drenched shirt sleeve, he said, "What are you asking me?!"

Ford was empathetic. "Frank, Jeanie will be physically unable to hold her children in her final days. She may not even know where she is at times," he explained. "The radiation will wreak havoc on both her body and her mind."

Frank was still a little lost. The fog of the diagnosis had shrouded his thinking. "You can't ask that of me!" he was beside himself.

"Frank, would you and your children rather have six good months with Jeanie or twelve horrific ones?" reasoned Ford. "It's an impossible decision to make, I know, and that's why you should let Jeanie make it." Ford wanted to make sure Frank understood what life would be like in Jeanie's final days. "I think you should take Jeanie home to her family."

"Okay, I will." At that moment, Frank wanted nothing more to do with being in a hospital. He needed to get his Jeanie back home to her children and the house that she would die in. Frank knew that Jeanie was the one in pain, and he would try to hide his until she was no longer able to see him cry. Frank Bruno would be strong for his wife in her remaining days so that she wouldn't have to.

Janine Louise Bruno died on Monday, August 26, 1974, on her thirteenth wedding anniversary. Frank and the kids buried her on September 1. Frank vowed to his children that he would work hard and that he'd give them the best life possible. Frank also promised Jessica and Maddie that he would never replace their mother and never remarry.

Frank would also try to fulfill Jeanie's request that he not mourn her death but rather celebrate her life and the time they had together. Frank would return to work and try as hard as he could to be the same old Frank. He would not tell anyone that Jeanie passed away because he didn't seek pity or sympathy from anyone. He would do his job and not let his broken heart fracture his future.

Frank also made one more promise to himself. He promised that he or his children would never celebrate the very God that took his Jeanie away from him ever again.

Chapter 8 – Sinners vs. The Saints

Frank and Penny were stunned. Garrison Winter had just mentioned the name of the retirement home in Pittsburgh that Polly Anne Steinman went missing from back in 1965. The two detectives thought that the utterance could not possibly be a coincidence. Frank Bruno was good at poker, especially when playing the game with a suspect. He would keep his cards close to his chest, but their suspect immediately caught him off guard in this case.

"Mr. Winter, I'm Detective Bruno, and I'm with the Philadelphia Police Department." Frank was monotone in his delivery. "We're investigating the disappearance of Victor Rogers and have some questions for you."

"Yes, I was expecting the two of you," smiled Winter.

Frank looked puzzled. "That's odd because the way you greeted us a moment ago indicated that you were surprised to see us here today."

"Not at all, Detective. It was merely a figure of speech."

"That seemed odd too," said Frank. "Never heard someone say, 'What in God's Glory?' before."

Winter laughed. "Well, you know," he paused. "again, simply a figure of speech. God is almighty, and I celebrate in his glory every day."

"Is that so?" asked Frank while Penny stood by quietly, still shocked by Winter's words.

"Let me ask you, Frank...." Winter stopped himself. "I'm sorry, may I call you Frank?"

"Mr. Winter, how did you know my first name?" Frank was puzzled.

"I think you told me just a moment ago." Winter looked confused.

"No, I didn't," said Frank, flashing Penny a curious look.

"Oh, then perhaps your partner here mentioned it to me when we met yesterday," Winter looked more convincing.

Frank looked at Penny for confirmation. Penny shrugged her shoulders, conveying that she may or may not have.

"Sure, you can call me Frank."

Frank looked over at Penny and, with a look, communicated that he now understood her description of her first meeting with their suspect. Frank, too, thought the old man was both charming and a mass murderer wrapped up in an eighty-three-year-old body.

"Frank, I was going to ask if you were God-fearing?"

Frank looked at Penny and then back to Winter and shrugged before saying, "Should I fear God?"

Winter smiled, "A poor choice of words, again. I'm sorry, Frank. What I meant to ask is that do you believe that God is great?"

"What I do or don't think of God is not relevant to why I am here today, Mr. Winter." Frank quickly dismissed the God question.

"My apologies, Frank." Winter paused for a moment and then offered the two detectives a seat. "Please do sit down, Detectives."

Frank and Penny obliged, and the three were now seated around the backgammon board and table located near the boarded-up windows at the south end of the solarium. Outside, the orange and brown leaves were swirling, with some leaves blowing up against the four by six-foot panes of glass.

"What happened to the windows, Garrison?" Frank's eyes went to the wood panels that covered two broken-out spaces.

"Oh, vandalism, I suppose," Winter looked sad. "Kids these days, they don't seem to possess the wisdom or experience to know what beauty lies in glass," offer Winter. "Glass is the window to the world, much like eyes are the window to the soul."

Winter just stared out at the rustling leaves, lost in his own world for a moment. "Few things are more satisfying than watching those leaves swirl, though."

Frank raised his brows to acknowledge the statement made by the old man, whom he started to believe might be a little nuts.

"Do you play backgammon, Frank?" Winter smiled, now looking down at the backgammon board as if it were an old friend.

"Mr. Winter, you seem to be asking all of the questions, but I was hoping to ask you some of my own. May I?" Frank was cordial.

"Yes, of course, Frank. And again, call me Garrison."

"I was wondering if you could tell me where Victor Rogers might be?"

"Oh, straight to the point of why you're here today, I see," Winter shrugged as if to say he was disinterested. "Well, in that case, no, I cannot tell you where Mr. Rogers is. But wherever Victor is, I'm sure it's just heavenly." Winter smiled again.

Frank and Penny looked at each other, perplexed by Winter's answer.

"By 'Heavenly,' are you suggesting that Victor Rogers is in Heaven?" Frank posed his question in an effort to trigger a response that could possibly trip up his suspect.

The smile ran from Garrison Winter's face, and he answered without emotion. "I never said anything of the sort, Frank, but you did. Is there something that you're not telling me, Detectives?" Winter now extended his gaze to both Frank and Penny.

"We don't have an answer as to the whereabouts of Victor Rogers. That's why we're here. But we believe that you might," said Penny, finally chiming in.

"Well, as I said before. I cannot say." Winter came off as evasive in his response.

"Cannot or will not?" asked Frank, looking right into the eyes of someone he thought could be the devil incarnate.

"Cannot, I'm afraid. Because you see, Detectives, I don't know where my dear friend ran off to," smiled Winter.

In the minds of the two detectives sitting before him, Garrison Winter looked and sounded very much like a man who was lying.

"Are you certain that you cannot tell us where Mr. Rogers 'ran off to,' as you say, Mr. Winter?" Penny sounded like a seasoned detective, trying to get her suspect to confirm what she believed was a lie from moments ago.

"Penny, I promise you that I CANNOT tell you where Victor is." Winter was matter of fact.

Frank jumped back in. "Garrison, I understand at the time of the disappearance of Victor Rogers you were an employee here at Heavenly Gates. Is that correct?"

"Yes, I was one of three custodians who worked here," responded Garrison.

"And how was it that you were such 'dear' friends with Mr. Rogers? Are you good friends with all of the residents here?"

Winter looked off into space before saying, "I'd like to think of everyone as a friend, but there was something special, something pure about Victor."

Winter exhaled and smiled with a blank stare as if trying to remember Victor Rogers' face. "This world was not meant for Victor, and he, not for this world." After his remarks, Garrison's eyes refocused on the two detectives sitting in front of him.

Penny and Frank again looked at each other and thought the comment was both strange and sinister. They were both a little uncomfortable by the whole conversation. If this was a mass murderer they were talking to, he was different from any other killer Frank Bruno had previously interrogated. But then again, Frank Bruno had never met a mass murderer before. As for his partner, Penny Bryce had never questioned a killer of any kind before.

"Garrison, I understand you no longer work for Heavenly Gates. Is that correct?" asked Frank.

Winter repositioned himself in his chair, crossed his legs, and dawned a smile. "Oh, no, I'm retired now. I'm afraid this will be my final stop."

"Final stop?" Frank asked with suspicious intonation in his voice.

"Yes, I have traveled extensively in my time here," Garrison exhaled completely, looking exhausted.

"Where else have you lived, Mr. Winter?" Frank, for the first time, removed his notepad and pencil from the inside left chest pocket. Penny followed her mentor and also removed her pad and pencil.

"Oh, you know?" he paused, "Here, there, everywhere," Garrison Winter was vague.

"Pittsburgh?" blurted Penny, hoping to have an a-ha moment. When she did, Frank gave her the stink eye as if to say, 'Shut up and don't show this possible mass murderer our cards.'

"Pittsburgh?" Garrison pondered for a moment, pursed his lips, squinted his eyes, and looked upward as if struggling to remember. "What state is that in again?" He shook his head and looked back at the detectives. "You'll have to excuse me, Detectives. I'm just a little old man, and my memory fails me from time to time."

Frank thought that the killer sitting before him was as prolific at lying as he was in getting away with murder. "Please excuse my partner, Garrison. She spoke out of turn." Frank again looked at Penny and, without words, conveyed to her that he would be asking all of their remaining questions.

Frank continued, "The question I would like very much for you to answer is how does a former custodian come to live out his remaining years in such a storied retirement home as this one? I'm certain that the cost of staying here is quite expensive."

Frank was dying to get that particular question answered, as it made no sense that Garrison Winter, the prime suspect in a possible murder, could live in the very home in which the victim also lived.

"Frank, I have to tell you, embarrassingly enough, I have no earthly idea how much it costs to live here."

"Excuse me?" Frank was perplexed. Looking at Penny, he saw that she was just as surprised as he was.

"It's true," said Winter. "I was asked to stay on and live here for free as long as I wanted. You'll have to ask Director Travers. He is a wonderful man, and I'm sure he can explain to you why they chose to allow me to live here at no cost."

"I'll be sure to do just that. We're meeting with the Director right after we're finished talking with you."

"Oh, please pass along my warmest regards," Winter smiled. "People have said that he reminds them of a younger version of me."

Penny spoke back up again even though she knew Frank had hoped she wouldn't. "Garrison, how long have you been here?"

Frank thought it was a good question and gave Penny a nod of approval.

Old Man Winter thought about it for a moment. "Hmm, I have been a resident since January of 1970 and have lived and worked here as a custodian since January of 1966." Winter shook his head, pursed his lips, and then said, "Yep, that sounds about right."

Frank wrote down the information, and when he did, jotted 'Pittsburgh, December of '65,' Philadelphia, January of 66'. Before his final question, he thought to himself, "*What are the chances?*"

"Garrison, we have just one more question for you today, if you wouldn't mind."

"Yes, Frank. Please, go ahead." Garrison was happy to have guests, and his enthusiasm showed it.

"So, you were the last person to see Victor Rogers before he vanished. Is that correct?" asked Frank.

"I do believe that's what witnesses told your dear departed colleagues," Winter nodded.

"Tell me. Why do you think a ninety-five-year-old man would walk out of this majestic home into the dead of winter, with neither shoes nor jacket and a foot of snow on the ground?"

"Well, I do remember playing backgammon with Victor that morning," Winter remembered with great affection. "Oh, how we loved to play backgammon together. And we talked about his life," recalled Garrison.

"It would have been too cold to play backgammon out here in the solarium, no?" asked Frank.

"Oh, heaven's no. We play in the main dining room during the winter," said Garrison. "Me, I personally love the snow, the cold, and the winter. That's why they call me Old Man Winter. But Victor? No, he hated the cold."

"Please, go on," encouraged Frank.

Detective Frank Bruno liked it when suspects talked too much. Many times they'd say something incriminating. Frank had hoped that on this occasion, his prime suspect would do just that.

Garrison continued, "I remember asking him if he would change anything about his life or how he lived it. He pondered for a moment and told me of all the wrongs he wished he could make right. All the things he could have done differently," recalled Old Man Winter.

"And what did you say to him before he just up and vanished, never to be seen again?"

"I told him that he'd lived a long and wonderful life but that it was time for him to go."

Frank and Penny looked at each other, trying hard not to reveal their shock to the mass murderer sitting across from them. Frank wrote down Winter's near confession in his notebook. Then, he and Penny stood up and thanked Garrison Winter for his time.

Frank thought that the two had gathered a great deal of information they didn't have before and wanted to ensure that Winter would be receptive to a future visit.

"Mr. Winter," Frank extended his hand, "thank you for your time today. I look forward to our next meeting."

Frank had it in the back of his mind that the next meeting might yield a confession. Guessing that the boys from Pittsburgh would likely offer up information that could possibly connect the three disappearances and perhaps enough evidence to arrest Old Man Winter.

"It was a pleasure meeting you too, Frank. I, too, look forward to our next meeting."

Penny also shook hands with Winter. He nodded and thanked her for coming. "Penny, always nice to see you."

As Frank and Penny showed themselves out, Garrison Winter yelled out to Frank. "Frank, when you used to go to church, did it help?"

Frank stopped in his tracks, looked at Penny, and turned around, furrowing his brow.

"Excuse me." Frank was taken aback. "Mr. Winter, first of all, you just suggested that I don't attend church. Why would you make that presumption? And second of all, what do you mean, did it help?"

Winter stood up and walked over to Frank and said, "Frank, I see that you're bothered by my question. Please know that I meant no offense."

Frank's nod was almost imperceptible. Not bothered as much as baffled. "Why would you ask such a random question? Additionally, a person's faith is their own business, and certainly not yours." Frank was now red-faced.

Penny had never seen him lose his composure but recognized that Garrison Winter had struck a nerve.

"Frank, there are no random things. I was merely asking if practicing your faith helps you cope with loss and the everyday struggles that life presents?" Winter was methodical in his delivery.

"Mr. Winter, again, my faith is not your concern. Nor will it ever be. I would respectfully ask that you never bring it up again."

"Yes, of course, Frank. May I ask you one more question, though?"

"I would be careful with what you ask, Mr. Winter."

"Alrighty then. I was just wondering how the girls were doing?"

Frank ground his teeth and went red again. "What in the hell does that mean?" he asked, clenching his fists.

"Frank, you impress me as someone who has children, and by your reaction, I believe that you do. Girls, I'm assuming. Two of them, I bet."

Frank started to lunge at Garrison Winter, who didn't flinch, but then looked at him and saw a little old man. A man that knew something, he thought. A man that knew too much. Frank needed to know how. He was beginning to realize that everything Winter said had a purpose. He guessed that every word was meant to draw a reaction. One that would help him to read the man who was interrogating him. Frank thought that Old Man Winter was playing a game of life and death. His gut told him that he was in the presence of evil.

Penny tugged on Frank's arm, urging him to just walk away without further confrontation. Frank pulled his arm away, aggressively escaping his partner's grasp, and then took one step closer to the old man. Frank stood a whole head taller than his suspect and was half his age.

"Mr. Winter, why would you assume that I have children, then assume that I have two and that they'd both be girls?" Frank was frightened all of a sudden, but anger helped to conceal his fear.

"Frank, by the looks of you; your age, personality type, your obvious physical and psychological attributes, along with the fact that you're a long-time civil servant, I see you with only little girls."

"You see, most strong men tend to have daughters, while strong women tend to have sons." Winter turned to Penny and smiled, giving her the creeps.

Looking back to Frank, Winter continued. "I'd surmise only two daughters, though, and that they're young. What with your busy professional life. I see you as a late bloomer. My guess is that they're close in age, too. That's a good thing!" Winter's eyes widened as he launched what Frank perceived as a sinister smile.

"Oh, and why's that?" asked Frank, whose strong exterior could not mask the terror in his heart.

"Oh, you know, should anything happen to you, they'd have each other to care for one another during the trying times in life. And oh, I'm sure those children do adore you. And you, they."

Frank was mortified. How could this stranger know anything about him? Frank looked over at Penny and said, "C'mon, let's go!"

"I will see you very soon, Mr. Winter," said Frank before turning to leave.

Winter held out his hand again to shake Frank's before he turned. Frank, seeing the gesture, looked down at Winter's empty hand and wanted to spit into it. Instead of shaking the old man's hand, he turned to leave without saying another word.

Penny attempted to say something as they were leaving, and Frank shut her down with a stare that told her to keep her mouth shut.

"All the best, Detectives. I look forward to seeing you both very soon!" Winter waved and smiled as Penny and Frank exited the room.

Once the two made it through the massive dining room and back into the long hallway that led to the front doors, Frank hunched over, placed his hands on his knees, and tried to collect himself.

Penny touched Frank's back to see if he was alright. Without warning, he stood up and grabbed her, pushed her up against the wall, and held her there for a moment before speaking.

"What in the fuck did you tell that old man about me?" Frank had kill in his eyes.

Penny was frightened. "Frank, I didn't tell him anything! Now please let me go!"

"He said that you told him my name in your first meeting!" Frank clutched Penny's jacket tighter. "Well, did you?"

"He lied. I never told him your name. I never even mentioned that I had a partner, he guessed. Now please, let me go." Penny was terrified and could barely catch her breath. With Frank still seething and tears in his eyes, Penny said, "Frank, take your hands off of me, now!"

Frank, seeing the dread on his partner's face, released her. In relief, Penny exhaled and stood there for another moment, frozen in fear. It would be several more seconds before she could summon the courage to address her partner.

Straightening her jacket and smoothing her lapels, she said, "Frank, what just happened in there?" Penny looked at her partner, who seemed paralyzed, his face white as a ghost.

"How did he know that I have two girls?" Frank looked frightened, thinking that the mass murderer knew who he was, where he lived, who his kids were, and where they went to school. He was scared, and at that moment, he didn't care that his rookie partner knew it.

"Frank, I didn't tell him anything. I swear to God!" Penny was frightened too. "He looked at me and smiled when he said, 'strong women tend to only have sons'!"

"Penny, he didn't mention anything about Jeanie. Or me having a wife. Why?" asked Frank. "That psycho only talked about the girls and me! He asked me if church helped cope with loss." Frank's anguish dripped from his eyes.

Penny could tell something else was wrong. It wasn't just fear that she saw in Frank's eyes. It was heartbreak.

"Frank, what is it?" Penny gripped Frank's right arm as if to console him. At that moment, Frank Bruno broke down and cried, running toward the front door of the Heavenly Gates mansion. Penny gave chase and, seconds later, found Frank doubled-over crying on the steps in front of the massive double doors.

"Frank! What is it?! Talk to me!"

Frank was inconsolable. "It's Jeanie," he sobbed.

"What about her? Frank, what is it?"

"Jeanie died, Penny! She died. She left me and the kids!" Frank cried. "They're all I have! And that son of a bitch in there somehow knows it!" Frank looked like a frightened child. "Somebody tipped him off. He may not be working alone. Penny, this is big. Something's going on here that we can't grasp."

Penny was shocked. Not knowing what to do, she hugged her partner and said, "Frank, I'm so sorry. When? When did Jeanie pass?" At that moment, she felt less like a detective and more like a friend.

"It was August 26. I took an extended vacation so that the kids and I could spend her final days by her bedside. Then, we buried her in Hood Cemetery on Germantown Avenue." Frank paused for a second and then continued, "Cancer took her, Penny. It was cancer."

"Oh, Frank. My god, what is happening in this world? What is going on?"

Penny realized that the day Jeanie died was just three days before she got promoted to Detective. She started to feel that the universe was in control; Jeanie dying, finally getting promoted, and now Old Man Winter. *"What in the hell is going on?"* she said to herself.

Frank tried to pull himself together. Rubbing his eyes, he said, "We need to talk to Travers!"

"Frank, no. We could do it another day." Penny was sensitive to her partner's emotional state.

"It has to happen today. Evil lives inside of this place, and we need to make sure that everyone in there knows it!"

"We can't just go in there and tell them the Devil is in their midst." Penny was trying to talk sense into her partner.

"Penny, this investigation needs to move forward. We don't have any time to waste. McClain may put an end to this when he gets back."

Penny looked Frank in the eyes. "Frank, why didn't you tell anyone about Jeanie?" She rubbed Frank's arm again. "Those poor girls. How are they coping? Let me help you. Whatever I can do," she said.

"We found out back in April. It was breast cancer," Frank shook his head and rubbed his eyes. "Penny, that poor girl didn't stand a chance. It had spread everywhere. She suffered, Penny." Frank looked forlorn and detached.

"Oh, Frank. I am so sorry. Bring those girls over to our house. Let them spend some time with my boys."

"Penny, he knows where I live. I can feel it. He did it. He killed those people. I can't put the girls in harm's way. We need to complete this investigation fast." Frank wore a look of urgency.

"If that man is a sinner, then we're the saints. And we need God on our side," Frank was feeling righteous. "Penny, do you pray?"

"Not so much anymore."

"Penny, pray. Pray tonight and tomorrow, and after that, pray some more. We have to prevail over the evil that lives in there. You pray for my girls and me, and I'll pray for you and your boys."

"You serious, Frank?" Penny wasn't sure because she never knew Frank to be a religious man. She'd never heard him mention church or God one time in the four years that she knew him.

"Penny, pray," Frank was afraid. "Good must prevail over the evil that lives inside of this place."

Chapter 9 – Victor Rogers

After their meeting with Garrison Winter, Frank and Penny composed themselves before going back inside. Both now felt convinced the old man was somehow connected to the disappearances of both Victor Rogers and Polly Anne Steinman. They didn't have enough information about the case in Indiana to make a third connection yet.

"Okay, so what's the plan when we get in front of Travers?" Penny asked a now calmed down Frank.

"Sorry that I lost it back there, Penny. I guess I really haven't had time to grieve." Frank was embarrassed by his meltdown in front of his rookie partner.

"Frank, I'm just so sorry for your loss. I only met Jeanie twice, and both times she seemed genuine and warm," said Penny. "The way you talk about her," she paused, "she must have been the same person at home that the rest of us knew. Like I said, anything Joe and I can do to help. You know, watch the girls from time to time, or have you guys over for dinner. Whatever."

Frank was uncomfortable talking about Jeanie's death and regretted bringing it up to Penny. "Thanks, Penny, but I may never mention my personal life at work again. That's just not me. It's not who I am." Frank tried to shake off how he was feeling personally and trying to get back into work mode.

"Frank, it's me, Penny. I'm your partner. I'm supposed to know stuff."

"Penny, say nothing to the guys at work. I'm not looking for their pity," Frank was serious. "Poor, pathetic Frank. The guy who lost his wife to cancer. That ain't me, Penny. Say nothing to no one."

"Whatever you say, Frank. But now I know, and I plan to help out when and where I can."

Frank shook his head and rolled his shoulders in an attempt to get his head back in the game. "Okay, let's talk about what's going to happen when we get back in there."

Penny looked like a trainee at Kinney Shoes, first day on the job. She looked at Frank like he was the teacher, and she, his student.

"First things, first. If we run into that psycho in there, please keep me from tearing him apart."

"Yes, sir. You and me both," said Penny, who looked like she wanted to fight someone.

"When we get Travers in a corner, we need to learn why it is that the Devil is living here for free. We also need to learn more about Victor Rogers. Let's try to acquire any files that they have on him."

Frank jotted down some notes while reviewing his entries from earlier.

Penny referenced her notes too. "Frank, from what I know about Rogers, he was an Army veteran and a medic during the first world war. It says here that he served in France and Germany, and get this, he was a passenger on The Lusitania when a German U-boat torpedoed it in May of '15. It says here that he lost his wife and three kids in the sinking and never remarried. Apparently, he'd saved dozens of lives that day but was unable to save his own family. Imagine living with that your whole life," Penny shook her head, exhaled, and mouthed the word, Wow.

"It turns out that after the war, Rogers went on to become a priest. Langhorne and Gaffney turned up no past criminal history. And that's it. That's all there is in the file."

"Wow!" Frank's brows rose high on his forehead. "The Germans killed his wife and kids, and he decides to become a medic and then a priest? If I had a gun in my hand, I would've had it pointed right at Germany if I was him. Instead, the guy tried to help people." Frank had a hard time reconciling what motivated Rogers to turn the other cheek.

"We'll probably learn more from Travers when we get in there," said Penny. "By the way, I feel terrible about something that happened earlier." Penny was hesitant to elaborate.

"What is it? Just say it." Frank pushed his partner.

"When I saw you flirting with that Gruber woman, I," Penny was tongue-tied.

"Just say it, Penny."

"I thought it was an act, but for a moment, I wasn't sure. I thought for a second that you were really flirting with her, and I was shocked because of Jeanie. Now I feel like shit for thinking it."

"Penny, Jeanie was the one," Frank was pointed. "There will never be another. I will never remarry. I will never love again."

Penny looked surprised. "Frank, Corinthians 7:8-9. You're allowed to remarry."

"Penny, it's not about what the bible says. It's about Jeanie. I'll never do it. That would be like me leaving her. I'd never do that to her or the girls. It'll never happen."

Penny hoped that Frank would eventually change his mind. She thought that those two little girls needed a female role model in their life. They would need a mom again one day. She stayed quiet about it, seeing that Frank hadn't mourned Jeanie's death yet.

"Well, Aunt Penny will always be there for those precious girls."

"Thanks, Penny. Now let's get in there and get more information than we already have." Frank shook off what happened earlier and put his game face on.

Now back inside, Frank and Penny made their way down the long foyer, unsure of where they were going. They knew that taking a left at the end of the hallway led them to the main dining area, kitchen, and solarium, so they'd take a right instead and see where they ended up.

"This place is amazing!" said Frank.

Penny shuttered, "Scares the shit out of me!" She walked just behind Frank, using him to shield her from the unknown. Penny was religious and could feel evil all around her.

"What kind of money did your family have back in the day. How did nothing get left to you when they all passed on?" Frank wondered aloud.

"The Great Depression. That's how," said Penny as she looked back and forth into what appeared to be sitting rooms flanking the hallway.

"I mean, look at these paintings. Good grief! They must be worth a fortune." Frank looked back at Penny, shaking his head in disbelief.

"That one there," Penny lifted her chin and motioned with her eyes to Frank's left. "That's my great-grandfather, his wife, and sons. The youngest one, there on the right, that was my grandfather."

"They possessed unimaginable wealth," Frank shook his head again.

"Remember, he was building railroads back then, Frank. It was his company that built the North Broad Street line back in 1867."

"No shit!" Frank was impressed. "I used to take that line every day when I worked downtown."

"That was a lucrative industry before air travel."

"Big Money, apparently! This place is way over the top!" Frank surveyed the home and its furnishings and thought that it must have cost a fortune just to maintain the place. He could only imagine what people spent to live out the rest of their lives there. He would try to get that question answered when they met with Dean Travers.

Just then, as Frank recoiled his thoughts, Bernice Gruber appeared at the end of the hall, exiting into the foyer from the right-side doorway, opposite the dining area. She looked excited to see Frank again.

"Well, there you are, Detective Frank! I was wondering what happened to you." Instead, Gruber didn't make eye contact with Penny, acting as if Frank was standing there alone.

"Well, I was looking for you too," Frank smiled. "After we met up with Mr. Winter, we went looking for you and got a little lost, I'm afraid." Frank laid it on thick again.

"Miss Gruber, if you could show us to Dean Travers' office, that would be greatly appreciated," said Penny, trying to make eye contact with a woman she'd come to dislike very much.

"Yes, of course, Frank, let me take you to him," said Gruber, again ignoring the fact that Penny was standing right there.

The three turned right into another long hallway with shorter hallways running toward the mansion's front and back. The halls appeared to lead to either studies, libraries, servants' quarters, or reading rooms for the residents. Penny imagined that when her family resided there, the children must have had fun playing hide and go seek with one another.

Gruber took the visitors left into a foyer at the end of the hall with a door that led to the estate's Northwest corner and the Administrative Ward. There, they saw little activity and no residents or staff members.

"Frank, this is the Administrative Ward for the estate. My office is right over here." Gruber pointed to the right, indicating that the second to the last door in the long hallway was her office. "Should you have a moment and can find some time away from your little detective friend here," she motioned to Penny while raising her nose slightly, "perhaps we can chat for a moment prior to your departure?" Gruber's face suggested to the detectives that she planned to make sure Frank understood she was interested in him.

"I'm sure I can break away from my partner here for a moment. Right, Penny?" Frank looked at his partner as the two followed closely behind Gruber, smirked, and rolled his eyes.

Penny gave Frank a little push in the back. She thought her partner seemed to be fully recovered from the emotional breakdown he'd had just twenty minutes earlier.

At the end of a hallway, lined with offices, Gruber stopped in front of a massive doorway. It was the last office on the right before exiting out of the back or western side of the mansion. The door's arch suggested to Frank and Penny that whoever occupied the room was clearly important. The doorway itself was three feet taller than the other doorways in the hall. Above it, crowning the arch's highest point, was a marble sculpture of a Falcon encrusted with gold trimming, its talons extended outward as if ready to pounce on its prey. The trim appeared to Frank to be either solid gold or gold plated. He thought that the sculpture's value alone could easily buy a new house for him and the girls.

"Frank, if you'd please wait right here for just a moment, I'll see if Mr. Travers is ready to receive you." Bernice Gruber suddenly seemed to act more professional and less flirty. Both Penny and Frank noticed the change and recognized that Gruber must have held a clear admiration and respect for her boss.

After Gruber disappeared through the massive doorway, Penny smirked and mocked the woman. "Ready to receive you!" she said under her breath. "I don't like that bitch! Just sayin.'"

Frank wore a sober look. "Listen to me, Penny. You need to get serious. When we get in there, you follow my lead and only ask follow-ups to questions that I ask Travers. This is important." Frank was all business. "If we blow this, then we may not be welcomed back in here without a court order. And if McClain shuts us down, we'll never get one. Got it?"

"I got it, Frank. Only follow-up your questions." Penny didn't want to make the same mistake twice in one day. She knew she'd pissed off Frank with the 'Pittsburgh' utterance in front of Old Man Winter.

After several moments, Gruber reappeared from Travers' office with a smile. "Frank, Mr. Travers will see you now. There is one thing, though," said Gruber. "You must address Mr. Travers as Director Travers."

"That won't be a problem at all," said Frank, nodding with a cordial smile.

Gruber flashed Frank a modest smile, looked both ways, and leaned toward his right shoulder, and whispered, "Don't forget to stop by my office before you leave today." Gruber made it clear that she'd be very disappointed if he left without saying goodbye.

Frank smiled and whispered back to Gruber, "That too will not be a problem, Miss Gruber."

"Call me Bernice," smiled Gruber as she walked away.

Penny felt a little nauseous but said nothing. She just stood there watching the never married, past her prime, Gruber make a fool of herself. As far as Frank was concerned, Penny thought that he was a damn good actor but again questioned whether he was acting or not. She again felt terrible for thinking such a thing.

Frank and Penny watched as Gruber turned into her office just twenty feet away before speaking again, not wanting to be overheard. "Director, huh?" said Frank with an unimpressed smile.

"Bernice, huh?" Penny looked at Frank, leaned in, and whispered in his ear, "You better come and see me before you leave, Stud." She then pushed his chest and chuckled softly.

Frank smiled and winked at his partner. "Alrighty now, it's time to get serious."

After the two shook off their smiles, they preceded through the massive doorway to find Travers standing behind his desk awaiting his guests. As Frank walked through the door, Travers said, "Welcome, gentleman!" he then stepped from behind his desk and noticed Penny. "Oh, please excuse my announcement. I was expecting two detectives. I'm so sorry, Madame."

Frank turned to Penny in an effort to let her stick up for herself, giving way to her slight stature.

"Director Travers, my name is Detective Penelope Bryce, and I'm with the Philadelphia Police Department. It's a pleasure to meet you." Penny then offered her hand to the Director.

"Yes, of course, Detective. You'll have to forgive me for my unfortunate assumption." Travers reciprocated Penny's gesture to shake hands.

Director Dean Travers stood six foot two, Frank's height, but was gangly and looked far older than his actual age. Frank and Penny guessed he was in his mid-fifties, but his eye wrinkles were pronounced and odd-looking to both making him look much older. Penny could see why he'd never been married. She could also see why Frank was so appealing to Bernice Gruber after she'd given the impression to Penny, on her first visit, that she found Dean Travers to be agreeable. It seemed to Penny that Travers now had competition in the eyes of Gruber.

Frank's eyes went wide and lips tight as his rookie partner handled herself more like a veteran. He then looked toward Travers, who now turned to face him. "Director Travers. Thank you for agreeing to meet with us. I can only imagine how limited your time must be. It's quite an operation you run here."

"Detective Bruno," Travers nodded in agreement and sighed, "yes, we are busier than ever. Residency and staff levels are at an all-time high." Travers' brows went high onto his forehead as he sighed.

Frank was confused. He looked back toward the door and cocked his head, and said to himself. *"Hmm, I didn't see any people walking around out there."*

Looking back at the Director, Frank responded to his claim. "Why do you think that is, Director Travers?"

"Well, the fact is, our country is getting older. With the advance of medicine, overall medical care, and the improved treatment of the elderly, folks are just living longer," offered Travers.

"I see," said Frank.

After an uncomfortable moment of silence, Travers smiled and said, "Yes, well then, won't you please have a seat, Detectives?" he then motioned for them to sit in the chairs in front of his massive desk.

Frank looked at Penny as if to say, "Ladies before gentleman."

Travers returned to his chair situated behind his desk. As Frank and Penny sat, they surveyed the room and the splendor that resided there. Frank looked down at the ruby red carpet and admired its elegance.

As Penny settled into the back of her chair, her eyes went upward to the massive cathedral ceiling that must have been fifteen to sixteen feet in her estimation. The ceiling rose in the middle of the room into a dome with a massive chandelier hanging down some six feet. The remainder of the ceiling was coffered with a fresco painting that depicted *The creation of Adam*, with God extending his hand and finger to touch Adam's.

Penny was impressed, but Frank's attention was focused on how he could get Travers to divulge as much information as possible without turning him off.

"Director Travers, this must be your wife and children," said Frank as his eyes went to a picture on Travers' desk.

Travers smiled with pride, "No, I'm afraid that's my dear sister Carolyn and my three godsons. They are all impressive young lads, and I'm very proud of her and them," Travers beamed.

"They are all striking young bucks, to be sure," said Frank. "And I can now see a resemblance between you and your sister," said Frank. "She, too, is striking."

Frank knew that Travers was not married as Gruber had made that clear to Penny during their initial meeting. He knew that complimenting someone on their family was a great way to start a dialogue and a way to get someone to loosen up and drop their guard.

Penny was still taking in the room's grandeur. Knowing that her great-grandfather likely used the room as his private office more than one hundred years ago, she felt nostalgic. She could almost feel his presence as she stared at the ornate wallpaper and gold sconces that ran around the perimeter of the room.

"So, Detectives, Miss Gruber tells me that you're here to discuss Victor Rogers. Are there any updates in his disappearance?" Travers seemed both curious and concerned.

"Yes and no," said Frank. "Yes, we're here to discuss his disappearance. And no, there are no breaks in the case, which is what brings us here today."

"Well then, how may I be of assistance to you?" Travers interlocked his fingers and leaned forward, planting both elbows on the desk in front of him.

"Unfortunately, the previous detectives have both passed on since the case went cold, which makes it impossible to ask them questions." Frank tried hard to look helpless, hoping to coax some empathy and assistance from the Director.

"Cold?" Travers looked confused.

"Oh, sorry," said Frank. "Cold Case is a term used when a case goes unsolved for an extended period of time."

"Well, that's very interesting. I thought you called it a cold case because he disappeared in the winter," Travers seemed to be impressed with himself for posing the thought. He pondered for another moment and said, "Yes, it was sad when Mr. Langhorne passed so suddenly. We were all devastated when it happened just days ago."

"So suddenly?" Penny slid to the front of her chair. "But Spencer Langhorne was very ill, no?"

Frank cocked his head to the side, also curious about Travers' comment.

"Why, yes, Mr. Langhorne was in good health, albeit suffering a stroke last fall. Our on-staff physician monitors the health of all of our residents weekly and, to the best of my recollection, even he was caught off guard by his passing," recalled Travers.

"Might we see his medical records at some point, Mr., I mean, Director Travers?" asked Frank, nearly botching Travers' title.

Travers overlooked Frank's slip-up and said, "I'm sure that won't be a problem, Detective."

"Director Travers, what can you tell us about Victor Rogers? What kind of man was he?" Frank pulled his notepad from the left chest pocket of his gray tweed jacket with black elbow patches.

Penny mimicked her partner, and when she did, Travers noticed his eyes following each detective's motion. It was clear to him that Bruno was senior to Bryce.

Travers pushed himself back into his brown leather chair and pondered for a moment before speaking. "Victor Rogers was the most well-liked and respected of all of our residents," Travers paused, "and staff for that matter."

Frank took advantage of the pause and asked, "Why do you think that was?"

Travers nodded, "For so many reasons. His pedigree to start with. Rogers descended from British Royalty. His family immigrated to Montreal just after the Civil War and then came to Philadelphia in the 1880s. They were very wealthy. I believe they imported and exported goods back and forth to England and Ireland. They had a small fleet of ships, from what Rogers once told me."

Frank jotted down the information, followed by Penny.

"He was a nice man, very kind. He was a Priest at *Immaculate Conception Roman Catholic Church* for nearly forty years before retiring here in '66." Travers continued, "And his family, those poor souls. Victor lost his wife and three daughters back in 1915."

Frank wrote the word 'daughters,' thinking of his two girls at home. He then underlined and circled the word.

"Yes, the Lusitania," Frank mumbled. "What else can you tell us about Mr. Rogers," asked Frank, who was now beginning to admire the man too.

"Well, he was a war hero," Travers offered before being abruptly cut off by Penny.

"A war hero?" Penny displayed a look of curiosity. "Our understanding was that Victor Rogers was a medic during his time in France and East Prussia."

"Detective Bryce, you don't just become a war hero for killing the enemy." Travers looked at Penny as if she were ignorant on the subject. "You can also be a hero for saving lives, which Mr. Rogers did. Hundreds of them, perhaps even thousands. Our Victor Rogers never killed anyone."

Frank detected a slight attitude from Travers toward Penny and quickly brought attention back to Travers himself. As a seasoned detective, Frank knew that people loved to talk about themselves and that whenever an interview or interrogation was heading south, he'd turned the conversation toward the subject who was being questioned.

"Director Travers, how long have you been here at Heavenly Gates?"

Travers was happy to answer Frank's question, now sitting erect in his chair, staring directly at Frank as if Penny had disappeared.

"Yes, well, I'm proud to say that I was the first Director brought on after the home re-opened as a retirement community. I came on in '66. I was the only candidate they interviewed."

"They knew they had their man," Frank smiled, flattering Travers.

"I'm not sure if you're aware, but from 1949 to 1965, these facilities were used for psychiatric care for only the most mentally disturbed patients." Dean Travers seemed to enjoy educating the detective sitting in his presence about the history of the estate.

Frank leaned in, "Yes, I was aware as I live just several miles from here and pass it daily to and from work."

"Then you're aware that it was formerly known as *The Allan Institute*," said Travers.

"Yes, and I understand they had some issues and had to close it down. Is that right?" Frank tried to look both concerned and curious.

"Yes, they did. It was down for nearly a year before reopening as Heavenly Gates." Travers was pointed, "And I'm not sorry either." The Director looked down. He appeared to Frank and Penny to be formulating his next thought, as if unsure he should be speaking on the subject. "This place was never meant to treat sick patients. The estate was originally built to care for the elderly."

Penny could not resist correcting the Director. Clearing her throat first, she interjected. "Director Travers, it's my understanding that this place was built in 1860 as a private home for Samuel Crenshaw, his wife, and their three children." Penny seemed defensive of her family history and the history of the estate. "It was called FalconClaw."

"Why, Detective Bryce, you do know your history, don't you? Impressive," said Travers, now turning back toward Penny, looking almost offended by her interjection.

Frank could see the conversation wasn't going to end well and immediately spoke up with a look of concern on his face. "Director Travers...."

Travers quickly cut off Frank, holding up his index finger in Frank's direction while focusing his eyes keenly on the female detective.

"Detective Bryce," Travers was now fixated on Penny and her presumed knowledge of Heavenly Gates, "what more can you tell me about this storied home? I would love to hear what it is that you know," Travers was sarcastic. He felt offended that a police detective would postulate knowing more about the estate than he.

Penny positioned herself in her chair as if ready to joust with the Director, who likely occupied the very chair that her great-grandfather once had.

"The original name of the manor was FalconClaw, and it was constructed between 1860 and 1863," Penny beamed. "Its original owner, Samuel Crenshaw, had it built to face slightly southeast so that from the home's four-story tower, he could watch the construction of his railroad that would help to connect North Philadelphia with the booming downtown area."

"Fascinating! Please, tell me more," Travers was now riveted by Penny's knowledge and seemed desperate to learn more.

Frank sat back in his chair as if to get out of the way of Penny and Travers. He quickly determined that Penny planned to win Travers over with her knowledge of the place that the Director loved working at. He surmised that Travers loved being a part of both the estate's famous and infamous history. Frank knew that Travers reveled in his role as Director of the historic mansion, and Penny's knowledge fed into his affinity for the place.

"Well, Director Travers, as Samuel Crenshaw grew older, and with his wife Rebekah passing on in 1895, along with the departure of his three sons, having moved on with their own lives, he no longer desired to live here alone."

"Fascinating." Travers was on the edge of his seat, hanging on to Penny's every word.

Frank now felt as if he was the one to have disappeared.

"Please, continue," insisted Dean Travers.

Penny went on to say, "Though Crenshaw no longer desired to live here alone, he had no plans to leave the mansion. So, in 1901, at the age of 75, Samuel Crenshaw donated the estate to the City of Philadelphia. He wanted the elderly to live with dignity in their final years and longed for company, choosing not to be alone in the vastness of FalconClaw. It was he who named the manor Heavenly Gates. He was the first retired resident of the home."

Travers shook his head in disbelief. Disbelief that there was so much he never knew of the history and disbelief that Bryce knew so much.

"Detective Bryce, I must say that I am so impressed by your historical knowledge of this wonderful estate. How is it that you've come to know so much about it?" Travers looked curious.

"Well, Director Travers. I am the granddaughter of Samuel Crenshaw's youngest son, Ernest." Penny smiled with pride and felt relieved to finally get the fact off her chest.

Dean Travers fell back into his chair, astonished by the revelation. "Oh my. I'm speechless." Travers looked white as a ghost. "I am sitting here in the presence of royalty."

"Far from it. I'm just a girl from Rhawnhurst." Penny's modesty was unable to conceal her pride.

"Detective Bryce, when we're done here today, might you consider staying for a short while so that we might speak further? I can arrange for a car to take you back to wherever you're going after leaving here." Travers almost begged Penny to stay behind.

Frank was in shock. Travers looked at him and said, "Detective Bruno, might you do without your associate for an hour or two? I would very much like to give Detective Bryce a tour of the mansion. After all, she is now considered royalty around here."

"Yes, of course, Director. That won't be a problem at all. But I do still have some questions to ask of you," said a flabbergasted Frank.

"Yes, Frank. After your questions, I'll have Miss Gruber show you out." Penny fought hard to withhold her smile.

"Yes, that would be fine," replied Frank, biting his lip after seeing his partner's pleasure.

Travers spoke back up. "Detective Bruno, please continue with your questions as I only have a few short minutes left before I steal Detective Bryce from you."

"Please, call me Penelope," Penny said as her eyes went from Travers to Frank, smiling along the way.

"Penelope it is," said Travers in the affirmative.

"Very well, Director. I will finish with one question but hope to pay you a follow-up visit in the coming days. We're working on a new lead in the disappearance of Victor Rogers, one that I am not at liberty to discuss but will need to gather more information from you. Additionally, we'll need access to the medical records of Spencer Langhorne if that would be alright." Frank again looked helpless in an effort to gain empathy from Travers.

"Yes-yes. I'm sure we can accommodate you, Detective. Please ask your question." Travers seemed eager to get the conversation with Frank over with so that he could continue his with Penny.

Frank hoped what he was about to say didn't upset Travers and ruin what was, in his opinion, a good first conversation. It was a question; however, that had to be both asked and answered.

"Director Travers, how is it that Garrison Winter lives here as a resident? How does someone who was once a custodian become a resident that lives here for free?"

"Hmm, I see," Travers stroked his chin. "So this whole line of questioning today was to again shine the light of suspicion on our dear Mr. Winter?" Travers demeanor changed suddenly. He now looked agitated and suspicious of his guests.

"No-no, Director. Not at all," said Frank. "However, the fact that he was the last person to be seen with Victor Rogers means that he will remain a person of interest." Frank was playing damage control.

"Our goal for this meeting was to learn more about the victim, not any persons of interest."

"Okay, so why then are you asking me about the resident status of Mr. Garrison? Which, by the way, is a personal and confidential matter."

"Yes, I can understand the privacy policies of Heavenly Gates...." Frank almost stuttered before being saved by Penny.

"Director Travers, the only reason we ask the question is that it was Mr. Winter himself who divulged that he lived here at no cost," Penny spoke with a softness in her voice as if speaking to a close friend. "He actually encouraged us to ask you the question."

Travers turned to Penny, and with her words, his stance on the matter softened. "Well, Penelope," Travers, too, spoke with a gentle tone. "Since Mr. Winter offered you that information, I can tell you that it is through the great generosity of Victor Rogers himself that Garrison Winter lives here for free. Incidentally, that fact is part of the public record as well as it is included in Mr. Rogers' will."

Frank and Penny glanced at each other with surprised looks.

"Victor Rogers left it in his will that Garrison Winter would live at Heavenly Gates for free until the day he died or no longer chose to live here," divulged Travers. "You see, Detectives, the two men were quite close, and Victor Rogers had no remaining relatives to leave his modest wealth to."

Frank shook his head and stood up. Penny then followed.

"Director Travers, your time and candor is much appreciated, and I look very much forward to our next meeting." Frank extended his hand to Travers as the Director walked from behind his desk to reciprocate.

"Yes, Detective Bruno, I too look forward to our next meeting. You'll be sure to bring along Detective Bryce, won't you?" Travers smiled at Frank and then at Penny.

"Penelope, you will stay on for a short while longer, correct?"

"Yes, if it's alright with Detective Bruno, of course."

Frank smiled as Penny poked at him. "Yes, I'm sure we can do without Detective Bryce back at the station for a couple of hours."

"Lovely!" exclaimed Travers. "Then we shall go on a tour then?" He smiled while looking at Penny with great enthusiasm.

"Director Travers, before we start the tour, would you mind if I see my partner to the door?" Penny wanted to quickly debrief with Frank before he left.

"Not at all," said Travers.

Frank and Penny exited the office, took a left, and then stopped midway between Travers' and Gruber's offices.

"Penny, that was amazing! I thought you messed the whole thing up before you won him over. I'm so impressed!"

"Frank, we now have a motive!" Penny was focused on the revelation about Rogers' will.

"Yes, that was quite a nugget of information." Frank lamented, "Get him to tell you more about the history of this place. I wonder if what happened here between '57 and '65 could have anything to do with Rogers' disappearance. Something stinks here, and we need to start turning over old stones to find out more."

"Will do. Now you go see your little friend, Bernice," Penny smiled.

"I sure will, Penelope!" Frank smiled as he jabbed back.

"Ha-ha!" Penny laughed and said, "I'll see you back at the 39th in a couple of hours."

Before separating, Frank looked at Penny and whispered, "I'll bet a slice of pepperoni pizza from Tony's that the remainder of Rogers' estate was left to Heavenly Gates."

Penny's eyes went wide.

"A slice of pepperoni!" Frank smiled as he walked away. "You'll see!"

Chapter 10 – Project MK Ultra: The Sleep Room

Before rejoining Travers in his office, Penny decided to snoop around before meeting with the director. After seeing Frank disappear into Gruber's office, and with Travers likely wrapping up his affairs in expectation of providing her with a tour, Penny walked back up the hallway to inspect a door that she and Frank had passed on the way to Travers' office. The door she remembered passing had a sign on it that read, 'Authorized Personnel Only,' which piqued her interest.

Penny approached the door with apprehension, not knowing what or who might be on the other side of it. Now at the door, she paused for a moment, looked both ways, and then firmly grabbed the knob in an attempt to turn it but found that it was locked.

At that moment, a young intern came around the corner and asked Penny, "May I help you, Ma'am?"

Penny was caught off guard by a woman who, in her estimation, appeared to be in her early twenties. Penny had to think quickly. "Ah, I was looking for the lavatory. Is this the way?"

"Oh, no. No one's allowed through that door. Only Director Travers has the key. The lavatories are in the hall just around the corner." The young woman pointed to the doorway she'd just walked through. It was the same door that Penny and Frank came through earlier. "If you entered through the front door and you're here now, you would've passed it along the way. Would you like me to show you where it is?"

"No-no. That won't be necessary. I think I remember seeing it now. Thank you for your help, though." Penny was cordial. "May I ask you a question?"

"Of course," the woman seemed receptive.

"How long have you worked here?" Penny asked.

"Only three months," said the young woman. "Everyone in the Administrative Ward are interns except for Miss Gruber and Director

Travers. We all work six-month internships, and then they replace us with new ones."

"Oh, you must be a student, then?" Penny guessed.

"Yes. I major in psychiatric medicine at Temple University. Several of us here are all in the same program at Temple."

"Psychiatry, huh?" Penny's wheels began to turn, and her gut was connecting the locked door, interns, and psychiatric medicine. Penny refocused on the woman's eyes and said, "Well, I'm sure your parents must be very proud of you."

"Yes, they are. They're both psychiatrists, and they used to work here. Well, I have to go. Have a nice day." The young woman then turned to walk back toward the admin offices.

Penny found the information to be quite curious. *"How long ago did the intern's parents work here?"* She thought to herself.

As the young woman disappeared into an office down the hall, Penny walked through the door to the long hallway that led back to the foyer and dining room area. She then entered the shorter hallways that she and Frank had passed earlier. Every door she tried to open was locked. The only room she was able to access turned out to be the bathroom the young woman had told her about.

Penny finally made her way back to Travers' office, passing Gruber's along the way. As she passed, she could hear Frank and Gruber laughing and again thought that her partner was a good actor. As she got closer to Travers' office, he walked out, startling her.

"Oh, there you are! I was beginning to think you had a change of heart. I'm so glad you stayed behind." Travers looked relieved and excited. "Please do come in, Penelope."

As the two entered Travers' office, Penny explained her absence. "I just needed to powder my nose before our tour."

Travers took the gesture as a compliment. Penny took a seat in the chair Frank had sat in earlier, with Travers now positioned behind his desk.

"Director Travers, I'm so excited to be getting a tour today. Knowing that my great-grandfather lived here at one time makes me feel somehow connected to the place."

Penny exaggerated but only slightly. She did feel a kindred spirit as she walked through the halls but never really felt connected. "Might we be touring the master suite? My guess is that it's on the upper levels?"

"Why surely, but it's no longer used for sleeping quarters, I'm afraid. It's now a recreation room for the residents. You will find the ladies playing bridge and the gentlemen playing canasta there, I'm sure."

"So, Director Travers, before we go out on our tour, may I ask you some questions that have nothing to do with the Rogers investigation?" Penny lied to the Director. Everything she was about to ask him was strictly intended to assist her in her investigation.

"What sorts of questions do you have, Penelope?"

"Well, you seem to have it all figured out. A man in his early fifties, holding an incredibly important position that provides so many elderly people with quality care in the years in which they need it the most. That's very noble," said Penny. "Additionally, with the large amount of responsibility you have on your shoulders, you seem to be in complete control. You're clearly highly educated, and..." Penny paused.

"And what, Penelope?" Travers seemed to hang on Penny's next words.

"Well, you're so refined," said Penny, almost embarrassed by the comment. "Now I know why Miss Gruber thinks so highly of you."

"Well, Penelope, dare I say, flattery will get you everywhere with me." Travers stopped short of blushing. "Believe it or not, I'm sixty-one years old," he smiled. "Now, please, go ahead with your questions."

Penny feigned a look of surprise. "Thank you, Director Travers."

"Please, call me Dean," Travers interrupted. "I would ask, however, that when we are in the presence of staff, you address me as Director. I wouldn't want those working here to feel as if I'm their friend. Best that they keep it professional. I'm sure you can understand."

"Dean, does that mean that we're friends?" Penny tried to blush but wasn't sure she was as good of an actor as Frank.

"I would like to think so, Penelope."

"Please, call me Penny."

"And if I prefer your given name of Penelope?" Travers tilted his head and raised his brows.

"Penelope, it is then," conceded Penny with a smile.

"Now, please, go ahead with your questions."

"Yes, well, as I was going to say. Because my father's grandfather likely sat in this very office. I feel like I should know you better." Penny slid forward in her chair. "Where were you educated, Director?"

"I am proud to say that I'm a graduate of Harvard. I have a Ph.D. in Social Sciences and a master's degree in Economics." Travers' eyes went to his diplomas on the wall to the right of his desk.

"Yes, I saw those as I took in the majesty of the room but was too embarrassed to stare." Penny was again acting. "If I may ask, Director, where did you work before coming to Heavenly Gates?"

"Of course. I am proud to say that I worked for the Federal Government in the Housing and Home Finance Agency. I left there just several months after it was renamed the Department of Housing and Urban Development or HUD for short." Travers wore a look of great pride.

"You'll have to excuse me, but I don't know if I've ever heard of either of those agencies." Penny avoided eye contact. "I'm so embarrassed."

"Oh, you shouldn't be, Penelope."

"So, that was '65, then?" Penny was taking mental notes.

"Well, it was renamed in September of '65, but I left in the Spring of '66 and began my role here almost immediately."

"Yes, quite impressive that you were the only candidate they spoke to before hiring you for the job," said Penny.

"Well, my old boss at the HUD recommended me for the position. His name is Robert Weaver. Director Weaver was the first Black man appointed to an executive cabinet position. LBJ placed him, but he also worked under JFK." Travers almost seemed to be boasting.

"Impressive!" Penny shook her head, "But I guess I don't understand why a man of your stature decided to come to work in North Philly, of all places. I mean, you should be in Washington, D.C. changing the world."

"Why, thank you, Penelope," Travers was modest, "but my place is here, continuing the good work of my predecessors."

Penny's back went straight, thinking that Travers slipped up with the admission. "Predecessors?" She interpreted his words as a mistake, revealing that he might be connected to The Allan Institute after all.

"Well, Penelope, you know that this was a retirement community prior to being a psychiatric hospital, with your great-grandfather being its first resident back in 1901, as you mentioned earlier."

"Oh, yes. Of course." Penny smiled, trying to make it look as if she was embarrassed.

"Okay, enough about me. Now, how about that tour?" Travers stood, indicating to Penny that he was finished answering her questions.

"Yes, I'm very excited!" Penny beamed.

After showing Penny around the administrative offices, the employee lounge, and medical facilities, the two headed down the hall where the locked door was. As they passed it, Penny asked, "What does that door lead to, Director?"

Travers shrugged and, without eye contact, said, "The past, unfortunately. Please come this way. I want to show you the library and the sitting room that your great-grandmother undoubtedly spent much of her time in."

Penny was taken first to a massive library with both mounted deer and boars heads positioned high on the walls above bookshelves, that in her estimation, were twenty feet tall. Rolling ladders could be rolled back and forth on three walls, with the fourth wall having an actual balcony. She was also overwhelmed by the smell of mildew. She'd guessed that the books lining the walls were more than one hundred years old and that the humidity in the room would've wreaked havoc on them over the many decades.

"Does that man look familiar to you, Penelope?" Travers pointed to an oil painting of a man with a shotgun perched on his right shoulder while prominently displaying a pheasant in his left hand.

"That would be Samuel Crenshaw," Penny nodded her head and displayed her family pride.

"If you look over there in the far corner, you'll see that very pheasant stuffed and on display," Travers smiled.

"Really? The exact one?" Penny looked surprised.

A modest Travers laughed, "Well, maybe not the exact one."

The Director knew that his tour would bring Penny great joy and happiness. What Travers didn't know is that Penny hoped to see the rooms in the home where psychiatric experiments had been conducted in the past.

"Can we see the basement?" asked Penny.

"Now, why would you want to go down there, Detective?" Travers looked a little curious and also seemed suspicious by the request.

Penny noticed that Travers called her 'Detective' instead of Penelope. She knew that her request caught Travers off guard and was quick to come up with a reason why she'd asked it.

"Well, I can only imagine that my grandfather, Ernest, played down there with his siblings. I'm quite certain that they would have had hours of fun chasing each other around the place."

"Well, I'm afraid that it's been closed off since 1965. I don't go down there very often." Travers again tried to brush aside Penny's question.

Penny could see that he was uncomfortable speaking on the subject. She also wondered if he'd just slipped up again by suggesting that he does, in fact, go down there from time to time. Penny wondered that if it had been closed off since 1965, why would Travers go down there at all?

After an hour of seeing all the mundane areas of the mansion, like the kitchen, employee housing, resident common areas, swimming pool, and horse stables, Penny asked, "Where are all of the residents, Dean?"

"My guess is they're in their private quarters. Most can be a bit bashful when I give a tour to an outsider."

"Can I see that wing of the home?"

"Oh, no, Penelope," Travers was apologetic as he shook his head. "That would be an invasion of their privacy, I'm afraid."

An hour later, Penny and Travers found themselves back in Travers' office.

"Whew, thank you for the tour, Director Travers. It was far more than I'd hoped it would be," Penny lied. "It's so much bigger than it looks from street level."

"Yes, it's quite large," Travers' nodded in agreement.

"So many stairs," said Penny, shaking her head.

"Yes, I only go upstairs when it's necessary for me to do so."

"Was that an elevator that I saw upstairs in the main hallway, Dean?"

"My dear Penelope, you miss very little. The City of Philadelphia is fortunate to have you. Yes, it was an elevator," said Travers. "It's needed as many of the residents can no longer climb the stairs at Heavenly Gates, but unfortunately, it hasn't worked for some time. We really must get it repaired soon."

"Does it provide access to each floor of the house?" asked Penny.

"Yes, it does."

"This place is one of the few grand old mansions left in North America," he paused. "Penelope, may I ask if you've ever been to Canada?"

"No, I haven't. But I understand that it's beautiful there."

"Oh, you must go some time!" Travers wore a look that revealed his affinity for the country. "If you do, you should go to Montreal. There, you will find one of the most beautiful mansions in the world. It's called Ravenscrag. It's on a hill that overlooks the St. Lawrence River and downtown Montreal. It's simply marvelous. They don't build them like that anymore." Travers' eyes went off into the distance for a moment. His blank stare indicated to Penny that he was feeling nostalgic. "I understand the same architect was responsible for both Ravenscrag and FalconClaw," offered Travers.

"Is that why they're both named after birds?" Penny wondered aloud.

"Ravenous birds at that," Travers flashed a sinister smile at Penny.

"Director," Penny caught herself, "I mean Dean, if birds have talons, I wonder why this place was called FalconClaw?"

"Yes, that is a wonderful little mystery, isn't it?" Travers pondered aloud. "I'm sure there are a great many more mysteries hidden within these walls." Travers again flashed a sinister smile.

Penny was starting to feel uncomfortable. She took a mental note of where her holstered revolver and the door were.

"Penelope, another wonderful mansion," Travers paused, "more like a gothic-style castle is Casa Loma. It's in the northern section of Toronto. Oh, it is magnificent." Travers' brows shot to the top of his forehead.

After a few seconds of Travers wandering off in his own little world again, Penny spoke up.

"Dean, I wanted to ask you something," Penny paused with purpose as if to give the impression that she was hesitant. "It's about this place."

"What is it, Penelope? You look as white as a ghost." Travers displayed concerned for his new friend.

Penny's voice crackled with hesitation. "Dean, since I was a little girl, I've known about this place. Though I've never visited, it was always private, and I had no business being here, though I'd always wondered, until today, what it was like on the inside."

"Well, I'm glad I was able to satisfy at least some of your curiosity."

"There's something else, though. It has nothing to do with Victor Rogers, you, Mr. Winter, or Heavenly Gates for that matter."

"Yes, Penelope, what is it?" Travers again seemed concerned.

Penny exhaled, looking nervous before speaking. "Dean, what happened here? There were rumors of crazy witchcraft and voodoo stuff going on here. Half of North Philly thinks this place is haunted or something. I mean, what in the world went on here in the fifties?"

Travers looked uncomfortable with Penny's question.

"Director, I feel I have a right to know as my distant relatives lived here. This place was always like heaven to me. I looked up to it," said Penny. "From the back seat of my parent's car when I was little, to driving by it myself as a young adult, I looked at this place perched high up on the hill as a utopia. But when the rumors started, I felt stripped of any pride I'd ever had. I would no longer tell people that my great-grandfather built the place. I haven't told anyone in years. My husband and family know, but I never even told my children. I only told Detective Bruno just before we got here," Penny lied. "I'm almost ashamed because of the rumors surrounding this place. I feel cheated out of my childhood memories, Dean."

Penny was starting to think that her acting skills were beginning to rival Frank's. "Then, in 1970, the news reports started coming out that they were doing mind-control experiments here, and that shattered my idea of the place. I just don't know what to think anymore."

Travers displayed empathy by saying, "Penelope, you poor thing. Your childhood has been tarnished, hasn't it? You should feel pride for this place, and instead, you feel shame."

Penny said nothing. She sat there acting like she was both sad and mad. It was an act, though. While Penny did feel a familial connection to the place, she certainly didn't feel cheated out of her childhood. FalconClaw may have been built by her great-grandfather, but she never felt like she had any rights or ownership of its memories or considerable worth. Penny was wearing her detective hat. She was trying her best to extract information about Heavenly Gates that could further her investigation into not only the disappearance of Victor Rogers but maybe even that of her great-grandfather, Samuel Crenshaw. In her mind, the two couldn't possibly be connected some forty-nine years apart, but in her heart, she couldn't escape the similarities between the two cases.

Travers spoke back up, feeling sorry for Penny. "Penelope, I'm afraid that I can't tell you much more than was reported on in the news," his eyes conveyed his regret.

"Dean, there must be something. You came here less than a year after the city shut it down. Is there nothing you can tell me about what went on here?" Penny tried again to look helpless.

"Well, I will tell you what I do know, and then you can reconcile that with any news reports that you may have seen. At least then, you'll be able to dispel any untruths or rumors that are neither truth nor fact-based," offered Travers.

"That would mean the world to me, Dean. It's the lies that I can't take. Any terrible truth would be better than any comforting lie." Penny gloated on the inside, thinking that that was a good line she'd just fed the director.

"Well, Penny, let me start from the beginning. Yes, you can indeed learn things simply by working here. Sometimes literally tripping over awful memories. Things that weren't reported in the news, and yes, I saw every last one of those damn news reports." Travers looked agitated. "All of that was preceded by the disappearance of Victor Rogers. The negative media attention we received in just an eight-month span nearly put us out of business." Travers looked tired all of a sudden. "As I told you and your partner earlier, residency and staff levels are at an all-time high, but after those reports came out in the winter of '69 and the spring of '70, both dropped to record lows. I thought for sure we would be unable to sustain this place."

"Going back to the Great Depression, this place closed down as no one could afford quality care for their aging loved ones. After thirty-one years, Heavenly Gates was no more," said Travers. "Your great-grandfather would have been broken-hearted. The place was vacant from 1931 until1940. It was the war effort that would eventually bring it back to life. The federal government leased the estate from the city and used it as a makeshift factory. These rooms were filled with women making uniforms for military personnel, while in the basement and horse stables, they made munitions of some sort. The smell of gunpowder still lingers down there, I'm afraid," Travers exhaled in resignation.

"I vaguely remember any of that," said Penny. "I was just a little girl. During the war, we never really left Rhawnhurst much. When we did pass those gates out front, it seemed that there was very little activity around this place."

"Well, after the war, the government still had it leased, so they tried to make it some sort of military academy, but by the time the Korean war began in 1950, they shut it down again, but only for a couple of years." Travers looked troubled by what he was about to divulge. Penny noticed that he went a little pale at that moment.

"Please, go on, Dean. It means so much to me to fully understand the history of this place. And coming from you, it doesn't seem as bad as hearing all of those awful rumors and news reports." Penny hammed it up.

"Well, what happened next nearly ruined this place," Travers looked sick. "Are you sure you want the truth, Penelope?"

"I do, Director Travers."

Travers got up and walked over to the door, and closed it. Penny again inventoried her revolver just in case Travers wasn't who she thought he was. In her mind, perhaps he, like her, was simply acting. She kept her eyes on him as he walked from his desk to the door and then back to his desk again. Her heart rate went up a few beats, but she didn't show it. Her time in uniform walking the beat in North Philly had prepared her well.

Travers sat back down, paused for a second, and continued. "Penelope, after the Korean War ended, many soldiers came home and exhibited signs of empathy for their communist North Korean captors. Many higher-ups in the military suggested that the men must have been brainwashed. Many suggested that communists were attempting to infiltrate our country through the minds of our returning soldiers. After the war ended in 1953, the military-industrial complex had no wars to fight, and the CIA, first formed by President Harry S. Truman in 1947, had a big budget."

"The CIA focused on the fight against communism and how mind control might help in the programming of their soldiers in both combat and secret spy missions. You see, the United States government thought that perhaps the Soviets, and the communist Chinese government, had developed advanced brain-washing methods."

"I'm confused," said Penny. "How does this place factor into the Korean War?" Penny was only half acting at that point. She was intrigued by Travers' account of actual events that she knew little about.

"You see, Penelope, the United States government still had a lease on this place, and it sat vacant. It had all the facilities necessary to take in patients that were suffering from some sort of delusions and study them," said Travers. "The CIA, working through a doctor named Cameron, would use any means necessary, either chemical or psychological, to influence people's behavior. They'd stop at nothing to crack what the Soviets were up to."

"Guinea pigs," Penny said under her breath.

"Yes, test rabbits, I'm afraid," Travers wore a vacant look, sitting upright in his chair, hands out in front of him, his fingers locked tightly.

"Director Travers, I want the truth." Penny implored the man in front of her, who looked like he was close to putting an end to the conversation. "Dean, please. I can handle it."

"Penelope, have you ever heard of a man named Dr. Donald Cameron?" asked Travers.

"Maybe," said Penny, "the name sounds vaguely familiar to me."

Travers continued, "Well, his name was in the news often back in '70. From 1957 to 1964, Dr. Donald Ewen Cameron, former head of The Canadian, American, and World Psychiatric Associations, was found to be far too controversial to work in traditional psychiatric care facilities. The CIA brought him in to conduct top-secret psychiatric studies on live patients here without their knowledge or consent. During those years, FalconClaw was known as, The Allan Institute."

Travers' face was placid. "Penelope, have you heard of the term *Sleep rooms*?"

Penny leaned forward. "No, I haven't," she responded with great curiosity, now finding herself on the edge of her seat. She felt that Travers was about to reveal something that wasn't reported on in the news.

"It seemed that patients were put into insulin-induced comas, and they would be asleep for days, weeks, and sometimes months at a time. The project was called *MK Ultra*, and it would go on for the entire time that Cameron was here."

"During that time, patients suffering from a wide variety of mental illnesses would be given massive doses of LSD and subjected to intensive shock therapy and light and sound stimulation, all while unconscious. This would go on twenty-four hours a day, seven days a week, and countless hundreds were impacted," confessed Travers, almost displaying a look of guilt and shame. "Penelope, it went on for years."

"But what does light and sound stimulation do to a person who is in a coma?" Penny was curious as she leaned in.

"Penelope, the goal was to wipe their brain clean of any memories."

"To what end?" asked Penny, now looking appalled by the revelations.

"They were trying to depattern the minds of the patients, wiping their thoughts and memories clear. The patients would be subjected to subliminal messages played on a loop as they slept and would be exposed to rapid strobe lighting that would print new and sometimes bizarre memories onto their blank minds."

"I'm confused," said Penny.

"They were testing the notion that they could wipe away memories and replace them with new ones," revealed Travers.

"And?" Penny leaned in again.

"When the patients awoke from their comas, days, weeks, and even months later, Cameron would test his theory. They would question the patients to see if the new memories stuck and if their existing memories were wiped away," he explained.

"Again, Dean, I don't understand what their goal was." Penny was baffled.

"Penny, do you remember the Frank Sinatra movie, *The Manchurian Candidate?*"

"Yes, it's been a few years, but I remember the general premise. Wasn't Sinatra a POW who was brainwashed by the North Koreans and sent back to assassinate the president or something?"

"Close, it was actually Laurence Harvey who played that person. In the movie, Harvey's character was brainwashed by his captors and sent back home to overthrow the government," explained Travers. "It's the same premise here. Only our government was conducting experiments on mentally ill patients to see if they could replicate what they were certain the Soviets did to our POWs over there."

"Under the guise of 'Day Patient Services,' they would admit the mentally ill to The Allan Institute, now and before, Heavenly Gates. They would conduct their experiments right here in this estate."

"Dr. Donald Ewen Cameron was given broad authority, and only when patients were released to their loved ones was any suspicion of wrong-doing reported. By 1970, families around eastern Pennsylvania hired a prominent attorney to represent them. The U.S. and Canadian governments settled before the case went into federal court. The recipients of the payout were required to sign non-disclosure agreements. The truth still hasn't been fully told or understood," revealed Travers.

"So, that's why you wouldn't show me the basement?" asked Penny. "That's where it all happened, isn't it?"

"That's an evil part of this mansion's history. I'd just as soon leave it buried," said Travers, looking almost relieved to get the information off of his chest. "The worst part of all is that their experiments were flawed from the start."

"Dean, how do you know all of this?"

"As I said, Penelope. By simply working here, you can learn things that you wish you never had," Travers again looked remorseful.

"Dean, please tell me why you believe the experiments were flawed," Penny asked.

"Because the human subjects were flawed," Travers explained. "They all suffered from some sort of psychosis. If their mental state was unsuitable for testing, then surely the experimentation would result in unreliable data," concluded Travers.

"My god. Those poor people and their families," Penny paused. "Dean, thank you. Like I said before, I would rather know the terrible truth than a comforting lie."

Penny was conflicted. She believed that Travers was truthful in his recounting of the facts as he understood them but thought he knew too much. She now believed that he was placed at Heavenly Gates by the U.S. Government. *"But why?"* Penny wondered. She couldn't reconcile the two. *"Was Travers a government agent sent here to continue the mind control experiments? Was Victor Rogers a test rabbit? Was Old Man Winter really Dr. Donald Cameron? And what about Polly Anne Steinman? Were the Feds doing experiments at other retirement homes too?"* Penny needed to know how Garrison Winter factored into the sordid affair. She needed to learn more, and the boys from Pittsburgh would likely shed some light on the mystery.

Penny rose from her chair and walked behind the desk where Travers was now standing. "Dean, may I give you a hug?"

"Why, Penelope," Travers seemed to blush. "I'm sure that would be just fine, seeing as we're friends now." Travers now looked at Penny as if she was somehow a family member to a man that had no family at all.

As Penny hugged Travers, she couldn't be sure if she was embracing an angel from heaven or one of the devil's mutinous flock. She would soon find out, though.

Chapter 11 – Witchy Woman

Penny took Travers up on his offer to have a car drive her back to the 39th District. Now inside, she opened the second-floor door at the top of the stairwell and could see and hear Frank on the phone. It sounded to Penny like he was on the phone with the boys from Pittsburgh.

Frank saw Penny and waved her over but placed his finger on his lips, indicating that she shouldn't say anything. She could overhear the men discussing dates and times for the upcoming meeting they were to have. Penny pulled her chair out from under her desk and hung her purse strap on the back of it. She walked over to the coat rack positioned on the wall just outside Ron McClain's locked office and hung her gray jacket. Still stained with the rust she got off the front gate at Heavenly Gates just two days prior.

Penny was chomping at the bit to tell Frank what she'd learned and anxiously paced the floor near her desk, waiting for his call to end. A moment later, Frank hung up the phone, and Penny began to speak. "Frank, you won't believe...."

"Gimme a second," Frank held up his finger. He finished jotting notes from his call and said, "Okay, so we've locked down a date with the Pittsburgh boys. We're meeting them in Lewistown on November 6. That gives us less than a week to get our act together." Frank looked up at Penny and said, "So, did you take the tour, or what?"

"You're not gonna believe what I found out, Frank."

"Bring it on!" Frank waved the information on with both hands.

"Care to take a guess where Travers worked before getting the job at Heavenly Gates?"

"The Federal Government," Frank blurted out with confidence.

"How in the hell did you know that?" Penny was surprised.

"I can smell a Fed a mile away. Besides, I was at the FBI conference last fall. Those guys all dress alike, same haircuts, same body language. Like I said, a mile away." Frank winked at his partner.

"Frank, he worked in the HUD."

"What's that?" Frank had no idea what Penny was referencing.

"It's the Department of Housing and Urban Development. How do you not know that?" Penny shook her head. "A mile away, huh?"

"Never heard of it," shrugged Frank. "So, what does that mean?"

"Frank, from 1940 to 1965, the Federal Government leased the place from the city. During that time, they used it as a factory to make uniforms, and in the basement and stables, they actually made bullets." Penny was going off her memory as she didn't take notes when talking to Travers privately because she wanted him to think their conversation was not police business.

"During that time, it was used as a Military Academy until 1950; then it was used as a federally funded psychiatric hospital. Then, and get this, in 1957, the CIA funded a program that was run by some kook named Dr. Donald Ewen Cameron. The program was called MK Ultra. Do you remember the news coverage back in '70?"

"Oh yeah, mind control shit, right?" Tapping his pencil on his desk, Frank tried to recall the story.

"It's worse than you think, Frank," Penny's look conveyed a cover-up. "The story died in the papers pretty fast because the government paid off the plaintiffs in the case. The Canadians were also involved."

"The Canadians?" Frank stopped tapping his pencil and shook his head.

"Apparently, this guy, Dr. Cameron, used to be a world-renowned Psychiatrist, and at one time, he was the head of The Canadian/American and World Psychiatric Associations. His theories and studies went too far for the mainstream but not for the CIA. During and after the Korean War, the Feds thought that the Soviets and Chinese were responsible for brainwashing soldiers held as POWs by the North Koreans. They needed to test the methods possibly used by the Soviets and needed live subjects to do it."

"Man, this Cold War shit never stops," Frank shook his head. "What else?"

"Well, apparently, FalconClaw had the facilities needed for the testing. They brought in this nut job, Cameron, from Montreal and began advertising 'Day Patient Services.' Because the place had been a well-known psychiatric hospital for several years, no one suspected a thing," explained Penny, almost tripping over her words, trying to give Frank the whole story in a hurry.

"Okay, okay. Slow down, Partner," said Frank. "So, the Feds were doing what now?"

"They were conducting radical shock and chemical treatments on mentally ill patients that had no idea they were being used as guinea pigs."

"Jesus!" said Frank.

"Frank, they put these people into insulin-induced comas for weeks and months at a time. They were subjected to strobe light treatments when they were under, and huge amounts of LSD was pumped through their bodies. They were trying to erase their memories and replace them with new ones."

"Mother of God!" exclaimed Frank. "Those people didn't know what they were walking into. They went in to get better, and they got worse."

"Far worse!" exclaimed Penny. "Those people came out of there without a memory of their past. They couldn't even remember their family members. They didn't recognize their own children. My god," Penny put her hand to her mouth. "Their kids, Frank," she said while shaking her head.

Penny exhaled and then took in a deep breath. "Then, in '65, they shut it all down. Like overnight. Cameron went back to Canada, and those poor people, some two-hundred and eighty, suffered lifelong brain trauma," explained Penny. "Then, in '70, that's when the shit hit the fan. Many of the families involved hired a big-shot lawyer. The governments of Canada and the U.S. settled out of court. The story went away quickly because the plaintiffs all had to sign non-disclosure agreements."

"Okay, so what does this have to do with Victor Rogers?" Frank was trying to connect the dots.

"This might sound crazy, but what if the experiments continued on after 1965?"

"Son of a bitch!" Frank rose from his chair. "The Feds put Travers in there to keep it going. So you think they were conducting experiments on Rogers and that something went wrong?"

"Frank, he had no family, no one came to visit him," reasoned Penny.

"No one would miss him if he disappeared!" said Frank. "I'll be damned!" Now Frank was pacing the floor.

"Frank, whatever went down, it happened in the basement," said Penny. "While you were in there hitting it off with Gruber, I got busy snooping around. I found a locked door and started asking around. Apparently, only Travers has the key."

"How do you know that?" asked Frank.

"An intern told me that no one is allowed in the basement and that only Travers has the key. When we went on the tour, I asked him what was down there, and his response was cryptic, 'The past, unfortunately,' is what he said." She paused before adding, "Frank, Travers knows more than he's letting on." Penny looked frightened.

"How does Old Man Winter fit into all of this; you think?" Frank wracked his brain.

"Frank, this is going to sound crazy," Penny paused and took a nervous breath. "What if Garrison Winter is really Dr. Donald Cameron?"

Frank's eyes went wide. "That would be some crazy shit, right there!" he paused for a moment. "Well, that old bastard was playing head games with us." Frank sat back down and immediately started writing on his notepad. "Penny, this is all too crazy! There's no way they could pull it off," Frank looked at her in disbelief.

"Frank, they fooled everybody for eight years before it all shut down in 1965." Penny was now sitting on the corner of Frank's desk.

"Write this down! Bad stuff happened, and they shut it down, and then less than six months later, they put a Fed in charge, who had no experience running a retirement home."

"Travers said it himself, he got the job immediately. They didn't even interview anybody else. Then, Garrison Winter shows up right after Polly Anne Steinman goes missing." Penny leaned over and tapped her finger down on Frank's notepad. "Frank, what if the government is doing this at other places around the country? There could be other people missing."

"Bloomington," Frank looked up at Penny, his eyes as wide as the hubcaps on his '67 Buick.

"There's got to be more victims, Frank. God only knows how many!"

"But how can they keep it from the staff? They can't all be government employees."

"What staff?" questioned Penny. "I've been there twice now and have only seen Gruber, Travers, and an intern. What's up with that?"

"And I found out that the admins are all college students. They're interns working for six months, and then they turn 'em over," said Penny, now walking back to her desk and sitting down. "Frank, get this! The intern I questioned said that most of the interns there study Psychiatry at Temple. And you'll never guess what her parents do and where they used to work?"

"Psychiatry?" Frank sat up in his chair. "They used to work at Heavenly Gates?" he was astonished.

"She didn't say when they worked there, but if it was 1965 or earlier, then that'd be something, right there."

"But still, how could they keep it quiet? Travers said staffing and residency levels were at an all-time high. Somebody would have seen something."

"Frank, I toured the whole facility, and guess how many residents I saw?"

"None," said Frank.

"Maybe Rogers saw something," Penny posed the thought. "Frank, there's an elevator, and it runs from the resident sleeping quarters down to the basement."

"No shit?" Frank couldn't believe Penny learned so much in her short time with Travers. "How in the hell did you get all of that information out of our boy Dean Travers? Does this guy have the hots for you or something?"

"No, but I think he was blown away by the fact that I'm a Crenshaw," said Penny. "I kinda felt guilty playing on his emotions. I was mostly acting, you know, kinda like you with Gruber." Penny smiled and threw a balled-up piece of paper at Frank. "So, what happened in there with you two anyways? I heard you two laughing it up in her office."

Frank went straight-faced. "We have a date on Saturday."

"What in the hell are you talking about?" Penny was shocked.

"I need to know what she knows about Rogers' disappearance, so I told her that I was unmarried when she asked, and then she asked me out for coffee on Saturday, so I said, yes."

"Is that even ethical?" Penny was stunned.

"I'm going undercover, Penelope!" Frank reminded Penny that she played on the emotions of Dean Travers.

"Touché," Penny laughed out loud. "Fair enough, Partner. Just don't muddy the waters." Penny purposely didn't mention the hug she'd shared with Travers. She knew that Frank was lonely, though, and that he missed his Jeanie.

"Frank, again, I'm sorry about Jeanie. I was so sad to hear that she passed."

Frank was stoic, "It's okay, Penny, me and the girls will be fine."

"Who's helping you take care of them? Who's gonna watch them when we drive over to Lewistown?"

"Jeanie's sister is looking out for the girls. She watches them during the day for me. Sometimes she even sticks around and cooks dinner for the three of us." Frank's eyes went off to nowhere. "I miss her, Penny. She was my best girl."

Penny was heartbroken for Frank. "I know, Frank. Like I said, whatever me and Joe can do to help out. Just let me know, Partner."

"Penny, say nothing to McClain or the guys," he paused, "I mean nothing!"

"You got it, Frank. Nothin!"

While jotting her memories from the Traver's conversation, the other four detectives walked in. Penny and Frank looked at each other, and without words, conveyed the message to say nothing about what the two were working on.

"Hey, Frankie Boy! We just got a big one!" shouted Jack Riggins.

"Oh, yeah! What's that, Riggo?"

"We just busted the kid who keeps stealing Old Lady Stanton's poodle."

"No shit?!" said Frank, looking at Penny and smiling. "Who was it?"

"It was the neighbor kid. Apparently, he liked messing with the old dame," said Doug Coons.

Penny chimed in, "Well, maybe tomorrow you'll catch the guy who stole a pack of gum down at the five & dime last week."

"Ha-ha! Whatta you know, Bryce?!" smirked Riggins. "At least we got cases to work on!"

"Just messin with you, Riggo!" Penny tried sounding like one of the boys.

"It's Riggins! Only my friends call me 'Riggo!' Got that?!"

"I gotcha!" said Penny, no longer smiling.

"C'mon, Penny. Let's grab a slice across the street." Frank saved his partner from the bullying of the guys.

Now sitting in the back booth at Tony's, the jukebox drowned out their conversation to the other patrons who were grabbing some pizza for lunch.

"Frank, going through my notes back at the office, I forgot to mention that everyone is an intern in the Admin ward at Heavenly Gates."

"Yeah, you mentioned that," said Frank, sprinkling hot seeds on his pepperoni pizza. "Everyone but Travers. I got it."

"Everyone except for Travers..." Penny paused and raised her brows, "and Gruber."

"Well, that would make sense," said Frank. "They probably got a tight budget."

Penny leaned in close and whispered, "So, what if she's in on it too?"

"Listen, if there's something to be 'in on,' then she'll know," said Frank, taking a bite of his pizza. Wiping his mouth, he added. "I'll lay on the charm and see what she knows."

"I gotta tell you, though," Penny shook her head as *Witchy Woman* blared from the jukebox. "I felt like Travers was truthful. I mean, yeah, he gave me the creeps a couple of times, but overall, I believed the guy. He was nice."

Frank was thinking about Gruber as he sang along with the Eagles. *"Well, I know you want a lover. Let me tell you, brother, She's been sleeping in the Devil's bed. And there's some rumors going round. Someone's underground..."* He swayed in his seat, singing to Penny.

"A real lady-killer, huh? Poor Bernice Gruber has no idea what she's in for, does she?" Penny laughed.

"Who knows..." said Frank. "For all we know, she's a cop-killer," he shrugged. "Just sayin..., if they don't find my body, you better be the one to arrest her and Travers."

"Don't even say shit like that, Frank!" Penny threw a crumpled-up napkin at her partner.

Frank laughed and sang out the last line of the song, "*Woohoo, witchy woman. She got the moon in her eye*!" carrying the last note a little too long for Penny's taste.

"Come on! Raven hair and ruby lips? That's Gruber to a tee. You gotta admit it," Frank joked with Penny.

"What can I say? I'm not an Eagles fan."

"How in the hell can you be from North Philly and not like the Eagles?" Frank joked, knowing that Penny rooted for the football team but not the band.

When Frank finished, he saw Penny's eyes go toward the front of the restaurant, where some patrons heard the 'not like the Eagles' comment.

Frank turned to see cross-eyed stares and yelled, "Whatta you lookin' at?! I was talking about the band," Frank yelled to the guys up front.

Frank turned back to Penny, and in an eerie moment of foreshadowing, *Evil Woman*, by Crow, started to blare from the jukebox.

"You hear that?" Frank motioned with his head to the jukebox just feet away. "I'm telling you, they're all evil!" he joked. "God's telling us to run."

Frank was acting sillier than usual. Penny laughed but was superstitious. She took the songs as a bad omen.

Still smiling, Penny said, "Just watch yourself, Frankie Boy."

"Don't worry about me. I'm pretty damn sure God almighty is gonna come for you before me!" Frank joked.

What Detective Frank Bruno couldn't possibly know at that moment was that in just fifty-five days, Detective Penelope Denise Bryce would be dead.

Chapter 12 – The Pittsburgh Boys

In the early morning hours of Wednesday, November 6, a loud horn from a '67 Buick sounded, ending one day and beginning another. Dogs, alley cats, neighbors, and Detective Penny Bryce were alerted that Detective Frank Bruno was down on the street waiting for his partner.

A minute later, the front door of 2125 Fuller Street opened. Stepping out onto the front porch were Detective Penny Bryce and her husband Joe, still in his pajamas. Joe waved to Frank, kissed Penny goodbye, and waited until his wife got into the car. It was still dark out, and flurries, illuminated by streetlamps and the Buick's headlights, filled the air, along with Frank's memories. The last time he saw snow, Jeanie was still alive. Frank barely even noticed Penny getting into the car.

Penny waved goodbye to Joe through the fogged window and then looked over at Frank and noticed him just staring out at the street, wiper blades flapping. Penny looked away and then down, inspecting the crease in her brand new beige, polyester slacks. She'd bought a new outfit the previous Sunday for the trip to Lewistown. Moments later, noticing that the car still hadn't moved, Penny looked over at Frank and said, "You okay, buddy?"

Frank looked over at Penny but saw Jeanie sitting there instead. Studying her face, he was confused when he heard Penny's voice coming out of his wife's mouth.

"Frank, you okay, partner?" said Penny, trying to get Frank to focus in on her eyes.

Frank snapped out of his fog and said, "Yeah-yeah. I'm good." He then grabbed the column shifter in his right hand and cranked it down into drive. The Buick rolled away, leaving tire tracks on the snow-dusted street.

Frank took Route 1 North up to Interstate 276 and took a left on the Westbound onramp. Penny sat quiet, uncomfortable that Frank hadn't spoken to her in the fifteen minutes since she got in the car.

"My fucking God!" Frank was in a bad mood. "What's up with the snow? I mean, Jesus, it's the first week of November, for Christ's sake."

Penny looked over at Frank, studying his eyes, trying to gauge where his head was. "You gonna tell me what's going on, or what?"

"Whatta you mean?" Frank brooded.

"Just counting how many times you used the Lord's name in vain in one sentence." Penny looked out her window, avoiding eye contact with her partner, who was having another bad day.

"Whatever!"

"Frank, you called off work Monday and Tuesday and didn't answer your phone since Saturday before your date with Gruber."

"It wasn't a date," Frank snapped at Penny.

"Whatever it was, I thought you were dead until you called last night. I almost sent a squad car over to your house to check up on you." Penny was irked.

The dawn came late that day as the two drove west toward central PA.

Frank squirmed in his seat. "I'm fine!" he said. "I'm right here. I'm not dead either!" Frank just kept staring at the empty, windblown, snowy highway. Now peeking from behind the Buick, the sun was trying its darndest to get Frank's attention in the rearview mirror.

"You gonna tell me what happened Saturday night or not?" Penny almost demanded to know what happened between him and Gruber.

"Nothing happened! And I told you, it wasn't a date."

"Got it! It wasn't a date," Penny repeated Frank's assertion. "Now, what happened?"

"Nothing, we just talked. We didn't go anywhere. She invited me in for coffee, and we just stayed there."

"Annnnd?" Penny prodded her partner.

"And nothing."

"Frank, did you find out anything that could help out with the case?"

"No," Frank was short with his partner.

"That's it? That's all you got for me? One-word answers?"

"Penny, nothing happened!" Frank was defensive and guilt-ridden.

"I didn't ask if anything happened. I asked if you gained any information that could help us with the case." Penny was pissed. "What the fuck's wrong with you today?!"

Frank shook his head, snapping himself out of his funk. He knew Penny didn't do anything wrong and knew that it wasn't fair that he took his guilt out on her.

"I'm sorry, Penny, I just haven't been feeling well. I think I caught a bug or something. I'll be fine."

"So, nothing to add to the case file?" Penny was skeptical. Raising her eyebrows, she tried to coax information out of her partner.

"She doesn't know anything. That poor woman has no life, no friends or family. She works endless hours and goes home. She worships Travers and Heavenly Gates. It's the only thing's she's got going, that place."

"Or maybe she's a good actor, just like you," Penny wondered aloud, staring at the snow now blowing violently across the highway.

"I don't know. If she does know something, she didn't give it up. And trust me, if Travers knew anything, she would never give him up, either."

Penny looked at the dashboard clock, it was 6:15 am, and she said, "You got any music in this crate?" She opened the glovebox and sifted through a small collection of eight-track tapes.

"What's all this shit? The Eagles? The Kinks? CCR? Chicago? You don't have any Beatles in here. What in the hell's wrong with you?"

Frank shook his head. "Not a fan, that's all."

"Who in the hell doesn't like the Beatles?" Penny exhaled loudly to make a point.

"Who in the hell doesn't like the Eagles?" Frank mocked his partner.

"Girls! That's who!" Penny was sarcastic. "Boys like the Eagles."

"Yeah, and chicks like the Beatles!" Frank mocked Penny again.

Penny closed the glove box and turned on the radio. She turned the dial, looking for a clear signal, and finally settled on Edison Lighthouse's 'Love Grows.' Both Penny and Frank seemed to like it and sang along.

"There's something about her hand holding mine, It's a feeling that's fine, And I just gotta say," Penny screamed, "HEY! *She's really got a magical spell, And it's working so well, That I can't get away,"* Frank screamed, "Hey!" The two laughed and sang along until the song ended.

When the next song came on, Penny turned down the volume and asked Frank, "Do you need to talk, Frankie?" she paused. "I'm your partner, and I got ears, too."

Frank shook his head, no.

"Cuz I'm here for you, buddy."

"First of all, I'm good. And second of all, I don't need saving, Penny," Frank lied to his partner.

"Well, just know that you've got a friend in me," Penny reached over and touched his hand.

"Whattaya, Carole King, or something?" Frank laughed. He then looked down and reciprocated by squeezing her hand and then looking at her. "Thanks, Penny! Everyone needs a friend like you in their life. Glad you're in mine."

"Okay, so how's it gonna go today?" asked Penny. "We haven't talked about the case since last week."

"Yeah, sorry about that. I figured that we had a few hours in the car this morning, and we could discuss it on the way there," Frank apologized.

Penny looked out the window. Wearing a blank stare, she said, "Yeah, well, I'm nervous. And the only thing that settles my nerves is being in control." She shook her head and said, "And right now, I don't feel like I know shit."

"Penny, you'll do fine. It's not a test," said Frank, trying to calm Penny's nerves. "We're just gonna share information with other detectives. That's it."

"So, what then?" asked Penny.

"We bring it all back and try to make a case that will convince McClain that we're on to something."

"So what do we know, anyway?" Penny was rhetorical in her question.

"We can't say shit about brainwashing experiments, that's for sure!" Frank was adamant.

"Why? That's our whole case so far!" Penny was confused.

"Penny, we don't give away what we think in a meeting like this. We give away what we know. Speculation will come after we have all the facts." Frank was trying to mentor his rookie partner.

"Okay, so what exactly do we know? Or what exactly are we going to say we know?" Penny was all ears.

"WHAT we know is the right answer," said Frank. "It's the What? The Why? And the Who?"

"What?" asked Penny.

"Penny, it's the three W's," said Frank. "The WHAT and the WHY should eventually lead us to the WHO. Got it?" asked Frank.

"No, I don't 'got' it,'" Penny was looking a little lost.

"So far, we know what happened. Victor Rogers disappeared in the morning hours of December 23. Last seen with eighty-three-year-old custodian Garrison Winter," said Frank. "We know there were two sets of footprints leading away from the retirement home and none coming back. What we don't know is the WHY or the WHO. Hopefully, we can shed some light on those two things."

"I'm getting it now," Penny's stress level was beginning to come down.

"When we get with the Pittsburgh Boys, we can also talk about means, motive, and opportunity. But not until we know what they've got, first."

"So, do we agree that motive could lie in Victor Roger's Will?" asked Penny, now consulting her notes.

"Absolutely! That's a big one, right there. It costs a lot of money to live in that place, even for just one year. I mean, what if Garrison Winter lived to be a hundred. That's thousands of dollars."

"That is a lot of money once you stretch it out like that." Penny pursed her lips and nodded.

Frank continued, "We also know that Winter must have had the opportunity because he and Rogers were known as early risers and would get down to the dining room before the other residents would get there. Gaffney stated in his notes that the two men would play Backgammon until breakfast was served," recalled Frank. "It's the means that has me confused. Winter is an old man. How could he convince another old man to just walk out of that house into the snow? And..." Frank paused, "Where's the third set of footprints making their way back to the house? I mean, Old Man Winter was there when everyone came down for breakfast."

"Frank, detailing all of this like you just did freaks me out. My great-grandfather's disappearance happened the exact same way from what I remember as a kid." Penny looked frazzled.

"Listen, we say nothing about that event." Frank was again adamant.

"But why? It's so closely related. It happened at the same place, Heavenly Gates."

"Because that was fifty-four years ago. It can't be the same person who was responsible for both men disappearing."

"No, but that doesn't mean that they're not connected." Penny looked off into the distance, seeing only trees and her suspicions.

"I'll make a deal with you," said Frank. "I'll bring it up if I think their case is connected to ours. If I don't bring it up, then you don't either. Deal?"

"Yeah, fine. But that doesn't mean that I agree with you, but it's a deal."

"And fine, I do like *Desperado*. If Don Henley ever went solo, I would buy his album."

"Well, he ain't never going solo because the Eagles are never breaking up like your Beatles. Hell would have to freeze over before that happens."

Forty-five minutes later, at 9:04 am, Frank and Penny pulled into a parking space in front of the Coleman House, a four-story hotel near the historic downtown area and just around the corner from the famous Embassy Theatre. Part of its lore was the fact that Franklin Delano Roosevelt stumped there back in 1932, during his Presidential run. It was a place Frank had once been to when he was a little boy back in the mid-thirties.

Frank mentioned to Ken Kowalczyk ahead of time that he'd be driving a dark blue '67 Buick, so when the detective from Pittsburgh noticed a car pull up in front of the hotel that he recognized as Frank's, he went outside to welcome him.

As the wind swirled and flurries turned to snow, Kowalczyk waved to the occupants of the car as it settled into its parking space.

"Frank, so glad to see you again!" Kowalczyk recognized Frank immediately as he exited the car.

Walking around to the front of the car, Frank extended his hand to shake Kowalczyk's as Penny got out of her side.

"Ken, nice to see you again." Frank showed respect though not recognizing the detective from the FBI seminar the year before. "This is my partner, Detective Penny Bryce." Frank motioned to his partner as she stood uncomfortably on the sidewalk, clutching at her lapels and the sudden gust of wind.

Penny extended her hand to shake Kowalczyk's. "Nice to meet you, Detective Kowalczyk."

"It's a pleasure, Detective." Ken Kowalczyk tipped his hat.

Penny appreciated that the Pittsburgh detective recognized her hard-fought job title.

As the three shielded their faces from the wind and the snow, Frank asked, "You guys get any snow on the way in?"

"No, we came in last night," said Kowalczyk. "The news kept saying snow, so we didn't want to chance it." Ken grabbed the hotel's front door handle and pulled it open, holding it for Frank and Penny as the wind tried to push it closed.

The three were met by Detective Harrison Lane. His burly stature and rugged jawline made an instant impression on the Philly cops. The four detectives then made their way down a long hallway to a small conference room with hideous-looking red carpet, marked with gold squares and what looked like Fabergé eggs. Brown stains littered the floor. Inside the room were two folding tables and five chairs set up in the middle of the room, with a smaller table against the left wall with a coffee maker, Styrofoam cups, creamer, packs of sugar, and plastic stirrers. Along the back wall were dozens of folding tables and chairs that were leaned up against the wall. Trashcans next to the coffee table overflowed with garbage.

Kowalczyk looked embarrassed and said, "Sorry, this is the best we could get on our budget. The local VFW had some kind of party here last night, and I guess the hotel staff didn't come in to clean it yet."

"How much did it cost us?" asked Frank, surveying the mess.

"It was free!" laughed Harrison Lane from across the room. His booming voice caught Frank and Penny off-guard.

After the four detectives sat down, Frank said, "Well, let's just dive right in then."

The detectives unpacked whatever case files they had on the table, and Penny joked, "Who's the fifth chair for? We thinking our suspect is going to walk in the door?"

The men all laughed, and Kowalczyk said, "Well, we do have a little surprise for you, Philly guys. Arriving shortly is a man named Shane

Jensen. He's a detective from Bloomington. After we talked with you guys on the 30th, we called the Bloomington boys and told them what we learned from you guys." Kowalczyk caught himself, "Sorry, Detective Bryce, I meant to say, the Bloomington Detectives."

"Don't worry about it, Detective Kowalczyk," said Penny with a smile. "I am one of the boys."

"I go by Ken!" said Kowalczyk.

"They just call me Lane!" Harrison Lane jumped in and shook Penny's hand.

They all laughed, and Penny said, "They call me Penny."

Ken said, "Jensen should be here soon. He flew into State College last night and was getting one of the locals from the University Park Police to drive him down."

"Well, that's just fine," said Frank. "Let's not wait though, more snow is coming, and Penny and I are driving back tonight."

"Roger that!" said Lane.

After thirty minutes of discussion, Shane Jensen finally arrived, and the five detectives started exchanging information. After another hour, they'd borrowed a chalkboard and started filling it with information.

By noon, the chalkboard was full, and the five detectives were all dumbfounded with what they'd come up with.

Frank stood at the head of the room near the chalkboard and said, "Okay, let's go over the similarities that each of our cases has in common." Across the top of the chalkboard were the names of each victim. Commonalities were listed vertically below each name.

Frank recapped the morning by stating only what the detectives knew, purposely not mentioning what each of them suspected.

"Okay," said Frank. "So we know that Victor Rogers was 95 years old and went missing on December 23, 1969. Polly Anne Steinman was 94 years old and went missing on December 21, 1965. And finally, Barbara Jo Tipton was 94 and went missing on December 19, 1957.

All were last seen with an 83-year-old custodian who was later dropped as a suspect due to insufficient evidence." Frank placed checkmarks next to each fact as they were pointed out. "What else do we know?" he asked the group rhetorically, arms folded, his chin cradled in his chalk hand.

He continued reviewing the listed facts. "We know that each victim was in their mid-nineties and that each was led away from their retirement home the morning after a significant snowfall the night before." He added, "Two sets of tracks leading away from the home and none returning. What else, fellas?" Frank turned to the group.

Ken Kowalczyk spoke up, "Guys, am I the only one that's made the connection of the retirement home names?" he looked around at the others. "They all have a connection to God or Heaven."

Everyone seated reviewed their notes.

"We've got *Heavenly Gates*," said Penny.

"I got *Valhalla Springs*," said Shane Jensen.

"And we've got *God's Glory*," said a nodding Kowalczyk, looking at Lane, who was also nodding his head.

"That's only a modest connection," said Frank. "Just in Philadelphia, there are count 'em, five retirement homes with names denoting God, Heaven, or the afterlife."

"That makes sense," said Lane. "If people are ready to die, they'd want to go to a place that feels like a gateway into Heaven. I mean, I would feel more comfortable, wouldn't you?"

Those in the group all nodded.

"Yeah, but," said Kowalczyk, "we can't rule it out. It's a similarity."

"Ken's right guys, that is a similarity," said Frank while writing the word *Heaven* in each of the three columns.

"Yeah, and look at the dates," said Jensen.

"What about 'em?" asked Ken, "1957, '65, and '69, and all in December."

"Look a little deeper than that," Jensen challenged the group.

"The dates are sequential if you throw out the year," Penny spoke up. "Descending from the last disappearance, 12/23, 12/21, and 12/19. Whatta you want to bet the next cold case that turns up will be another December victim?"

"Cold case?" Shane Jensen looked confused. "Why are you calling them 'cold cases?' Because they're all in December?"

Penny only smiled while the other three men broke out into laughter.

"Guess your phrase didn't make it that far west, huh, Frank?" Ken joked.

"What? What did I miss?" Jensen looked at the others, not understanding why he was the only one not laughing.

"Shane, the term *Cold Case* is new. It means a case that is shelved after a certain amount of time due to lack of leads," explained Frank.

"Frank's being modest," interjected Ken. "Last year, the FBI held a seminar in Harrisburg and Frank, and I were there. The seminar covered things like how to reapproach unsolved cases, forensic science, psychological profiling. You name it."

"Yeah, and?" said Jensen.

"Our boy, Frank over here, used the term *Cold Case* to describe cases that were dead, sitting on shelves in storage closets. Like the stiff on the paper, they're cold," explained Ken.

"Not quite," explained Frank. "The word cold actually refers to the leads in the case. If you've got a new and promising lead, it's hot. After a while, they cool off and become warm leads, and after that, they...."

"Become cold," Jensen finished Frank's sentence. I get it now," Jensen paused. "So, you came up with that, Frank?"

"Yes, he did! And I was there," said Ken Kowalczyk. "It's a term that seems to have stuck. Detective rooms up and down the East coast are using it. Hell, even the FBI has adopted it last I heard."

The group nodded their approval in Frank's direction while Penny beamed with pride. She felt lucky to have Frank as a friend and a partner. Frank, on the other hand, was modest, blushing almost, standing at the head of the room a little red-faced.

"Okay, let's keep going," said Frank, looking back to the chalkboard. "What else can we come up with?"

"All of the victims were born in the 1800s," Penny spoke up.

The group turned to her and wondered why she was stating the obvious.

Penny looked over her notes and blurted out, "And so was my great-grandfather!"

Frank's head dropped with the utterance. He'd made it clear to her not to mention the fact that her great-grandfather's disappearance was similar.

Without Frank's blessing, Penny rose from her chair, walked over to Frank, and smiled, holding up her palm to her partner. Frank looked her in the eyes, without expression, and reluctantly handed her the piece of chalk he was holding.

Penny grabbed the top of the chalkboard and flipped it over, spinning it around to its blank backside. Then, she began scribbling dates as the four men in the room just looked at each other and then to Frank as if to say, "What gives?"

When Penny was done scribbling, the chalkboard listed the following dates: 12/23/1969 - 12/21/1965 - 12/? - 12/? - 12/? -12/? - 12/?- 12/? and 12/7.

Penny put down the chalk and rubbed her hand together, wiping the chalk away. "Gentleman, we have a serial murderer on our hands."

"A serial what?" said Jensen, as the others chimed in.

Frank just dropped his head and began shaking it from side to side.

"What in the hell are you talking about?" asked Ken Kowalczyk. "I've never heard of such a thing. He then turned to her partner and said, "Frank, whatta you got to say about this?"

For the second time in a week, Frank cleared the way for Penny to defend herself, just as he had at the beginning of the Travers interview. "Don't look at me," he threw his hands in the air in a motion of surrender. "She's every bit the detective that we are."

The group turned back at Penny, looking for an explanation.

"Gentleman, In 1930, a German investigator, working a case that spanned years, and included eight victims, first used the word, 'Serial' to describe the unknown suspect in his case. He then married it with the word 'Killer,'" explained Penny.

"Like, you mean a box of cereal?" said Lane, chuckling.

"Serial, with an S," said Frank. "As in a series of murders."

"Exactly!" Penny pointed an animated finger in Frank's direction.

"Okay, I get the serial part, but what are you talking about with regards to your great-grandfather?" Ken enhanced his annunciation of the word 'grandfather.'

Penny picked the chalk back up and circled the date 12/7 on the chalkboard. She turned to see Frank covering his mouth with his right hand as if fighting back the words that might save his partner from an embarrassing moment in front of senior detectives.

Penny continued, "My great-grandfather disappeared on December 7, 1920. He was last seen with a custodian. He walked right out the front door of Heavenly Gates retirement home in North Philadelphia, never to be seen again."

"Holy shit!" Ken Kowalczyk was astonished. His words were echoed by the other detectives.

"But, Penny," said Jensen, "while I'm sorry your family had to go through that horror back in the day, that was 1920. No way these murders are part of a series."

"Look at the dates!" she drew a vertical line down the side of the nine dates. "I'll bet anyone of you they're connected." Penny was trying hard to connect dots that the others couldn't see yet.

"What about them?" asked Lane. "Most of them are question marks," Harrison Lane pointed out the obvious. "That means you're guessing!" He now seemed to judge her credentials. "We're here to discuss facts, Detective."

"Go on, Penny," Frank jumped to his partner's defense. "Let her finish, guys."

Penny filled in the question marks with numbered days, starting with the one at the top; she wrote 17, 15, 13, 11, 9. "These are the missing dates. I got money that there are at least five more victims out there, and these are the days in December they went missing."

Penny's comments were met with skeptical moans and groans.

"So, you're saying that there are nine total victims simply because you're great-grandfather went missing back in '20?" asked Lane.

"Penny, no disrespect," Ken Kowalczyk butted in. "But I'm beginning to think that you're a rookie detective. Am I right?" he asked. "How long? Six months on the job, maybe?"

"Six weeks," said Penny.

"Hey! Wait a second! You're that broad that sued the City of Philadelphia," said Jensen. Looking at the other guys hoping they agreed with him, he wondered why a woman was sent to do a man's job.

Frank said, "Watch your words, Jensen! That 'broad' is my partner, and she's as smart as any one of us."

Jensen threw up his hands and said, "Okay, I'm sorry." He eyeballed the much larger man and knew he didn't want to piss off the grizzled homicide detective from rugged North Philadelphia.

Ken stuck up for Penny too. "That woman right there," looking at Shane Jensen while pointing to Penny, "took on the City of Philadelphia," he paused. "and won. Philadelphia's got almost as many people living there as the entire state of Indiana!"

"Alright, alright!" Jensen threw up his hands again. "I was out of line. I'm sorry."

"Yeah, you were," said Harrison Lane, trying to look ominous.

"Penny, I think what Jensen was trying to say is that police officers, detectives, judges, just about anyone who's required to think objectively about a case should recuse themselves when a family member is involved," said Ken.

"Ken, my great-grandfather went missing fourteen years before I was even born. I'm not emotionally invested in the man; I barely knew his youngest son, my grandfather." Penny fought off the notion that she somehow wasn't being objective. "I'm looking at the numbers and the facts."

"But they can't be related. There're forty-nine years between the two Heavenly Gates disappearances," said Jensen. "That's too long for one guy to pull off."

Frank agreed and wished Penny hadn't brought it up. He felt she wanted the cases to be connected to her great-grandfather so that she might somehow feel she belonged in the investigation. Frank was starting to wonder why any of them were there at all.

Penny went back to Jensen's question from a couple of minutes prior and said, "Ten!"

The four male detectives chorused, "Ten, what?"

"Shane asked me if I thought there were a total of nine victims in this case," she paused. "I'm suggesting that there're either ten victims or there will be."

Jensen threw his hands up in disgust and said, "This broad's got a big set of crystal balls on her!"

Frank stood up, "Watch it, Jensen!"

"Penny, where are you coming up with this stuff?" Kowalczyk shook his head. "I mean, what in the hell are you talking about?"

The others, not including Frank, all nodded in agreement with Kowalczyk's comment.

"Guy's, listen. If we have a serial murderer, then he's killing with a purpose," explained Penny. "No serial murderer would kill just nine people and stop there. He might stop at ten, or twenty, or thirty, but not somewhere in the between."

"That's some fantasy horseshit right there, Doctor Penny," said Harrison Lane. "You're just making this shit up as you go. I'm starting to agree with Jensen over here."

Penny shook her head, "I think our guy has a god complex. The number 10 is all over the bible."

"The bible?! What the fuck are you talking about?!" Kowalczyk got up from his chair and walked away from the table. Running his fingers through his hair, he groaned, "We're getting nowhere here!"

Frank spoke up, "Penny, you're losing all of us right now. Don't just throw shit out there. Spell it out for all of us. Pretend like we're in seventh grade for a minute."

"Listen, guys, this is just a hunch, but we don't have much more to go on," said Penny. "The number 10 is used hundreds of times in the bible. Ten generations of man lived on earth before the flood; the Ten Commandments; the ten patriarchs before the flood; the ten plagues sent upon Egypt by God," she explained.

"So, all of that might mean something if this nut job is a God freak, but we don't know that," said Jensen. "And what if your great-grandfather was the second victim? Just cuz you think there might be a tenth victim doesn't mean they're not already dead."

Penny defended her stance. "The tenth victim will fall on a Christmas due to the obvious religious significance."

"Yeah, but, Penny," said Lane, "there's been four Christmas's since our last known victim in '69. Like Jensen said, they may already be dead."

"Either way," said Penny, "A recent Christmas or a future one, there's a tenth victim. I'm sure of it."

"Holy shit! Hang on a second, guys!" Frank spoke up after spotting something in the case files on the table. "Penny, we got a name on the custodian back in 1920?"

"No, but I think I can figure it out," Penny's thoughts went to Dean Travers and how he might be able to help.

"Jensen, you got a name?" asked Frank.

"A name of who?" Jensen still seemed a little embarrassed from his 'crystal balls' comment minutes before.

"A name of the custodian that Steinman was last seen with?" Frank seemed impatient.

Flipping through his notes, Jensen said, "Um, um, got it! It was George O' Doyle. Why?"

Ken Kowalczyk sat erect in his chair and wondered where Frank was going with his line of questioning.

"Our guy was Glen Duncan, middle name Olen," said Ken. "Frank, what's your guy's name from '69?" he asked.

"Both Frank and Penny said, 'Garrison Winter' at the same time."

"You guys sure that Winter is a real name?" asked Kowalczyk. "That name seems a little fake to me. I thought that the first time you mentioned it to me, the first time we spoke."

"That is weird," said Jensen. "Our guy was nicknamed Old Man Winter," he said as he flipped through his notes.

Frank and Penny turned to each other in shock.

"Wait a second!" said Lane, "Our notes indicate the same thing; Old Man Winter!"

"Holy shit!" said Frank, still staring at Penny.

The thought had never occurred to either Frank or Penny that Winter might be an alias. At that moment, Penny's eyes went wide. Snapping her fingers, she raced for the door, running down the hall to the front lobby.

Frank headed back to the chalkboard and began writing down the names of the custodians in question.

Minutes later, Penny ran back into the room, out of breath. "His real name is O'Donnell!" Penny yelled. "It's Garrison O'Donnell!"

Frank wrote the name O'Donnell next to the crossed-out name 'Winter' on the chalkboard. He then turned to the group, now standing aside from the chalkboard revealing what he'd been writing. The initials of each of the three custodians were G.O.D.

Chapter 13 – Just Close Your Eyes, Frank

On Saturday, November 2, Frank parked his Buick in front of Bernice Gruber's duplex at 6230 Magnolia Street in the North Hills section of Germantown. The street was tight, maybe the width of three cars, no more in Frank's estimation. The duplexes were even tighter. Every single home on the street was connected to another on both sides. Frank noticed that the continuous row of houses on the entire block shared a common roof.

"Jesus Christ!" said Frank, out loud. "How do I know what door to go to?"

Frank sat in the car past the 8 pm time he was supposed to pick up Bernice. He was hesitant. *"It's just coffee, Frank,"* he told himself as his left hand struggled to find the door handle. Minutes later, Frank got out of the car, looked up to the sky, and mouthed the words, "I love you, Jeanie."

Frank considered the notion of even walking into the home of another woman as cheating on his best girl. He was fighting both his nerves and his guilt.

Now standing at the front door of Gruber's house, Frank's hand struggled to reach for the doorbell. He stood for a moment, trying to get the nerve to ring the bell when the door opened abruptly, catching him off-guard.

Bernice Gruber pushed open the screen door and said, "Well, there you are! I watched you pull up. It took you forever to come to the door!" Gruber stepped back and waved him in. "Get in here!"

"Um, I really shouldn't. We could just go now if you want," Frank almost stuttered over his words.

"Don't be silly! Come in for a second. I just put on a pot of coffee. Are you hungry?" asked Bernice.

"No, I just ate," Frank lied. He hadn't eaten anything all day due to the nerves that had paralyzed him.

"Can I fix you a coffee, or maybe a cold beer?" offered Bernice.

Frank thought a cold one could possibly be the remedy to his nerves. "You got any Schlitz?"

"I took you for a PBR guy!" smiled Bernice as she led Frank into the kitchen.

Frank hated Pabst Blue Ribbon with a passion. "Sure, I could go for that!" he flashed a nervous smile.

"You okay, Detective Frank?" asked Gruber. "You look like you've seen a ghost. Been a while since you been in a woman's house?" she poked at his stomach as she went for the drawer containing the bottle-opener.

"Yeah, no, um," Frank mumbled. "I guess it has been a while."

Gruber pulled out a bottle of Pabst and popped the top off, handing it to Frank.

"Thanks, Bernice. That's mighty kind of you."

"It's just a beer, Sailor!" Bernice tilted the top of her bottle toward Frank's, wanting to toast the occasion. "Here's to us!" she said as they tapped bottles.

"Whatta you mean?" Frank asked Gruber.

"You know, boy meets girl?" Bernice raised her brows, smiled, and winked.

"Oh, I gotcha," Frank let out a nervous chuckle.

Bernice walked out of the kitchen and into the cramped living room of the tiny home. Frank stayed in the kitchen for another moment, trying to gather his wits before Gruber yelled, "You coming?!"

"Coming," said Frank, taking a deep breath before he proceeded into the room that could barely fit a couch, coffee table, reading chair, and television stand that all sat crammed in the front room of the house.

Frank walked in and sat down in the reading chair, positioned next to the window in front of the house and close to the door. He figured it would be an easy escape if he had to run.

Bernice launched a seductive smile at Frank, flashing a look that conveyed to him that she was questioning why he didn't sit next to her on the couch.

"Detective Frank, now why in the world are you sitting way over there? It's getting cold out, and this girl needs warming up."

"Well, I just figured we were getting ready to leave soon and, you know," Frank babbled his words.

"Oh, I thought about it, by the way," Gruber paused. "Would you mind if we just stayed here this evening instead of going out for coffee?" Bernice had a flirtatious look in her eyes. "It was a long week, and I just don't think I have it in me to go out tonight."

"Um, yeah, sure." Frank hesitated before saying, "We could stay here. That's fine."

Two hours and a six-pack later, Gruber got up to close the door. "Burr, it's getting cold out there. They said it's supposed to snow next week. Can you believe it?" she asked Frank.

"No kidding!" Frank's heart raced, and his nervous smile showed it. "Winter seems to come earlier and earlier each year."

"Um, Frank," Bernice tried her best to look sexy. "I said it's getting cold in here." Gruber batted her eyes and motioned her head down to the sofa next to her, hoping that Frank would get the not-so-subtle hint.

A trembling Frank reluctantly joined Gruber on the couch, sitting just six inches from her while holding his beer in both hands between his legs.

Gruber sighed and said, "What's a girl gotta do?!" before sliding closer to Frank, grabbing his right wrist, and throwing his arm around her like a scarf. "Detective Frank, you need to loosen up. I'm not gonna bite you or anything." She smiled and said, "Well, maybe just a little nibble."

"Listen, Bernice. There's something I gotta tell you." Frank recoiled his arm back down to his lap.

"Frank, I'm guessing that you just got out of a long relationship with someone, and you're not quite over her yet," said Gruber. "Does that sound about right?" Bernice slid her backside to the edge of the couch, swiveling to look at Frank.

"Well, yeah, that's just it, you see...."

Before Frank could finish his sentence, Gruber got down on her knees and wiggled her way in between his legs. Frank was a little drunk and a little scared and was rendered speechless.

In that moment of hesitation, Gruber said, "Just close your eyes, Frank, and pretend that I'm her." Frank's head fell back, and Gruber leaned in, reaching for his exposed neck; she began kissing it.

Frank closed his eyes and lowered his head to kiss Bernice, but in his mind, he was kissing Jeanie. Frank could feel Bernice's hands reach for his belt buckle as they kissed passionately, and he panicked. He stood abruptly and pushed Bernice out of his way, knocking what was left of her first beer onto the floor.

Frank made it to his car and started the engine. Sitting there for a moment, he pounded the steering wheel and began wailing. His anguish echoed down the crowded street. His face was drenched with guilt before he'd made it to the end of the block.

Twenty minutes later, he arrived at his house and looked up at the window and the bedroom he and Jeanie once shared. He sat there for two hours, the guilt preventing him from going into the house where Jeanie's spirit was still very much alive.

Frank slept on the couch for the next three nights, feeling unworthy of sleeping in the bed he'd shared with his best girl, Janine Louise Bruno.

Chapter 14 – A Numbers Game

It was 8:00 pm, and Frank and Penny were halfway back to Philly from Lewistown. The trip revealed obvious connections to at least three missing persons but nothing concrete to present to Ron McClain. Frank knew that he and Penny would have to lay everything out for their Chief and make the case as compelling as possible without using hyperbole. Their boss would demand facts, and if those facts didn't justify the manpower, Ron McClain would shut down the cold case investigation.

Frank looked over and saw Penny asleep, leaning up against the door jam. From the side, she almost looked like Jeanie for a second. In Frank's mind, though, anyone sitting next to him in the front seat of his Buick would remind him of the only woman he'd ever loved.

It didn't immediately hit Frank why he'd given Penny such a hard time earlier that morning. He knew that the guilt of kissing a woman, who wasn't his Jeanie, was too much for him to handle, but he unfairly resented Penny for just being in his life. Whether Frank liked it or not, Penny was Jeanie's replacement, which was hard for him to wrap his head around. He didn't look at Penny the way a man looks at a woman, but she filled a void in his life, and instead of resenting her for it, he decided to be thankful instead.

Driving through the snow, Frank felt free and his head clear. He recounted the day's events and let his gut work out the new wrinkles in the case.

In the driving snow, Frank started seeing numbers. The victims were all in their nineties, all born in the 1800s. The custodian in each case was an 83-year-old man. He was starting to see the number eight, and when he saw the age of the custodians, he didn't see the number 38. Instead, he saw three eights. He didn't know what it meant. He just knew that it meant something.

Looking back at Penny, he was impressed with his new partner and how she carried herself in Lewistown. He was a little pissed off that she brought up Samuel Crenshaw's disappearance prematurely because they'd made a deal. Penny wasn't supposed to mention her great-grandfather's case from 1920. In the end, though, he was glad she did. He was starting to wonder if the reason why he was so upset with her was that she beat him to it. Frank thought that Penny's great-grandfather's disappearance had to be connected. How? He wasn't sure. What he was sure of, though, is that they were on to something, and whatever it was, it was big.

The revelation that four cases could somehow be connected was no longer a theory, the facts in the case were too similar, and not one detective in the earlier meeting thought otherwise. Now, if Frank could just convince his boss.

Adjusting the rear-view mirror so that he could see himself, Frank was again feeling guilty about his encounter with Bernice Gruber. He couldn't understand what possessed him to agree to coffee with her. Perhaps he was truly lonely and needed someone to fill the emotional void left by Jeanie. He knew in his heart that going to Gruber's that night had little to do with the Rogers' case. Maybe he was just subconsciously testing himself to see if he could remain faithful to his Jeanie. No matter, in his heart, he failed the only woman he'd ever loved. But he would never do it again.

Adjusting the mirror back into place, Frank saw Jeanie sitting in the back seat smiling at him. Startled for a moment, he swerved just as they were passing a Mack truck. The sudden jolt and sound of the truck's horn knocked Gruber from his mind and Penny from her sleep.

Now awake and staring wide-eyed at Frank, Penny looked alarmed. "Everything okay?" she said while rubbing her eyes and sitting up in her seat.

"Yeah, we're good." Frank acted as if nothing had happened.

"We almost home?" Penny yawned.

Frank responded, "Still got about an hour to go."

It was dark, and the snow was falling heavier now. The darkness and the weather seemed to match Frank's life. He was cold inside, and his world was dark. Penny seemed to be the only bright spot in his life.

In the springtime of his life, his youth, Frank was mostly alone, a young man trying to figure it all out. In the summer of his existence, Jeanie was his light, his warmth, and his energy. Now, he was entering into the fall of his life, and he indeed felt like he was falling. Frank hoped that he'd live long enough to see the winter, or the last part of his life. He knew in his head and heart that it would be cold and lonely without his best girl by his side.

He looked over at Penny and was again thankful. Her friendship helped to fill the void of not having a woman in his life. Frank was happy to have her as his partner. Sure, she made mistakes and would continue to do so, but her instincts were good, and Frank knew that good detectives had good instincts. He made the decision at that moment to begin trusting those instincts more.

"Damn, I was out that long?" Penny yawned again.

"You deserved it. You did good today, Detective."

Penny immediately perked up with Frank's comment. Looking apologetic, she said, "You mean that, Frank?" she paused. "I know I broke our deal. It's just that when I saw the dates of the disappearances, my gut was screaming at me."

"Yeah, you broke our deal, but this time, you were right to trust those instincts," said Frank, looking at Penny and nodding with approval.

"Penny, I don't know what it is, but you have something. Your abilities are innate, and I'm sad the city didn't promote you four years ago. Hell, six years ago, for that matter!" Frank was passionate. "I can't imagine if you were around for The Boy in the Box case, or the Dresden Murders, or the Federal Savings heist. I mean, man, you could have given so much insight to those cases!" Frank looked exasperated.

"Well, there'll be many more cases after this one," thought Penny aloud. "I just hope we find out what happened to Rogers and the others. And what happened to my great-grandfather."

The conversation died down for a few minutes when Penny, staring out the window, said, "Have you ever seen snowflakes that big before?"

Frank was also impressed. "They're like the size of baseballs!"

After another minute of silence, Frank said, "Penny, I'm starting to see numbers."

"Whatta you mean? Like right now?"

Penny sounded concerned. "You want me to drive?"

"No, I mean in the case," clarified Frank. "When you started bringing up that 'Ten' stuff, I started seeing eights."

"How do you mean?" Penny seemed intrigued.

"Well, all the victims were born in the 1800s, and the custodians were all 83 years old. But I keep flipping their ages around for no particular reason to 38, or three eights," revealed Frank.

"You religious, Frank?" asked Penny.

Frank just stared at the snow filling his headlights, shaking his head side to side, "Not since Jeanie died, I'm not."

"Frank, 888 is the sign of the angels."

"Wow, I hadn't heard that since Catholic School. I must've been twelve," recollected Frank. "Penny, you wanna hear some shit? The address for Heavenly Gates is 888 Bedford Street!"

Frank and Penny chorused, "Holy Shit!"

The two sat for a minute and pondered how religion might be associated with the case. They were still having trouble believing that someone could kill in the name of God. But those thoughts were quickly dashed by the thought of all the Holy Wars that had ever taken place.

"Penny, what if this guy's a God-hater. What if he's killing true believers just because they believe?" asked Frank, turning to look at his partner.

"That would be a hell of a thing," Penny responded without turning to look at Frank.

"Well, we've got a problem," said Frank.

"Just one?" smiled Penny, now reaching for some music in the glove box.

"We can't say anything to the Chief about what we think might be the religious motivations of our killer."

Penny slammed the glove box shut. "What in the hell are you talking about? That's the only theory we have! This morning you said we couldn't tell the boys from Pittsburgh about MK Ultra, and now you're saying we can't bring up religion to McClain. What the fuck, Frank? How in the hell can we present a case without a theory?"

"Penny, Ron McClain is the most religious person I know. On top of that, he's old-school."

"So, you're saying that he doesn't have an open mind?"

"That's exactly what I'm saying!" exclaimed Frank. "If he did, he'd still be cracking cases with us."

"How'd he ever get promoted to Chief, anyway?" Penny shook her head.

"His people skills." Frank looked at Penny straight-faced before they both broke out into laughter.

"That's a good one, Frankie Boy!"

After a moment of reflection, Frank sighed and said, "I like it when you call me 'Frankie.'"

"Oh, yeah. Why's that?" Penny smiled at her partner.

Frank looked solemn, "Because Jeanie always called me that."

"I'm so sorry, Frank!" Penny was mortified. "I've been calling you Frankie since we became partners. I'm so sorry."

Frank looked at Penny and said, "Penny, it's okay. I like it. Every time you do it, I'm reminded of her. I always want to be reminded of her. The day I stop remembering her is the day she really dies."

Penny didn't speak. She felt awkward at that moment and so sorry for her friend.

"I kissed her, Penny," Frank was guilt-ridden.

"Kissed who?" Penny looked perplexed. "Jeanie?"

"Gruber," said Frank, his white knuckles choking the steering wheel. "I cheated on my Jeanie, Penny! I broke my vows!" Frank's eyes began to glisten. Each of the passing cars from the westbound lane lit them up like Christmas trees. First, the white and then the red lights reflected the guilt Frank was living with.

Penny was shocked by the confession as she didn't think Gruber was Frank's or anyone else's type, but then her empathy took over. She understood that Frank was lost without Jeanie and was probably just looking for companionship. "Frank, you didn't cheat on Jeanie. It was just a moment of weakness. That's all."

"Tell that to my kids! Tell that to my heart!" Frank slammed his hands on the steering wheel. "How am I supposed to live with that!" he cried.

"Frank, God will give you the strength to carry on."

"God?!" Frank looked over at Penny with disdain in his eyes. "It was your God that took her away from me!"

"Frankie, that's not true. God welcomed Jeanie into Heaven because it was her time. He didn't take her." Penny truly believed what she was saying.

"You might not be saying that if he took someone you loved." Frank was angry.

"He doesn't take, Frank." Penny shook her head, "He welcomes."

Frank shook his head and went silent for a while.

Penny opened up the glove box and pulled out an eight-track tape that would improve Frank's mood. After inserting it into the tape deck, she pushed Play. 'Take it easy,' started playing, and Frank was lifted from his funk.

"Good song choice, Penny. I see what you did there," said Frank, now smiling.

"I didn't have a choice, it's the first song on the tape, and you were being pissy."

The song came to an end, and Frank said, "Now this is my favorite Eagles' song."

'Witchy Woman' started to play, and Penny rolled her eyes. "God, I hate this song! Ever since I met you, it's all I hear on the radio."

"Come on, Penny! Sing it with me!" Frank started to sway and tapped out Henley's drumbeat on the steering wheel. *"Raven hair and ruby lips...."*

Penny gave in and sang along. *"Sparks fly from her fingertips. Echoed voices in the night, she's a restless spirit on an endless flight...."*

Twenty minutes later, the Buick pulled up in front of 2125 Fuller Street, and the passenger door opened.

Stepping out into the snow, Penny stuck her head back into the car and said to Frank, "Don't be trying to kiss me now, Frank. Joe will have none of that," she grinned.

"I ain't messin with Joe. He's too big for me," said Frank, laughing. "My fightin' days are over! And besides..." he paused.

Penny asked, "Besides what?"

Frank laughed, "You're not my type!"

"Thanks a lot, Frankie!" Penny laughed though her feelings were slightly hurt. "You always know what to say to a girl! Now I know what Gruber sees in you," Penny was sarcastic.

Penny laughed and shut the passenger door. As she walked up the front steps to her house, she whispered under her breath, "Not his type? Huh? And Gruber is?" Penny shook it off and spotted her two boys looking out the front window, anxiously waiting for their mother to be home.

The '67 Buick rolled down Fuller street replacing the tracks in the snow that it'd left sixteen hours earlier.

Chapter 15 – Vietnam Vic

It was Monday, November 11, and Ron McClain was due back today, so Frank and Penny had worked the day before developing a synopsis of their case.

It was after 9 am, and the two detectives were a little nervous ahead of McClain's arrival. They needed to make a compelling case so that their boss would authorize the resources and manpower that investigating an interstate, multi-jurisdictional case would require. McClain was not the end-all, be-all though. He too had higher-ups, and they'd also need to be persuaded.

It was a quiet Monday morning, and Penny and Frank, along with the other four detectives working out of the 39th, had time on their hands. They were all shootin' the shit when their boss finally walked in at 10:05 am.

"What in the hell are you guys doing just sitting around?" McClain barked as he came through the door of the Detective Room.

"Chief! How'd the vacation go?" asked Frank.

"Screw the vacation! My Eagles lost again! I'm pissed!" McClain hung his hat and coat on the rack outside his office and then unlocked his door and went in.

Frank got up and looked at Penny as if to say, "Here goes," turning towards McClain's office.

"God damned Eagles!" Penny mumbled under her breath as the other four detectives were shuffling papers on their desks, trying to look busy.

Frank stuck his head into his chief's office and said, "Hey, Boss! You got a second?"

"What is it, Frank? I'm gonna be busy for a while. I'll need a day or two to catch up."

"I figured as much," said Frank. "But sometime today, we'll need to sit down and talk. Something's come up, and Penny and I are running down some leads, and we need your blessing."

"Great!" McClain rolled his eyes. "I can hardly wait!"

"Well, let me know, Chief."

"Will do, Frank. Now close the door behind you. Would ya?"

As Frank stepped back out of his boss's office, McClain called out to him. "Frank, answer this for me..." he paused.

"Sure, Chief." Frank stepped back into the tiny office.

"How in the hell do the Eagles start the season 4 and 1 and then lose four goddamned games in a row?!"

"That's a tough one, Chief," Frank shrugged. "I could see losing to the Steelers last week but losing to the Skins always hurts."

"Don't even get me started on those boys from Pittsburgh. I'm glad I was out of town for that one." McClain looked like he wanted to break something. "27-0! What a debacle that was! At least we threw up 20 against the Skins."

Frank was taken aback by McClain's reference to the 'Pittsburgh Boys' and being 'out of town for that one.' "Well, I'll let you catch up. Let me know about later, would ya?"

"Sure. Will do, Frank," McClain motioned to Frank to shut the door on his way out.

Frank went back to his desk and sat down. With eyebrows raised he said, "Did you hear that last part?"

"I heard something about Pittsburgh," said Penny.

"He said, and I quote, 'Don't even get me started on the boys from Pittsburgh.' Now, how's that for a bad omen?" Frank looked deflated.

"What does that even mean?"

"The Steelers kicked our asses last week. Remember?"

"You guys with your football," Penny shook her head. "Just let me do the talking when we sit down with him later," joked Penny.

"Ha-ha! I might not even let you in on the meeting," Frank joked back. "You'll start talkin' God and the Devil, good versus evil, and he'll transfer both of us to the southside."

"I'm shitting my pants right now," said Penny. "When are we meeting?"

"He'll let us know."

Everyone's desk phone rang in the background. It was a call from downstairs. Tubbs was first to pick up, and he could be heard saying, "No shit, Vic's out on the ledge? Yeah-yeah, we'll get right over."

Everybody heard 'Vic' and 'ledge' and perked up in their chairs.

"What was that?" asked Frank.

"We got a possible 10-56!" Tubbs shot out of his chair. "Vietnam Vic, across from the porno theater, he's out on his window ledge threatening to jump." Tubbs and the others jumped from their chairs and headed for the coat rack.

"No shit!" said Frank. "Come on, Penny! Let's get down there!"

Everybody in the 39th knew Vietnam Vic. He lived right across the street from the Cinema One movie theater. The Cinema One was a target for local community organizations and church groups that wanted it gone. Since 1970, it'd showed only triple X-rated movies after being hailed as a historic landmark, first built in 1920.

Originally called the Wellman Theater, the building was once used as a playhouse, a musical theatre venue, a small concert venue for local acts, and even a church for those religious groups that didn't have a brick and mortar building to worship in.

No matter its use, the building had seen better days. The theater itself was part of a city block with a Ben Franklin's Five and Dime store, a coffee shop, a bank, a restaurant, an unemployment office, and a barbershop. The entire block was in disrepair, and while some called it historic, others called it the ghetto.

Victor Perry was born in 1951 and drafted into the U.S. Army on his birthday in August 1969. He was one of 2.2 million young men drafted to fight in Vietnam.

Earning the rank of Private First-Class, he was anything but that to the ladies that worked at the Cinema One. After two tours of service in Vietnam, Vic Perry was dishonorably discharged in 1972 under code Section 8. Section 8 is a category of discharge for a service member who is deemed mentally unfit to serve.

While the military blamed troubled soldiers for their mental state, Victor Perry blamed the military. He'd often walk around barefoot on the sidewalk just below his second floor, two-room apartment, situated above a drug store, about what his "country did to him." Wearing only his pant fatigues, dog tags, and no shirt, he usually had an opened can of Schlitz Malt Liquor in his hand as he chatted up every passerby.

When Vic wasn't harassing the pedestrians down on State Street, he was up in his apartment getting high. For the ladies working the ticket counter at the Cinema One, that meant a personal peep show would be happening, courtesy of Vietnam Vic.

Victor Perry had been arrested for indecent exposure no less than twelve times in the eighteen months he'd lived above the drugstore. Sitting behind the candy counter, where the tickets were sold, the ladies had a direct view into Vic's apartment. The women working at the theater regularly called the 39th District to complain. Vic was hauled down to the station so often that he knew just about every single uniformed officer and detective who worked there. After being booked and spending a night in jail, Vic would be released and not seen again for several weeks. After a while, the ladies at the theater stopped calling the police and just tolerated the harassment. Some workers at the Cinema One thought it was harmless as Vietnam Vic was known to be crazy.

"So, what's the big deal that we're all rushing over there?" asked Penny of Frank.

"We haven't heard from that crazy bastard in a while, and he's never done anything like this before," said Frank, as he rounded the corner of Brooke and Lenox.

"The rumors are true, you know?" said Penny.

"What's that?" asked Frank.

"His dick size." Penny stopped short of blushing.

Frank shook his head and smiled. "No way that guy's got a ten-inch prick!" He'd heard the rumors of how well-endowed Vietnam Vic was.

"I don't know about ten, but it's big," Penny's eyes got wide.

"Whatta you know about it?" Frank laughed.

"I got called down there once and went up to his apartment to arrest the crazy S.O.B., and there he was, naked as a J-bird," recalled Penny. "It was just flopping in the breeze. He just laughed and danced in all of his God-given glory."

"There you go again, giving God all the credit."

"Trust me, Frank, that boy is blessed," sighed Penny.

"Well, he's crazy. I hope he's not naked out on that ledge! He's gonna scare some of the old ladies walking by."

"Or, make their day," Penny chuckled.

"Good one, Penny."

As Frank looked for a place to park the Buick, Penny said, "Still not sure what all the fuss is. If he jumps, maybe he breaks his ankle. It's only about fifteen feet from his window to the sidewalk."

Frank parked the Buick about ten cars down the street as Vic's stunt had caused a traffic jam. As he and Penny walked upon the scene, they heard Vic screaming at the spectators and Police below. As they got closer, they understood the magnitude of the situation. People on the street covered their mouths in horror as Vic was shirtless, had a rope tied around his neck, and was nearly incoherent in his ramblings.

The two ladies working at the Cinema One were standing on the sidewalk across the street in tears, while a drunk, who'd lost a bar fight with Vic the year before, was encouraging him to jump.

Uniformed officers tried to talk him down while three others tried to get into his barricaded apartment door.

"You see what they did to me?!" Vic screamed and cried. "They ruined me! I was just a kid, and they made me go!" His tears streamed down his face.

"It's okay, Vic!" yelled back a uniformed officer that Penny recognized.

As Penny approached the officer, she addressed him, "Hey Tony."

"Oh, hey, Penny."

"How long's he been up there?" she asked.

"Well, we've been here about fifteen minutes," said Tony, "and he was out there for probably five minutes before we walked up on the scene."

Penny had walked the beat with Tony Palumbo a few months before her demotion to Juvenile Aid.

"Hey, Vic! It's Penny!" she shouted up to him. "I hauled you in last March. Get back inside, man! It's way too cold! You're gonna get sick."

"I'm already sick, and ain't nobody makin' me better!" Vic yelled down to Penny, with Frank at her side. "Those kids over there...they didn't have to die!" he screamed.

"Jesus Christ! That guy's in bad shape!" Frank said to Penny.

"Yeah, never seen him like this before. Anytime he was brought in to be booked, he was always happy and smiling. In a crazy way, you know?"

"Come on, Vic! Get inside! It's too cold for this shit!" said another officer on the scene.

"Fuck you! And fuck the government! I'm nobody and ain't nobody gonna miss me when I'm gone!"

After another minute, two officers came down the stairs that led to the second-floor apartment and yelled, "He's got the door blocked! We need a battering ram or something!"

A minute later, Vic was shivering and had his arms crossed over his chest, rubbing his shoulders, fighting off the cold.

"Okay, this is good," said Frank.

"How so?" asked Penny.

"He's getting cold up there. That means his drug-fueled adrenaline rush is coming to an end," said Frank. "He's gonna come around and get his ass back in that apartment pretty damn quick."

A minute later, Penny exclaimed, "Holy shit! Look at that! You're right, Frank! I think he's heading back to the open window."

Penny yelled up to him, "Atta boy, Vic! Get warmed up in there, and we'll talk!"

After Vic disappeared through the window, the boys in blue started to disperse the crowd, with some going back inside their businesses.

"Okay, let's get out of here! We got a meeting with McClain," said Frank.

"No, I wanna stay and talk to him. He needs help, and a warm jacket ain't fixing his problems." Penny looked concerned. "I'll catch a ride back with one of the boys. You go ahead," she encouraged her partner.

Frank said, "Okay, Penny, you go ahead and save that kid, but don't be late."

A split second later, and without warning, a single gunshot exploded inside of the apartment. The sound heard coming from the open window echoed off the Cinema One and surrounding buildings, taking everyone standing below by surprise, with some seeking shelter behind parked cars on the street.

Penny's face went white, while Frank, without hesitation, ran for the door leading up the stairs to Vic's apartment. Penny followed in hot pursuit. People on the street were all in shock, now realizing what'd happened. The ladies from the Cinema One were sobbing while embracing each other.

At the top of the stairs, Frank kicked in the door that seemed to be less barricaded now, as Vic had moved away some furniture blocking the door before pulling the trigger.

Frank, Penny, and two uniformed officers entered the tiny apartment. Inside they witnessed Vietnam Vic sitting on the sofa, naked. The rope was still around his neck, with the other end tied to the refrigerator. His head was lying on the back of the couch, while the wall behind him was splattered with his insanity and the memories he'd returned home with from Vietnam.

"Jesus Christ," said Frank, as Penny and the other two officers looked away, with one of them vomiting up his breakfast.

Frank walked over to Vic's body and picked up the gun. Looking at him for a moment, lost in thought, he ripped the dog tags from his neck and said, "This boy's got a mom and dad out there somewhere, and they deserve to get these tags back."

Penny teared up a little bit and said, "The war never ended for that poor boy."

"It did today," said Frank. "It did today," he repeated himself.

Victor Daniel Perry, born on August 8, 1951, died November 11, 1974.

Chapter 16 – Making the Case

Ron McClain welcomed the detective corps after making their way back to the 39th District Detective Room.

"So, Vic offed himself, huh, Frank? Poor bastard. Vietnam did a number on that guy." McClain shook his head. "Well, he's in a better place now."

"Yep," Frank was solemn. "He put a .38 in his mouth."

"Jesus Christ!" McClain looked down, shaking his head.

"Me and Penny, along with Palumbo and Wells from downstairs, were first on the scene," said Frank. "It was pretty bad."

Penny said nothing upon arrival. She was shaken up, having never seen anything like it. She just hung up her coat and took a seat at her desk.

"Well, if you were first on the scene, I'm gonna need to see a police report," said McClain. "Make sure you guys get it written up and on my desk before end of day tomorrow."

"Will do, Boss," said Frank.

Ron McClain looked over at Penny, and in a rare show of empathy toward the woman the city stuck him with, said, "Bryce, you okay?"

Still in shock by the suicide scene, Penny was caught off guard, surprised that McClain even spoke to her at all. "I'm good, Chief."

"Well, let me know if you need to take a day or something."

Penny was thankful until she'd realized that her boss didn't ask Frank if he'd needed some time off. She chose not to confront McClain after the realization at that moment.

Frank motioned to McClain's office, indicating to his boss that he wanted a word with him.

McClain waved him in, and Frank closed the door behind him. "Listen, Chief, that was a pretty rough scene. Penny's pretty shaken up as she'd made a call to Vic's apartment earlier this year."

"So, she knew the guy?"

"She collared him once but didn't know him personally. It was seeing his brain splattered all over the walls that got to her, I think."

"Tell her to go home then," McClain said as he organized some papers on his desk. "There ain't shit goin' on around here, and I got six detectives out there doin' nothing right now. We won't miss her." McClain's offer was genuine.

"Nah, she'll be okay," said Frank.

"Then what is it exactly that you need from me, Frank?" McClain set his papers down and interlocked his fingers, staring at Frank, begrudgingly giving him his full attention.

"Boss, it's about the case I mentioned to you earlier."

"You didn't say shit about a 'case,' Frank. You told me you were running down some leads."

"Yeah, well, that's why I'm here. When can we talk to you about it?"

McClain looked bothered by the request and said, "Fine, whatever. Give me an hour, and I'll have some time for you guys."

"Thanks, Boss. I'll tap on your door after lunch," said Frank, turning to leave. "Oh, and Ron, I need another favor."

"And what's that, Frank?"

"I need Riggo and the other guys out of here for an hour when we talk," said Frank.

"What in the hell are the two of you up to?" McClain looked pissed. "You want me to send these guys out for a joy ride or something?"

Frank shot his boss a look like what he had to say was important.

"Forget it, Frank. If those guys aren't here after lunch, then it's because they're out on calls. I ain't sending the guys anywhere. If nobody's here when the phone rings, then I gotta answer the damn thing!" McClain picked back up the papers on his desk and said, "Now beat it! I'm busy!"

"That's fine, Boss. But this one's big, and I'm not sure you want the whole office to hear what we have to say." Now it was Frank that looked perturbed. "But that's your call."

Frank turned away from McClain, not waiting for his reply, and closed the door behind him as he left.

As Frank walked the six feet back to his desk, he heard McClain shout, "Bruno! Get your ass back in here!"

Frank smiled and winked at Penny. He knew how to deal with the Chief, and he knew what McClain was about to tell him.

Frank opened the door and said, "Yeah, Boss?"

"Don't, 'Yeah Boss,' me! Shut the door!"

Frank stood at attention in front of McClain's desk, and his boss said, "Sit your ass down!"

Frank sat on the edge of his seat, awaiting a concession by his long-time boss.

"First of all, Smartass, don't pull that shit with me. You think you know me laying that bullshit psychology on me," McClain balled up a piece of paper and shot it at his best detective. "Well, I know you, too."

"Chief, I didn't mean anything by it," Frank lied.

"Bullshit. If it's important, then don't ask me; tell me." McClain was irked. "You got me from one to two o'clock today. Just you, me, and Bryce. I'll clear these guys out of here," he paused. "But it better be big, Bruno!"

"Roger that, Chief. We'll see you at 1!" Frank smiled and stood to leave. Before exiting the office, he stopped, turned, and looked back at McClain and said, "Hey Boss, it's good to have you back! Things were a little quiet around here."

McClain was dismissive, "Fuck you, Bruno!" launching another balled-up piece of paper, narrowly missing Frank's head.

"I'm serious!" Frank smiled and quickly turned to see where the paper ball landed.

"Bullshit! Now get out of here." McClain motioned with his hand for Frank to leave. "And shut that damn door! Would ya?"

Ten minutes later, Frank and Penny sat in the back booth at Tony's and talked about what happened with Vic.

"How you doing, Penny?" Frank seemed concerned with his partner after the suicide scene they'd witnessed just an hour earlier.

"Give me a break, Frank!" Penny was pissed. "I'm fine! Let me guess. You think I need a day off too? Because I'm a broad, right?!"

"Penny, that's bullshit!" Frank lashed out at his partner. "We were both there. That was an awful scene! It would be normal for any of us to request a day off after what we saw."

"Did you hear that son of a bitch? He asked me if I needed some time off but didn't say a word to you about 'taking a day.' That's some shit right there!"

"Penny, give it up. You knew what you were getting into when you got into this racket. You're the first female detective in the city's history and one of the first in the country. What'd you expect? Cotton candy and balloons? Suck it up, and don't ever lay shit like that on me again!"

"It's exactly what I thought it would be, but that doesn't mean it's not infuriating," Penny fumed.

"What are we eating?"

"Really?" Penny looked at Frank in disbelief. "I'm gonna eat after seeing that shit?"

"Fair enough. I lost my appetite too." Frank placed the paper menu back behind the hot seeds and napkins. "Let's just go over the case, then."

The two detectives pulled out their notes and laid them out on the table in the back of Tony's. The jukebox was blasting the Rolling Stones, and Frank was in no mood for it. He hated the Stones and had a headache. "I can't concentrate with this shit on." He slid to the end of the booth and got up. "Gimme a minute."

Frank walked over to the jukebox, reached around its back, and pulled the plug, silencing it. The people in the front, including Tony, voice their objections, with Tony saying, "Hey Frankie! What gives?"

"Police business, Tony. Gimme twenty minutes, okay?"

"Yeah, sure, Frankie. Whatever you need," Tony said while flipping a white towel over his left shoulder with his right hand.

"Thanks, Tony!" Frank yelled to the front.

"Hey, Yo, Frankie!" Tony yelled back. "Yuz want a slice back there?!"

"Nah, we're good, Tone!" Frank waved him off.

Sitting back down, Frank said, "Okay, we got one shot at this, Penny. If we can't convince McClain today, we got no chance later." Waving his finger, he said, "You follow my lead, and no throwing out religious theories."

"You sure, Frankie? Our theory makes a lot of sense."

"Penny, I told you. McClain is very religious, like Old Testament shit. If we hit him with that angle, he'll think it's blasphemy and throw us out of there."

"Okay, I'll follow your lead, then."

"Alright, let's lay it out then," Frank took off his coat and rolled up his sleeves. "We got three cases of old folks disappearing, last seen with an old custodian nicknamed Old Man Winter, and all having the same initials."

Penny interjected, "That right there should be all we need," said Penny. "No?"

"Penny, Ron's been around for some big ones. This ain't a big one yet," explained Frank. "This is all speculation unless we can link one guy to Bloomington, Pittsburgh, and Philly."

"So, how do we do that?"

"That's the problem." Frank raised his brow and nodded. "We need time and resources, and only McClain can give that to us."

"Okay, well, what if we tell him that we have a fourth missing person?"

Frank shook his head in frustration. "Dammit, Penny! You're just not gettin' it! Stick to the facts...."

Cutting off her partner, Penny said, "That is a fact!"

"Penny, you got a missing person's case file on Samuel Crenshaw laying around somewhere that I ain't seen yet?" Frank looked at Penny as if he'd said enough to shut her down.

Penny smiled at Frank like she knew something he didn't.

"What're you smiling about?" Frank was dismissive.

Penny fished a file folder out of her bag and threw it up on the table.

Frank grabbed the 10x15 envelope and began to unwind the string closure. "What's in here? Whatta you got?"

"Just open it, Frankie Boy!" Penny's smile was big.

Frank removed the contents and found what looked like copies of old newspaper clippings. "Penny, is this what I think it is?" Frank's brow collided with his salt and pepper hairline, and his eyes opened wide with anticipation.

"I spent my Saturday in The Philadelphia Public Library, and one of the old ladies there found some old newspaper articles on microfiche from December of '20 and January of '21 about the case." Penny's smile went from ear to ear. "Apparently, it was in The Philadelphia Inquirer for just a short while and then nothing after that January."

"Why didn't you show me this yesterday when we were working through the case file?"

"It's my silver bullet," Penny shot Frank a sly grin. "I didn't want you to shut me down before McClain got back today. And besides, I knew how you would react."

"Penny, we're partners. Don't spring shit on me at the last second. That's some Lone Ranger bullshit right there. You can shove your silver bullet shit!"

After a minute of flipping through the envelope's contents, Frank said, "Holy shit! They got stuff going back that far," he shook his head while studying the black and white copies more closely. "They just let you take this stuff with you?" Frank looked to be adding up how many pages were in the stack. He guessed around twenty.

"Hell no, that cost me 68 cents!" sighed Penny. "If this case goes forward, I'm taking it out of petty cash. That stuff ain't cheap!"

"Penny, we still have a problem, though."

"What's that?"

"It's implausible to think that McClain will believe that a case from fifty-four years ago could be related to ours. He just won't buy it," Frank had a 'tough luck' look on his face.

"Why don't we just keep it in our back pocket and see how it goes?" suggested Penny.

"Oh, shit!" said Frank looking at his watch. "We gotta get back over there. It's almost one!"

The two put their coats on and gathered their notes, then started to head for the front when Frank said to Penny, "Hold on, Pen! I almost forgot."

Frank walked over to the jukebox and plugged it back in. As he and Penny passed the owner, Frank said, "Thanks, Tony! I owe you one!"

"Hey, Frankie, fuhgeddaboudit!" Tony yelled while tossing pizza dough high into the air from behind the counter.

As the two detectives walked out the front door, the jukebox dropped a 45, and Glenn Frey's whining guitar led into Witchy Woman.

Five minutes later, Frank and Penny set down their stuff on their desks back in the Detective Room, hung up their coats, and took a deep breath. The place was empty, and McClain's door was closed. Frank and Penny could hear their boss finishing up a heated call.

"Great!" said Penny. "He's still in a pissy mood."

Frank said, "That's okay. We're on to something here, and we'll convince him to see things our way."

After Frank heard McClain slam the phone down, he looked straight at Penny and silently counted down from five using only his fingers. He mouthed the words, "three, two, one," and then turned toward McClain's door and knocked twice and asked, "Boss, you in there?"

"You're late, Bruno!" McClain yelled through the door. A second later, it opened with Ron McClain emerging. Tugging his belt upward to adjust his trousers, McClain said, "This better be good!"

Frank said, "Here, Chief, sit in my chair." He then pulled his chair out for his boss as an anxious Penny stood nearby.

"Save it, Frank! Just start talking," barked McClain as he sat on the corner of Frank's desk instead.

"Okay, Ron," Frank paused. "Since the day you left on vacation, Penny, over here, did some reorganizing of the 'Unsolved Crimes Closet,' ..." said Frank before McClain chimed in.

"It's about time somebody got in there and cleaned it up," said McClain, looking over at Penny.

"Good Job, Bryce," he gave her a begrudged nod.

Penny smiled as Frank continued.

"Chief, do you remember the old guy going missing up at Heavenly Gates back in '69?"

"Yeah, what about it?" McClain looked annoyed and impatient.

"Well, Penny read through the file and got curious." Frank looked at Penny and nodded his head. "She had questions for me that only Langhorne and Gaffney would've been able to answer, but they're both deceased...." said Frank before being cut off again by his boss.

"Langhorne ain't dead! He had a stroke last fall, but he ain't dead last I heard," professed McClain.

"He died on October 29, I'm afraid." Frank looked somber.

"No shit!" Ron McClain shook his head and said, "He was a good cop. We worked together for twelve years."

"Anyway, Boss. While Penny and I were looking through the case file, there wasn't much to see, but right around that same time, we got a call from our counterparts in Pittsburgh, who had a similar case back in '65."

"So what!" McClain shook his head again. "What's your point?"

"The point is, Boss. We got a series of disappearances that look to be connected," Frank tossed a manila file folder he'd been holding onto his desk and motioned to it as it fell.

"Frank, two in four years don't make it connected." McClain looked unimpressed. "Please tell me you got more than this."

Frank looked at him and said, "How about three in twelve years?"

McClain seemed only mildly interested. "What's in the folder, Frank?"

Frank grinned, "We may have a serial murderer on our hands."

"Okay, you just lost me!" The Chief of Detectives looked irked. "You telling me that you have evidence in that envelope connecting three missing persons to one guy?"

"Evidence? We got some, but what we have more of is probable cause that would warrant further investigation," said Frank.

"Frank, the guy from '69, was in his nineties if I recall...."

Frank shook his head and said, "Ninety-five."

"Great! Ninety-five," said McClain. "You telling me you're chasing a ghost, Frank? Is that what she's got you up to?" McClain used his thumb to point in Penny's direction.

Penny sat unbothered, shrugging off the insult.

"Boss, we think a serial murderer is snatching up old folks from retirement homes. We got three, one here in Old Germantown, one in Pittsburgh, and another one in Indiana."

"Indiana?" asked McClain flashing a curious look. "What the hell you know about what's happening in Indiana?"

"The Pittsburgh Boys got a call from Bloomington P.D. who were sniffing around old files. It turns out they'd heard of the case in Pittsburgh, and Pittsburgh heard about ours. Looks like one of their detectives used to wear a uniform here in North Philly. It raised a red flag with them because the Indiana case and their case read almost word for word," said Frank. "And get this, it's almost verbatim what Gaffney and Langhorne came up with."

"What year was the case in Indiana?" McClain looked curious.

"1957," said Penny.

With intended sarcasm, Ron McClain looked over at Penny and said, "Well, she speaks! I was beginning to think you left the building or something." McClain chuckled, looking back at Frank, trying to get a laugh out of his most senior detective. Nothing came back from Frank, who stood stone-faced.

Penny half smiled and looked at her partner, wanting him to get McClain's head back in the game.

"1957?" McClain shook his head. "There's no way they're connected, Frank,"

"Boss, we met up with the Pittsburgh boys, and we exchanged notes."

"And when was this?" McClain looked at Penny with disdain and then back to Frank. He was waiting for an answer he knew would piss him off.

"Last week. We met them halfway, in Lewistown. I told them no way we were driving all the way to Pittsburgh."

"You went chasing a ghost all the way over to Lewistown?" McClain rose from the corner of Frank's desk. "And who in the hell authorized that?"

"It was a hunch, Chief, and it paid off," said Frank.

"Paid off, huh?" McClain pursed his lips, and his eyes went tight. "Well, the next thing that comes out of your mouth better convince me it 'paid off,' or both of you will be suspended for two days without pay."

Frank was about to speak when Penny chimed in. His eyes flashed an 'Oh shit!' look before his head went down.

Penny stood tall and with confidence said, "Chief, we got a guy abducting old people from retirement homes, and he's using God's name while doing it. I'm a practicing Catholic, and I gotta tell ya," she paused, looked both ways and shook her head, "that really pisses me off!"

"Excuse me!" McClain erupted, getting into Penny's face. Frank stepped forward, ready to come to her defense. "What in God's good grace are you talking about, Bryce?"

"Boss, wait a second. What Penny's trying to say is...." Frank looked at Penny in disbelief that she spilled the beans.

Penny, bucking Frank's advice, jumped back in, and said, "And we got a fourth victim, too!" Penny almost had a look of relief on her face as she exhaled.

"Let me get this shit straight," McClain was in disbelief. "I go on my first vacation in two years, and I come back to this crap?! What in the hell has gotten into the two of you?" he shouted.

Ron McClain stormed into his office, slamming the door so hard that the glass making up the top half of the door cracked. Frank looked at Penny and said, "What've you done?! I told you to keep your mouth shut about that stuff."

"Fuck!" Penny said under her breath, avoiding any eye contact with her partner. She walked around her desk and fell into her chair, looking defeated. There, she pondered the repercussions of her revelation to Ron McClain.

"We're fucked, Penny," Frank said under his breath. He was pissed that his rookie partner ignored his advice for the third time in two weeks.

In his mind, the Lewistown utterance paid off, and giving up the Pittsburgh connection to Garrison Winter didn't come back to bite them yet. But he was sure the case would go cold again and never come out of the Cold Case closet. All of a sudden, Frank Bruno was reconsidering taking the rookie detective under his wing.

Penny got up and grabbed her coat, then said, "I'll see you Thursday, I guess."

Frank started putting the file back into his desk when McClain emerged from his office.

Penny nervously pulled her hair out from under her jacket collar, swallowed hard, and stood at attention. Frank also stood to accept his punishment.

McClain looked at Frank first and then at Penny and asked, "How is our suspect using God's name?" McClain was calm, and his curiosity seemed genuine.

Frank started to talk, and his boss, without looking in his direction, held up his index finger and said, "Uh! Don't say a word, Frank. I'm talking to this one over here." McClain stared at Penny, anxiously awaiting her answer.

A look of relief and excitement came over Penny's face as she leaned over and grabbed the folder from Frank's desk.

"Chief...." said Penny as her boss cut her off.

"Be careful what you say next, Bryce." McClain looked her up and down. "Or you'll be transferred to the 109th down at the airport."

Penny took a deep breath and collected her thoughts. "Alright, Chief. Here's what we're looking at...."

Frank was now a spectator and didn't say a word for the ten minutes that followed.

"Boss, did you know that Heavenly Gates was once called FalconClaw?"

"Maybe. Why?" McClain was skeptical of Penny.

"The construction of FalconClaw began in 1860 and finished in 1863. My great-grandfather, Samuel Crenshaw, built it and lived there with his wife and three sons, one of which was my grandfather, Ernest."

McClain looked impressed. "That place belongs to your family?"

"Not anymore," said Penny. Pulling out copies of old newspaper clippings from 1920, Penny said, "I have information here that proves Victor Rogers isn't the first elderly person to go missing from Heavenly Gates."

Ron McClain took the copies of newspaper articles from Penny and gave them a cursory once-over. "What's 1920 got to do with anything?"

"Frank and I believe that's where it all started." Penny then said to her Chief, "You might want to sit down for the rest of this."

Frank offered his chair to McClain for the second time. This time the Chief accepted his offer, looking at both of his detectives before sitting down.

As the three sat, they heard talking in the stairwell, and seconds later, the door opened. It was Tubbs and Taylor.

"Get the hell out of here!" shouted McClain to the two. "Can't you see we're in a meeting over here?"

Tubbs was apologetic. "Sorry, Chief! You said we could come back at two."

"Make it four! And if you see Riggins and Coons downstairs, tell 'em I said four!" McClain shouted as the two detectives were walking out the door.

"Alright, you need to jump to the part where this guy's using God's name in the process. And then tell me how in the hell an old guy from the twenties is still alive in '69 and killing old people."

With excitement, Penny pulled the remaining contents from the envelope containing case notes and spread them out onto Frank's desk.

"Okay, Chief, from the time I was a little girl, I'd always heard that my great-grandfather was abducted, never to be seen again. But by the time I was old enough to understand what it all meant, the details were sketchy and harder to remember for my grandfather and father," Penny laid out the case.

"Bryce, it's the details that I'm interested in, not your childhood," McClain rolled his index finger in Penny's direction in an effort to get her to speed things up.

Frank knew his boss better than Penny and jumped in to save her.

"Ron, in 1969, a man named Victor Rogers went missing from Heavenly Gates, last seen with an 83-year-old custodian named Garrison Winter, real name, Garrison O'Donnell. Before that, in 1965, a woman named Polly Anne Steinman went missing from God's Glory retirement home just north of downtown Pittsburgh, last seen with an 83-year-old custodian named Gabriel Olen Duncan. She was never seen or heard from again. And, get this, eight years before that, a woman named Barbara Jo Tipton went missing from a retirement village called Valhalla Springs...."

"Let me guess," said McClain, "she was last seen with an 83-year-old custodian?"

"You got it, Boss. His name was George O' Doyle."

"What do you mean, 'was'? The guy's dead or something?"

"Missing," said Penny.

McClain looked over at his rookie detective. "So, no one knows where any of these custodians are?"

Frank jumped back in. "We know where one of them is," he paused and looked at Penny, "He's still up at Heavenly Gates."

"And you talked to this guy?" McClain looked at Frank.

"We both did," said Frank, "but Penny got to him first."

McClain looked over at Penny wanting more information.

"Chief..." Penny said before being cut off.

McClain interjected, "It's okay to call me Ron."

"Okay, Ron," Penny continued.

As she started talking, Frank knew that she'd just made a breakthrough with McClain and was determined to keep her moving along with facts and not speculation.

"The custodians were all questioned and released after the investigators found no evidence that they were involved," said Penny. "That includes our guy, Garrison O'Donnell."

"So, where does the 'God' part come into this thing?"

Frank waved off Penny, who was about to speak. McClain saw Frank's hand gesture and looked back over to him.

"Ron, on the surface, it looks almost unreal...."

"What does?! For the love of God, get to the point, would ya?"

"Their names, Chief," said Frank, while Penny began to scribble something on her notepad.

Penny held up what she'd written and got McClain's attention. The word GOD was written in all capital letters on the notepad.

McClain threw his hands up in the air. "What in the hell are you guys getting at?"

Penny recoiled the notepad and then put periods between each letter and revealed it to McClain for a second time.

McClain rolled his eyes and said, "You've got to be kidding me! Their initials spell GOD, and you guys take the enormous leap and think they're all connected and using religion as a backdrop? That's rich!"

"Boss. Boss," Frank touched McClain's arm to calm him down. "I told you that that was just on the surface. There's more."

"There damn sure better be!" McClain took a deep breath, "Or we're all gonna get back to work doin' other shit."

"Ron, the dates the elderly folks came up missing are peculiar as well," said Penny.

"Enlighten me, Bryce." McClain looked sarcastic and was running out of patience with his veteran and rookie detectives.

"Victor Rogers went missing on December 23, Steinman, December 21, and Tipton on December 19," explained Penny.

"I see a coincidence there, but hardly a reason to open back up an investigation of dead people," McClain stood up from his chair as if getting ready to call a halt to the meeting.

"Chief, my great-grandfather went missing on December 7."

"So," McClain shook his head, waiting for the big reveal.

"We think there are more victims," revealed Penny.

Frank grimaced with Penny's words because he wasn't convinced that was the case.

Ron McClain looked over to Frank and asked, "Is that right, Frank? You think there're more victims out there?"

"I do," said Frank as he lied to his boss with a straight face.

"Keep talkin', then," said McClain, returning to his chair.

"So, all of the retirement homes have religious connotations to their names," said Frank. "The four victims were all in their nineties, they all disappeared in December on odd days, ending on the 23, and all of the custodians were beloved by the residents and nicknamed Old Man Winter."

"So, what does all of this mean?" McClain stood again. "The missing people are all dead! Nobody's making a fuss, so why are we?"

"Chief," said Penny, who'd been writing stuff on her notepad again. "This is my opinion and not Frank's. I believe that there're more disappearances that we don't know about yet," Penny paused, "and they'll continue."

"Okay, Detective Bryce, now how do you figure that one?" McClain backed up one step closer to his door.

Penny flipped her notepad toward McClain and said, "The open dates between my great-grandfather and the Tipton woman in '57 are the 9th, 11th, 13th, 15th, and the 17th. I believe we have other victims on each of those dates."

"Okay, just for laughs, let say you're right," said McClain. "That's a total of nine people, so what leads you to believe there'll be a tenth?"

Penny jotted something else on her notepad and revealed it to McClain.

"Christmas Day?! That's the big finale here?!" McClain was finished. Throwing his hands up in the air, he said, "I've heard enough of this mumbo-jumbo. You two are crazy! And obviously bored, might I add? I'm done here!"

McClain walked into his office.

"Boss," Frank yelled, "there's something else."

"And what's that?" McClain stuck his head back out the door.

"I'm seeing eights, Ron. They're everywhere!" Frank realized that he put his job in jeopardy by divulging that he was seeing things, but it was a last-ditch effort to save the case, but at that moment, Frank was willingly rolled the dice.

McClain walked back out and said, "Eights?"

"Yeah, eights," Frank nodded. "The sign of angels."

"The eighth sign is also the resurrection of Jesus." McClain wore a blank stare and added, "What else you got?"

"Heavenly Gates resides at 888 Bedford Street. The victims were all born in the 1800s, and the custodians were all 83 years old," revealed Frank.

"So, what does that mean?" asked McClain.

"Well, the custodians were all eighty-three, but when you turn the number around...."

"Thirty-eight," said McClain. "So what," he shrugged.

"I look at it and see three eights." Frank looked serious.

"Okay, so this guy's messing with the scripture, and that ain't right!" McClain paused for a moment as if to collect his thoughts and said, "So, Bryce, you think there'll be another victim, and that'll make ten? And it'll happen on a Christmas Day?" asked the Chief of Detectives.

"I do," said Penny.

"And which Christmas Day, in particular, might that be?"

"Not sure, Chief," answered Penny.

"So, we're supposed to sit around and wait until Christmas of '79 or something to make a bust?" McClain came to his senses. "Okay, I think you're both crazy, but I'd like to meet this old man from Heavenly Gates." McClain didn't believe everything was connected, but he was deeply religious and was curious enough to continue the charade a little while longer.

Penny and Frank were shocked by their boss's request. They knew that if McClain met Garrison Winter, he'd agree that the old man was peculiar and suspicious.

"Have him here tomorrow at noon. I want to lay my eyes on this guy. Now, get over to Heavenly Gates and ask him to come down here."

McClain returned to his office while Frank and Penny stood in shock. Penny wore a big smile, while Frank was dumbfounded.

After Penny left a message on Travers' answering machine, informing him that they were coming, the two detectives grabbed their coats and headed to 888 Bedford Street.

Chapter 17 – Crazy Eights

Frank pulled out of the police parking lot onto Yelland and took a right turn instead of a left.

"Where we headed, Germantown's that way," said Penny while pointing.

"We're taking the long way," said Frank.

"Ooo-kay," Penny was confused and suddenly nervous. "Everything alright there, Partner?"

Penny noticed that Frank seemed to be lost in thought when the two walked through the parking lot minutes earlier.

"No, everything's not okay!" barked Frank, shaking his head. "Penny, you keep fucking up, and it's gonna cost us at some point."

"What'd I do now?" Penny played innocent.

"You know exactly what you did!" yelled Frank. "This is the third time you revealed something I told you not to. First, telling Winter that we knew of the disappearance in Pittsburgh, then bringing up what happened in 1920 to the boys in Lewistown, and today with McClain. I asked you not to bring up the religious aspects of our theory, and you just couldn't keep your mouth shut!" Frank was red-faced.

"But I saw an opening, and my gut told me to take it." Penny defended her instincts.

"Fuck you and your instincts!" Frank slammed his hands on the wheel. "The next time you open your mouth after I told you not to, I'm going back to working alone. You can take the bus to your next case. Are we clear?"

"Yes, we're clear," said a frightened Penny. The last time she saw Frank that upset was back at FalconClaw after Winter got under her skin. She knew she was in trouble.

After twenty minutes of complete silence and watching Frank take wrong turn after wrong turn, Penny spoke up, "Frank, where in the hell are we going? We're nowhere near Germantown."

"We're going to church," said Frank. "Before I sit down with the Devil again, I want some advice from a priest."

"Are you shitting me?" said a stunned Penny. "I mean, you're joking, right?"

"No, I'm not joking!" Frank turned the Buick into the parking lot of St. Ambrose Catholic Church on East Roosevelt Boulevard. "We're here. Father Maloney's expecting us."

"Well, I never took you for a church-going guy," Penny shrugged. "The place is probably going to burst into flames when you walk through the front doors," she laughed.

"This is where Jeanie and I were married and where we baptized the girls." Frank paused, "And where we held the church service before burying my Jeanie. I haven't been back since."

Penny was mortified, "Geez, I'm so sorry, Frank."

"Get out of the car and let me do the talking this time. Got it?!"

"Yeah, sure, Frank, I got it."

As the two entered the massive church, Penny was in awe and felt a sense of calm after she'd passed under the stained glass which rose high above the double-door entrance. As they walked in, the two witnessed Father Brian Maloney kneeling behind the church's pulpit, crossing himself in front of a fifteen-foot statue of Jesus Christ, positioned high up on the back wall of the church. Out of respect, they stood in silence, and both crossed themselves.

After Maloney rose from reciting the lord's prayer, he turned to see Frank Bruno and a female guest standing in the center aisle near the rear pew. "Ah, Frank, welcome back. It's been too long since we've prayed together," said Father Maloney as he walked to greet his long-time parishioner and acquaintance.

Father Brian Maloney was a sixty-seven-year-old Catholic priest who'd been the Church's head Priest for twenty-six years after being its curate for seven and a deacon before that. All in the St. Ambrose parish. Father Maloney was tall and thin with grayed-over, red hair. The congregation at St. Ambrose and the community around it all knew Father Maloney, as he was an active part of his parishioner's lives in and out of the church, attending school events, sporting events, and even delivering prayer at local homeless shelters regularly.

Father Maloney took Frank's hand into his and provided a warm, comforting handshake to his grieving friend. "How are the girls adjusting, Frank?" asked Maloney. "And how are you adjusting, Frank?"

"We're all doing as good as we can, Father, considering." Frank was solemn. "I'm sorry I haven't been around much. I'm just working through some things."

"Yes, I understand, Frank. You'll return when you feel it's the right time," said Maloney. "Just don't forget to let God and our Savior, Jesus Christ, show you the light and return you from the darkness hanging over your soul."

It was an uncomfortable time for Frank as his faith was being tested in both his personal and professional lives. He blamed God for taking his wife and leaving his children without a mother, and at the same time, he feared that the man he would encounter later that day could very well be the Devil or the incarnation of evil. All Frank knew for sure was that he was a lost soul and had never been more vulnerable than he was right now.

"And who might we have here?" Maloney looked Penny Bryce up and down and offered his hand.

"Oh, I'm sorry, Father, this is my partner from work."

Penny extended her hand to meet Maloney's and said, "I'm Penelope Bryce. Frank and I work together, and we were in the neighborhood, and he very much wanted to show me the place where he worshipped." Penny exaggerated the truth because she wasn't exactly sure why they were there. Penny did know one thing, though, she felt safe in the church in which they stood and agreed with Frank's comments earlier about who they were about to meet again, both thinking that Old Man Winter was either the Devil himself or at the very least, one of his mutinous flock of angels.

"Are you also a detective, Penelope?"

"Yes, I am." Penny's chest swelled with pride. "Thank you for that assumption. Female detectives are pretty rare around these parts, I'm afraid."

"Well, if I'm being honest," Maloney smiled. "I read about you in the newspapers on many occasions. Your fight against the establishment will serve as an inspiration to all the young women that come after you." Father Maloney was sincere. "In the past year, I've baptized several baby girls named Penelope. I'm quite certain there will be more to come after your incredible victory for women's rights. Again, you are truly an inspiration."

"Thank you, Father," Penny was both surprised and grateful for his kind words.

"And Penny, if I may ask, did you travel the long road alone, or did you have God to lean on through the darkest of your days?"

"No, Father, I did not walk alone. The light of our Savior was the flame that carried me through."

"Ah, so you're Catholic then?" Maloney smiled and exhaled in relief.

"Yes, Father, since the day I was baptized into the church."

"And in what parish do you worship, young Penelope?"

"I am part of the massive congregation at St. Williams in Lawncrest."

"Ah, yes, Father Keagan delivers a powerful sermon each Sunday and Wednesday." Maloney knew him well. "He has long been a mentor of mine. I only hope the Lord sees fit to help him through his recent health struggles."

"As do I, Father," Penny concurred.

Maloney's attention went back to Frank.

"So, Frank, what brings you here today?" asked Maloney. "I can see it in your eyes that you're fighting off some sort of evil in your life. Have you come to me for guidance?"

"Father Maloney, you're a very wise man, and yes, it is your wisdom that I seek," said Frank. "But before that, I need to ask you some questions if you have time for us."

"Yes, when I received your call a short while ago, I set aside some time in my schedule, as I could sense that you were in need."

"Is there a place we can sit and talk, Father?"

"Yes, of course."

Moments later, Frank and Penny sat with Maloney in his modest office in the back of the church.

"Please do sit down," said Maloney, motioning to the two chairs in front of his desk. "It's not often I counsel people in my office. I'm embarrassed that it's not bigger than this."

"This will be fine, Father," said Frank. Penny nodded in agreement.

"So, what can I do for the two of you today?"

"Father, I'll cut right to the chase. Penny and I are investigating the disappearances of several people, and our prime suspect is, for lack of a better word, evil."

"Oh, I see," said Maloney. "The world is filled with evil, and it comes in many forms. We must combat that evil with an undying faith in our Lord, Jesus Christ."

"Yes, I agree." Frank didn't have time for a lecture but rather sought to have his questions answered. "Father, I have specific questions whose very answers might assist my partner and me in dealing with this man."

"Yes, of course, Frank. Please ask your questions then."

"Father, I'm seeing the number eight everywhere I go. Billboards, television commercials, shop windows, you name it. Can you tell me what that means?" asked a frustrated Frank.

"I'm guessing that you're seeing them in your job as well. Would I be correct, Frank?"

"Yes, Father, that's why I'm here." Frank was eager to hear what Maloney had to say.

"Well, as both of you are aware," Maloney sat back in his chair. "Bible numerology has been somewhat controversial over the years, as many agree that numbers used repeatedly in the bible convey meanings that have little to do with the actual numeral. The number six, for example, represents imperfection, and the numbers 666 represent the Unholy Trinity; the Devil, the Beast, and the False Prophet."

Maloney then leaned forward in his chair and said, "The number eight, in contrast, usually means something good. For example, if an angel were to send you a message, it would likely come in the form of the number eight or multiples of eight. The literal number eight appears seventy-three times in the bible."

"The number eight signifies the number of new beginnings. And less we forget, eight men wrote the New Testament: Matthew, Mark, Luke, John, James, Peter, Jude, and Paul."

Maloney continued, "Eight is also the number of Jesus, whose name in the Greek language adds up to 888."

"Furthermore, God saved eight people on Noah's ark to ensure a new beginning for mankind after the floodwaters receded. Since the meaning of four is derived from God's creation of everything, the number eight, or four plus four, pictures the new creation after the great flood."

"Shall I continue?" asked Maloney.

"Yes, please do, Father. This is all very important." Frank was looking for something, anything he could use to try and see through Garrison Winter's façade.

Maloney continued, "Jesus showed himself alive eight times after his resurrection. He first appeared alive to Mary Magdalene in Mark 16:9 - 11. Then he showed himself to two disciples traveling to Emmaus in Luke 24. After that, he appeared to all the disciples except Thomas, in John 20:19 - 24, and then again, a week later to all of them when Thomas was present, in John 20:26 - 29."

"The Sabbath, is the seventh day, so the Lord's day must be the eighth. Christ, rising from the dead on Sunday, initiated a new creation. In Luke 24:1, Matthew 28:1, Mark 16:2, and John 20:1, he pushed through the Sabbath, the first day of the week or seven days plus one, meaning eight. On the 8th Day, God said, 'Let the Church begin,' and so it began."

"Furthermore, Frank," explained Maloney. "the most joyous feast period of the year is the eight-day period of *the Fall Feast of Tabernacles*, followed afterward by the *Last Great Day.*"

"And lastly," explained Maloney, "Abraham is the father of the faithful, and he had eight sons: Ishmael, Isaac, Jokshan, Medan, Midian, Ishbak, Shuah, and Zimran."

"Frank, there are many more examples in the bible that make eight a powerful and meaningful number, but as you can see, they are all positive symbols and quite the opposite of evil."

Frank sat back feeling conflicted. He reasoned that Old Man Winter was mocking the bible.

"Frank, are you sure that this person is evil?" asked Maloney.

Frank leaned forward in his chair and said, "Father Maloney, the man in question may be responsible for as many as nine murders over the course of many years. This man is evil, and he's mocking God and the bible."

Maloney sat back in his chair, his eyes wide open, "Oh, I see. Well then, Frank, and Penny, I shall say a prayer for each of you and ask God to assist you in your fight for good and the riddance of evil."

The three stood, and Maloney offered his hand to Frank and Penny, then asked Frank a pointed question. "Frank, would you like to make a confession while you're here today?"

Frank smirked and was candid when answering his priest, "No, I would not, Father. But thank you for your time today."

After Maloney saw Frank and Penny to the door, the two detectives stood outside and spoke for a moment.

"Penny, I think it's important that we rattle the cage of Garrison Winter today. I want to try and scare him out of coming down to the 39th tomorrow."

"That's the stupidest thing I've ever heard," said Penny. "We need him there tomorrow. If he doesn't show, then McClain might balk and not allow us to continue our investigation."

"Well, now it's my gut that's talking, and I'm taking a baseball bat to that mother-fucker's cage!" Frank walked around and got into the Buick and revved the engine several times, illustrating his mood. Penny shook her head in doubt several times before joining him in the car.

Thirty minutes later, Frank parked the Buick on the street outside of 888 Bedford Street. It was now after 4 pm, and Frank and Penny chose to show up unannounced again.

After climbing the hill, the two stood at the front steps of Heavenly Gates and formulated their plan for their interaction with Winter.

"So, is there any way I can change your mind about the whole baseball bat thing?"

Frank was clear, "No God damned way. That guy killed Rogers, Steinman, and Tipton, and maybe more. I need to see if I can rattle him because if I can, he might be innocent of all three disappearances."

Penny was confused by Frank's statement, shaking her head in astonishment. "What in the hell are you talking about? You completely lost me on that one."

"Penny, if I can pierce the phony exterior of this psychopath, then he's not a psychopath at all, and he wouldn't be cunning enough to get three people to follow him to their death," explained Frank. "I need to see if he can hold up. If he does, then he could very well be guilty of killing those people. Or, at the very least, be in on it. There's a good chance he's not alone in the disappearances. How else can you explain no footprints coming back to the homes?"

"Are you nervous?" asked Penny.

"About confronting Old Man Winter?" clarified Frank.

"Yes, of course! What in the hell else would you be nervous about?" Penny was sarcastic.

"Hell! I'm more worried about seeing Bernice Gruber than I am seeing that serial murderer." Frank looked nervous all of a sudden.

"Big tough Police Detective!" Penny shook her head, laughed, and started up the stairs. Now standing in front of the doors and before ringing the bell, she asked, "So, am I allowed to talk, or should I be a good little 'Broad' and just shut up unless I'm spoken to first?"

"Penny, my dear, you can say whatever you want this time. The gloves are off." Frank climbed the steps, now standing behind Penny. "Just protect me from that predator in there." Frank shook his head and sighed.

Penny had to stop for a moment before knocking and wondered to herself, *"Is he referring to Gruber or Winter?"* She shook her head and smiled, looking back at Frank before turning to the door and ringing the bell.

After two minutes of agonizing consternation on Frank's part, the door opened, and it was Bernice Gruber. Opening the door to find the two detectives standing there, Gruber said, *"Well, if it isn't Philly's Finest!"*

Penny reveled in Gruber's disdain of her and smiled at the thought of Frank, standing behind her, shitting his pants.

"He's in the solarium," Gruber was dismissive. "I'm guessing you remember how to get there?"

Before the two could acknowledge Gruber's question, she abruptly turned and walked away.

"Well, that was brutal!" Frank tried to regain his wits.

Penny laughed. "You're about to be face to face with a stone-cold killer. Get it together, Detective!"

Frank shook off the butterflies before he and Penny made their way down the long foyer.

"Man, every time I come here, I get all freaked out," said Penny.

"I really like this place!" countered Frank. "Except for the Devil, of course." Frank lied to Penny. FalconClaw scratched away at his psyche. He knew that evil lived there and that he was about to face the very source of that evil. In his mind, he would need to show strength in the face of Garrison Winter, or evil would triumph over good.

Moments later, standing just outside the solarium, the two could see Old Man Winter sitting in front of the backgammon table, rolling the dice, and moving the checkers.

"Okay," Frank turned to Penny and whispered. "Like I said, the gloves are off, but let me start the conversation."

"Sir, yes, Sir!" Penny saluted.

Frank rolled his eyes. "Keep it up, Smartass!"

He and Penny entered the cavernous solarium without another word, their steps muted by the thick brown carpet beneath their feet.

The two were startled when, without turning in his chair, Garrison Winter said, "Good afternoon, Detectives. So good to see you again!" Only after finishing his sentence did he turn around to see the two approaching.

With only a look, Frank communicated to Penny that he was unsettled that Winter somehow knew they were there.

"Good afternoon, Mr. O'Donnell!" Frank nodded to Winter, revealing for the first time to the old man that he and Penny now knew his real surname. "If that is your real name?" Frank widened his stare.

"Well, you are a good detective, aren't you, Frank? It's been several years since I went by that name, though, I'm afraid."

"I'm guessing since January of 1966," said Frank, now in command of his nerves.

"Yes, that sounds about right," Winter nodded in affirmation. "Well, hello, my dearest, Penny." Winter stood to meet his favorite detective.

"Hello, Mr. Winter," Penny was cordial and terrified at the same time, fighting her trembling hands to shake Winter's.

"Why Penny, you're hands are so cold. Can I offer you a cup of hot tea on this brisk, late November afternoon?"

"No, thank you. I'm fine."

"And you, Detective Bruno? Would you like some tea?"

"No, we're both fine." Frank was focused on getting under the skin of the suspected murderer. "The reason why we're here...."

Winter cut off Frank, "I know why you're here, Detectives."

"Oh, and why's that?" asked Penny.

"Well, I'm sure by now you figured out that I worked at other retirement homes around the country, and you would have more questions for me."

Frank and Penny looked at each other, surprised by the admission.

"I'm sure by now you've likely shared your speculation with your boss and piqued his curiosity a bit," said Winter. "Please sit down and ask me whatever questions that you might have."

Frank and Penny did not expect Winter to be so forthcoming. The fact was that he had made both of them very uncomfortable. Frank removed his notepad from the left chest pocket of his tweed jacket after removing his overcoat first and then sat down across from Winter, with Penny sitting to his right.

"Yes, well, thank you for your time today, Mr. Whatever your name is." Frank's words dripped with sarcasm.

"You can just call me, Friend," smiled Winter, now seated back in his chair.

"Friend, huh?" Frank smirked.

"Yes, Friend," Winter smiled. "Now, what can I do for you, Detectives?"

"Mr. Winter, can you tell me how old you are?" asked Frank, his pencil ready to jot down the responses of the old man.

"I'm eighty-three years old, Detective."

"Eighty-three, you say?" asked Frank.

"Yes, the last time I checked." Winter looked off into the distance as if to ponder his actual age. "Yes, I do believe that I'm eighty-three years old."

Penny interjected, "Mr. Winter, after speaking with Dean Travers, he revealed to us that your real name is Garrison O'Donnell. Is that, in fact, your real name?"

"Oh my, I've had so many names over the years. I do prefer Garrison Winter, though."

Penny's brow, like Frank's, shot up with the admission.

Winter's eyes went to the massive solarium windows, and he began to ramble.

"The snow is so white and so pure. It cleans the dark scab left by evil men and purifies the darkness that can sometimes reveal itself in humanity. Good things happen after a healthy snowfall."

Penny continued, trying to get the old man to focus. "How is it that you can be eighty-three years old in 1974 when you were also eighty-three in 1969, Mr. O'Donnell?" Penny was now on the offensive.

"Oh, was I? Silly me," Winter shook his head. "I'm no good with numbers, I'm afraid," said Winter.

Frank and Penny looked confused. They didn't expect the conversation to take such a turn.

"Perhaps you can tell us what year you were born in, Mr. O'Donnell?" asked Frank.

"1888," said Old Man Winter. "Yes, that sounds about right." Winter squeezed his lips together, nodding as if to convince himself that the year was correct.

Frank quickly jotted down 1888, his pencil clawing at the number as he underlined and circled it several times.

Penny looked curious when doing the math in her head. "Mr. O'Donnell, that would put your age at 86 years old."

"Oh, would it? Hmmm, I'm sure of the year, though," he scratched his head, looking confused.

"Mr. O'Donnell," Frank addressed the old man, "Where are you from originally?"

"Oh, I came over from Ireland, such a beautiful place. Have either of you ever been?" Garrison asked the two detectives.

"No, I'm afraid I haven't," said Frank as he and Penny both stood shaking their heads, indicating no.

"When did you come to America?" Frank continued his questions.

"That would have been in 1912."

Frank wrote down the year in his notepad.

"That was a bad year for journeying across the Atlantic," Frank looked up after writing. "What with the Titanic going down in April of that year," he added.

"Oh, yes, what a terrible disaster," Winter shook his head. "It was frightfully cold that night! Oh, and the water, so cold."

Frank immediately looked at Penny; his mouth hung open. He then looked at the old man and asked, "You were on the Titanic?!" Frank was stunned.

"Oh, yes, I saved many people that night."

Frank was aghast, almost stuttering his next words. "So, you, you, helped to save some of the 700 survivors."

"Survivors? Oh no, I was speaking about the other 1517 souls on board."

"I'm sorry," said Penny, "What exactly are you saying?" Penny was baffled. When looking at Frank, she could see that he was too.

"Yes, I saved those poor souls. What a terrible way to go," said Winter. "But I can assure you that they're in a better place now."

"And where's that?" asked Frank.

"Why, Heaven, of course," Winter flashed a curious look. "Where else would they be, Detective?"

Frank needed a minute to collect his thoughts before he continued his line of questioning. He stalled by reviewing his notes out loud. "So, Garrison, may I call you Garrison since you apparently have so many last names?"

"Oh, yes, I'm very fond of that name," said Winter.

"Okay, so," Frank paused. "So you were born in 1888 and came to America aboard the Titanic in 1912. What did you do once you got here?"

"Immediately after leaving New York City, I traveled here to Philadelphia...."

Penny sat up in her chair and started to feel nauseous, awaiting Garrison's next words.

"And then I started working here, at Heavenly Gates," revealed Winter.

Penny looked sick, her complexion white, and she was unable to comment.

"So, you were twenty-four years old at that time, then?" asked Frank, who was now in full detective mode, locking down Old Man Winter on every word he revealed.

"Twenty-four?" Garrison looked confused. "Oh no, Detective, I was 83 back in 1912." Winter was puzzled, looking back and forth to both Frank and Penny.

Frank wrote the numbers 8-3-1-9-1-2 and then added them all together and wrote 24. Then multiplied 2 times 4 and got 8. He circled the number several times.

Penny, now visibly ill, was close to excusing herself when Frank looked up and asked Winter, "Garrison, how old were you in 1920?"

Winter again looked confused, taking turns looking at each detective, and said, "I was 83 in 1920. I've always been 83."

Frank stood up and said, "Garrison, will you please excuse us for a moment?"

"Why certainly," said Winter. "Penny, can I get you some water? You look ill, my dear."

Penny waved him off, saying nothing, then shot out of the room ahead of Frank. Frank followed closely behind her.

Moments later, in the foyer, Penny said, "I'm going to be sick." She then made her way down another hallway to the bathroom near the Admin Ward.

Frank waited outside and could hear Penny vomiting in the lavatory.

Minutes later, Penny emerged with tears in her eyes. She leaned back against the wall and collected herself before finally speaking. "Frank, did you hear that? He's the same Garrison O'Donnell then and now."

"Penny, what are you talking about? That old guy is off the rails crazy! He wasn't on the Titanic any more than he was 83 years old back in 1920. Everything he said validates that he's crazy," said Frank. "He's not our guy, Penny! We can't put him in front of McClain. We'll lose all credibility."

"Are you crazy!" Penny snapped. "We're absolutely putting him in front of McClain. That guy might be just crazy enough to kill old people. Don't forget that!" she wiped her mouth. "I've got more questions for him, and we're both going back in there." Penny was adamant.

"Penny, you heard what you wanted to hear in there. All you needed for that crazy old man to say was that he was 83 years old in 1920 and that he worked here. It's crazy on its face, not to mention impossible!" said Frank. "He's crazy and lying! Either way, putting him in front of McClain is a bad idea."

"You're going back in there with me!" demanded Penny. "That guy terrifies me, but he knows what happened to Rogers and Steinman, and maybe even Tipton. I get it, he's not one hundred and thirty-something years old, but he knows what happened to Rogers. That, I'm sure of!"

"Fine, we'll go back in there," conceded Frank. "But putting him in front of McClain is my call, not yours. Understood?" Frank made himself clear.

"Fine!" Penny rubbed her eyes and wiped her chin again.

"Now, get your act together, and don't lose it again, or you're off this case," Frank was direct with his rookie partner.

The two detectives made their way back into the solarium to find Old Man Winter again rolling the dice on the backgammon board.

"I just rolled a number three," Winter yelled just before he turned to see the detectives approaching.

"That's wonderful!" said Frank. "What's the significance of three, though?"

"Frank, I do love that you're so fascinated by numbers and their meaning."

Frank swallowed hard with Old Man Winter's comment. He was consumed with numbers and the number eight and multiples of the number. They kept him up at night. His fascination had turned into an obsession, and it was beginning to impair his judgment.

"The dice reflect the three of us, here in this room. And the snow that began to fall since the two of you left the room," explained Winter. "You see, the single spot on this die indicates me, and on this one, the two of you." Winter pointed to the die with the two dots on it. "You see? And the white that surrounds each of the dots is snow."

"Very good," said Frank. Now convinced that he was talking to a crazy person.

"So, Frank. How did your visit go at the church before you came here today?" Winter's question was a gutshot to Frank and Penny, catching both of them completely by surprise. It was Frank who now looked sick.

"What makes you think I went to church before coming here?" Frank played dumb. He didn't plan to admit that he visited Father Maloney.

"Just a guess. That's all," said Winter.

"A guess, huh?" Frank was rhetorical. He now believed that it was he in a cage and that Old Man Winter was on the outside, banging it with a bat.

Penny was again ready to leave the room. In her mind, the psychopath sitting in front of her was winning the head game that Frank was trying to play.

"Mr. Winter or O'Donnell," Frank paused. "Hell, I don't even know what your name is anymore. You're clearly out of your mind, and I'm beginning to think that coming here today was a waste of our time."

"Oh, that's so disappointing, Frank. Does this mean that I won't get to meet your boss?" Winter looked disappointed.

"Meet my boss?" Frank purposely looked confused, when in reality, he was terrified and losing the battle of wits with the evil in his presence. How could Garrison Winter possibly know why he and Penny came today and that they went to church prior to their arrival? Frank was now convinced that the old man in front of him wasn't crazy but calculating. He was also sure that Garrison Winter wasn't working alone. What frightened him the most was that Old Man Winter likely had somebody following his and Penny's every move. More determined than terrified, though, Frank was going to find out the truth, and Ron McClain would have to help.

"Mr. Winter, would you be available to come down to our station house tomorrow at noon?" asked Frank.

"I would absolutely love to!" said Winter, now perking up. "I don't get out much, as you can imagine, what with my old age and all."

Frank and Penny rose, dawned their jackets, and turned to go.

As the two detectives were walking away, Penny turned and asked Garrison Winter one final question. "Mr. Winter, did you know Samuel Crenshaw?"

"Oh, yes, I did. I also knew your grandfather, Ernest. What a wonderful man. He was the only one of Samuel's three sons who came to visit their father regularly. He was your great-grandfather's youngest and favorite child," Winter smiled.

"All the best to you, Penny. I shall see you both tomorrow at 12 pm sharp." Winter nodded his head as the two exited the room.

By the time Penny got to the foyer, she was crying. "Penny, he's fucking with you!" said Frank. "Don't let that monster beat you!"

"He knew my grandfather, Frank. He was there!" Penny cried. "He wasn't eighty-three years old, but he was there."

Frank agreed with Penny's assertion but also knew that the psychopath was playing head games. He thought about Penny's earlier assertion that Garrison Winter might actually be Dr. Donald Cameron from The Allan Institute. And that this was some kind of psychological experiment that everyone was in on except for him and Penny. Frank was beginning to trust no one except for his partner and friend, Penelope Denise Bryce.

Later that night, Frank was working late to finish the police report on the Victor Perry suicide. After running one last check on Perry's age, Frank was suddenly frozen in fear. A prior police report revealed to Frank that Vic Perry was born on August 8, 1951. Abbreviating the date, Frank wrote 8/8. He felt sick to his stomach. As he looked closer, he noticed that the numbers in Perry's birth year added up to sixteen. He wrote (1+9+5+1 = 16) on a scrap piece of paper. Looking more closely, all Frank saw was 8/8/8+8.

Frank looked around the empty detective office and suddenly felt alone and afraid.

Chapter 18 – 1927 to 1951

It was 12:05 pm on Tuesday, November 12, and Garrison Winter was late for his meeting with detectives at the 39th District. Frank and Penny had arrived early and briefed their boss, Ron McClain, on their interview from the previous day with their prime suspect. Frank made it clear to the Chief of Detectives that Old Man Winter was likely trying to appear mentally unstable so that the police wouldn't take him seriously and maybe, not investigate him further than they already had.

"He's not coming," Frank was nervous as he paced the Detective Room floor.

"I don't know," said Penny. "I think the old man likes the attention. You see the way he perks up every time we show up unannounced?"

"He's crazy but not innocent," said Frank, nervously tossing paper balls into the metal wire trash bin under the clock to the right of McClain's closed office door.

"Frank, that guy terrifies me." Penny wore the look of a battered wife just before her abusive husband returned home from work. "If this meeting was happening at Heavenly Gates, I might not be part of it."

"Penny, he freaks me out too, but what kind of detective runs away from an interview with a murder suspect?" asked Frank. "If McClain ever heard you talk like that, your career would be over. Now get it together, and keep your voice down," he whispered, not wanting McClain to overhear their conversation.

Penny took a deep breath and said, "I'll be fine."

Frank wasn't convinced. "If McClain removes you from this case," he paused, "you might never get another one," he said while looking her straight in the eye, his head cocked.

"What's McClain doing in there anyway? Winter's going to walk through the door at any second."

Frank said, "He gave Tubbs and Taylor a job to do, and now I think he's talking over another case with Riggins and Coons. Looks like a floater was found washed up on the banks of the Schuylkill, under the Route 1 Twin Bridges, just off Kelley Drive."

"On the River Trail?"

"Yeah, right down the hill by the water." Frank looked troubled. "It's a kid, Penny. A little boy."

"Oh, man. That's awful!" Penny grimaced. "I bet McClain's not taking it too well."

"He looked pretty shaken up about it when he told me earlier." Frank opened his desk drawer and grabbed a couple of number two pencils and his notepad. "I bet he's got the Boy in the Box running through his head like the North Broad Street Line. He'll never get over that one," said Frank.

"I hope somebody figures that one out someday. It's tough when it's a kid," Penny said, looking over at the clock as Frank's last balled-up piece of paper missed the wastebasket altogether.

At that moment, McClain's door flew open, and he walked out. "So where is he?" said McClain looking at his watch. "It's 12:12, for Christ's sake!"

"He'll be here," said Frank, though he wasn't so sure.

Just then, the phone rang, startling Frank and Penny, both staring at their phones as the rings chorused from every desk. Their faces couldn't hide their anxiety, looking at the phone like it was grim death.

"One of you two gonna answer that? What the hell's wrong with you?" asked McClain as he grabbed the receiver from Frank's desk. "McClain," he yelled into the mouthpiece. "Yeah, send him up! But pat him down first." McClain slammed down the phone. "Cat got your tongue, Frank?"

Frank was anxious, knowing that evil was walking up the steps at that very moment. Penny immediately switched positions from her desk, which backed up to the door, to where Frank was standing.

"You two idiots look like you've seen a ghost!" McClain made a face. "How bad can he be?"

Penny and Frank just looked at each other and reserved comment. A second later, the doorknob rattled as if someone was attempting to pull instead of pushing the door open. The three detectives looked at each other, trying not to chuckle. It wasn't the first time someone visiting the Detective Room on the second floor thought to pull instead of pushing the door open. When they did, the detectives who saw it would label the visitor an idiot.

The door began to open with a sudden push, and a little old man appeared, hiding behind a grey fedora and a black wool overcoat. It was Garrison Winter.

"Why, hello, Detectives," Winter removed his hat and unbuttoned his coat. "May I hang these, please? They're a bit wet from the snow, I'm afraid."

"Sure you can," said Frank, now seeing his suspect in a different light. Outside of Heavenly Gates, Frank thought that his prime suspect didn't look like a suspect at all, but rather a little old man that couldn't hurt a fly.

Frank could tell that Penny felt the same, watching her walk over to Winter, taking the garments from his hand and hanging them on the rack to the left of her desk. "Thank you for coming, Mr. Winter." Penny acted as if he were an old family member over for coffee and a visit.

"So this is the infamous Garrison, whatever your last name is," said the Chief of Detectives.

McClain had planned on being the bad cop during the interview. One in which the three had prepared to conduct in the middle of the Detective Room. Earlier, Frank and Penny had repositioned desks and chairs to give the three detectives and their suspect room to spread out a little.

"So, what is your actual name these days, might I ask?" McClain was snarky.

"Why, you can call me Garrison Winter," said the old man. "That's what my friends call me."

"Oh, so now I'm your friend?" asked McClain, towering over the old man in an effort to intimidate him.

"Oh, I would very much like to think so," said Winter. "A man of your standing and merits, Chief McClain, would enhance my standing in the community if I were able to call you friend."

McClain smiled, admiring the old man's charm. "Well, let's just say that the jury's still out on that one." McClain looked impressed with himself after the one-liner.

"Oh, I do value a good sense of humor, Chief McClain. I do believe that laughter keeps us young, don't you?"

"Again..." McClain and Winter smiled and chorused together, "the jury's still out."

"Yes, of course," smiled Garrison Winter.

Frank and Penny looked at each other, unsure of what they were witnessing. It appeared that their Chief was already stepping out of the 'bad cop' role.

Without offering his hand to shake the old man's, McClain instead motioned for him to take a seat in the middle of the room where four chairs sat, awaiting their guest.

"Have a seat over here, old-timer." McClain pointed to the chair directly across from where he'd be sitting. He wanted to look his suspect right in the eye as he questioned him.

Frank and Penny then walked to their pre-determined seats and sat down.

"So, Frank, why don't you kick us off and tell Mr. Winter over here why we asked him to come down to the station," said McClain, happy to be a spectator for a few minutes before he'd begin his line of questioning.

"Sure, Chief." Frank looked at Winter and readied his pencil. "Mr. Winter..."

"Please, call me Garrison," nodded Winter, hoping to set everyone at ease with the polite gesture.

"Garrison, it is then. Would you kindly explain the discrepancy between your purported age and your actual age? You threw Detective Bryce here and me for quite a loop yesterday," Frank grinned.

"Oh yes, and for that, I am sorry. I'm afraid it was late in the day, and I was a bit tired."

"So, how old are you, Garrison?" Frank leveled the question again.

"Well, let's see. If I was 83 in 1969, and this is 1974, then I must be 88." Garrison Winter appeared to be working the math out in his head. "Yes, 88. I'm certain of it."

Frank gulped when he'd heard 88 and then jotted down the number and circled it several times before looking back at Winter. "And in what year were you born?"

"1888, as I told you and Detective Bryce just yesterday."

Ron McClain did the calculation in his head. "Your math doesn't add up, Mr. Winter," he said while leaning forward in his chair. "If you were born in 1888, you would've been 81 in 1969, or 86 today. So either you're lying about the year you were born, or you're lying about how old you are today. Which is it?"

While McClain grilled Winter on his age, Frank was scribbling numbers on his notepad. He wrote the year 1974 and then drew a line between the 9 and the 7. After that, he subtracted the numbers from either side of the line and got an 8, from 9 minus 1, and then got a 3, from 7 minus 4, for 83. Staring at the 83, he circled it and then wrote, '3 - 8s.'

The sound of McClain and Winter bickering about age muted away until Frank only heard his own voice doing the math in his head. Penny noticed that he was lost in thought but tried to stay focused on Winter.

Frank then circled the two middle numbers, 9 and 7, added them together, and got 16. Dividing it by two, he got 8. He circled the number and then looked back up at Old Man Winter.

"As I said, I am 83 years old and have always been." Winter was relentless in his claim and now avoided eye contact with the three detectives in his audience.

McClain extended his elbow, placed it on his knee, and then pointed at Winter and said, "Listen here, Old-timer, I don't have time for your games...."

Winter cut off McClain by saying, "Perhaps you'll have time then to go down to the river and see that little boy they found washed up on its banks. Maybe you can help determine his identity before that case goes cold, too." Winter's smile was cryptic.

McClain shot to his feet, knocking his chair back several feet, startling both Penny and Frank. Old Man Winter didn't flinch, though. He just sat calm and unaffected by McClain's visceral reaction.

"What in the hell did you just say to me, old man?!" McClain was incensed.

Winter continued to smile while Frank and Penny were taken aback. "I was simply trying to say that I wouldn't want that poor child to go to his grave and remain nameless for all of eternity."

McClain was appalled that Winter would reference the one case that haunted him more than any other. Ron McClain looked over at Penny and Frank as if to ask if they'd mentioned the Boy in the Box case to the old man sitting before him. He also wondered how Garrison Winter could know about the child found down by the river. The press hadn't been notified yet, and the police were still on the scene.

"Mr. Winter!" raising his voice, McClain sat back down. "What did you do with the body of Victor Rogers?!"

"Why, Chief McClain, I'm not sure what you're asking me." Winter leaned back in his chair. "Victor Rogers was a wonderful man and a very good friend of mine."

"Yeah, well, your friends seem to keep coming up missing!" McClain raised his voice again. "How about Polly Anne Steinman and Barbara Jo Tipton? What did you do with them?"

"They were also very wonderful people. I adored both of them." Winter looked off, staring at nothing. He smiled as if recollecting a fond memory, his words stunning the three detectives.

Frank launched in with a question. "Mr. Winter, are you saying you knew the two women that Chief McClain just mentioned?" Frank thought this might be the moment that Winter implicated himself in the murders of the three missing persons.

Penny's gaze was transfixed on Winter's face. She knew that if he confessed to the three disappearances, he would likely confess to his involvement in her great-grandfather's disappearance, too.

Winter appeared to snap out of his daze. "I'm sorry. What was the question again?"

McClain instinctively reached for his handcuffs though he had none on his belt and hadn't for more than a decade. With the admission that Winter knew all three victims, he would be arrested immediately for suspicion of murder and held for further questioning.

"I asked if you knew Polly Anne Steinman and Barbara Tipton?" Frank rephrased the question.

"I'm sorry," Winter looked confused, "I can't say that those names ring a bell."

The three detectives sighed in frustration. They were all sure they had their man. Now, none of the three knew what to ask next.

After several moments of Garrison Winter studying the faces of the three perplexed detectives, Penny spoke up.

"Mr. Winter, yesterday you told me that you worked at Heavenly Gates back in 1920 and that you knew Samuel Crenshaw. Is that true?" asked a desperate Penny.

"That is true, Detective Bryce...."

Ron McClain sat back in his chair, arms folded across his chest, revealing massive, vein-riddled forearms that were intended to intimidate his suspect. He sat stoic and was eager for the old man to incriminate himself. If he did, he would be the first to walk him downstairs and book him. Frank knew better, though. Detective Frank Bruno knew that the old man was cunning and smart and that he was simply toying with them as if it were a sport to do so.

"Your grandfather and great-grandfather would sit around and talk about you and how they loved the name Penelope," Winter smiled at Penny.

"Mr. Winter, I wasn't born for another 14 years after my great-grandfather, Samuel Crenshaw, went missing. They couldn't possibly have talked about someone who wasn't born yet." Penny's emotions were on display while refuting Winter's assertion.

"Oh, Penny," Winter smiled and shook his head. "I told them all about you and the life that you would lead." Winter's smile grew and, for a moment, seemed to freeze the faces of the three detectives. They all seemed unable to comprehend the depravity of the monster they'd invited to their office.

McClain jumped from his chair and yelled, "Okay, I've had enough of this crazy son of a Bitch! Get him out of here!"

Frank and Penny rose from their chairs, signaling the end of the interview.

Before McClain disappeared into his office, he said to Garrison Winter, "Listen here, you sick son of a bitch! I know that you're guilty of something. And I know that you're not alone. When I have enough information to have you arrested, I will be the one slapping the cuffs on your wrists!" he then turned and walked into his office and slammed the door.

Old Man Winter looked surprised and disappointed. Turning to Penny and Frank, he said, "Oh, is that all for today, then? I'd hoped you would have more questions for me?"

Penny and Frank looked at the old man and then at each other. Penny deferred to Frank, who said, "You're free to go, Mr. Winter. But you're not free to leave the City of Philadelphia. We will need to speak with you again very soon."

"Leave Philadelphia?" Winter seemed surprised by the statement. Shaking his head, he said, "Oh no, this will be my final stop this time, Detective Bruno."

Frank looked spooked and turned away from Winter and began nervously moving the chairs and desks back to their original places. Penny was speechless and tried to avoid eye contact with Winter, hoping he'd disappear through the door just ten feet away, never to return.

Before walking out the door, Winter stopped, turned, and said, "Penelope, my dear, if you want to know what happened to your great-grandfather, you might want to first investigate the cities of St. Louis, Portland, Spokane, Barrington, and Youngstown. 1927 to 1951."

Penny's mouth hung open. She looked at Frank to find him staring back at her.

"Have a good day, Detectives." Winter smiled, dawned his fedora, draped his coat over his right arm, and disappeared down into the stairwell.

Frank rushed to look for his notepad as Penny scrambled for hers. Both recited the cities that Winter referenced aloud to avoid forgetting them before jotting them down on paper.

"What city was first?!" yelled Penny to Frank.

"I got it! I got it! I got it!" Frank yelled back, feverishly scribbling on his notepad.

Ron McClain's door opened. He'd heard the commotion just outside his office. "What happened? What's going on?"

Frank and Penny didn't even know their boss was standing there. Penny said, "What was the order, Frank?" Frustrated that she couldn't remember exactly what Winter said.

"St. Louis! Portland! Spokane! Barrington! And Youngstown! In that order!" yelled Frank. "1927 to 1951!"

Ron McClain stood scratching his head while Frank and Penny got to work.

Chapter 19 – Quantico

In the week since Garrison Winter was interviewed at the 39th District, Ron McClain, Frank Bruno, and Penny Bryce impatiently awaited word from the police departments in the five cities Winter mentioned before leaving that day.

Ron McClain had become incensed by Winter's subtle reference to the Boy in the Box case. How did the old man know that McClain worked the case? And how could he have known about the young boy, whose lifeless body had just washed up on the north bank of the Schuylkill River just two hours earlier? Both of those questions troubled McClain so much that he became certain something was amiss with the old man. It had been years since the Chief of Detectives took a case personally, and after meeting Garrison Winter, he wanted to know what involvement the old man might have in the disappearances. His involvement in the case ensured Penny and Frank would have access to approved resources. Just hours after the Winter interview on November 12, McClain allowed Frank and Penny to telefax to police agencies in St. Louis, Portland, Spokane, Barrington, and Youngstown. But word coming back would be slow as inter-agency communication was almost non-existent in 1974, except for intra-state communication of neighboring agencies.

To bide her time, Penny listed out the dates and cities where the known disappearances occurred, as well as those cities mentioned by Old Man Winter, on a chalkboard that backed up to the Schuyler Street side of the Detective Room.

The list included: victim's name, age, date of disappearance, city, and the name of the retirement community. Samuel Crenshaw was listed at the top, along with his age of 94, the date December 7, 1920, the city of Philadelphia, and the Heavenly Gates retirement home. Beneath Crenshaw's name were question marks in place of a name, the date December 9, a question mark for the year, the city of Youngstown, and more question marks in place of the name of the retirement home.

The list continued, and there were far too many question marks than Penny's patience would allow for. Penny stared at the board for hours and was sure when the other agencies around the country looked into their old unsolved case files, they'd surely call the 39th District and share what they had. Penny was desperate to replace the question marks with names and dates. Looking at the list, the only thing she wasn't sure of was what city was second. Was it Youngstown, Ohio, or St. Louis, Missouri? She'd figured Youngstown would be the first city a person would arrive in after leaving the western side of the state.

Penny and Frank set up a map of the U.S. on the wall near the chalkboard and used pushpins to denote the eight cities named in their case. Using red yarn that Penny brought from home, she tied one end to the pin marking Philadelphia and then extended it west to Youngstown, Ohio, Bloomington, Indiana, and Barrington, Illinois. Stretching the yarn further, she strung it out to the west coast, marking Spokane, Washington, down to Portland, Oregon, back east to St. Louis, Missouri, and then Pittsburgh, with it finally coming back to Philadelphia. Penny was sure that was the route her killer took. What she wasn't sure of was why it all started and ended in Philadelphia.

As Penny read about Youngstown, she noticed that it resided on the Pennsylvania/Ohio border, making it a booming small city, with steel production as its main export. The city was situated on Interstate 80, which ran East to West, connecting New York City to Northern California. It was a major shipping and transportation route connecting twelve states.

Steel mills lined the Mahoning River along Route 422 and served as one of the city's largest sources of employment. Those living in the Youngstown area either worked in the steel industry or knew someone that did. The same could be said for the auto industry, with General Motors operating its Lordstown Assembly Plant, which first opened in 1966.

Youngstown, also known as the armpit of crime, was geographically positioned halfway between Chicago and New York City, roughly 400 miles from each city. The location made it a beehive of activity for the mafia, who had businesses established throughout the city and would house, employ, and host events for traveling crime family members who'd meet halfway between the two larger cities. Looking at the census data that Penny got from the library, she learned that Youngstown was founded in 1796, and by the 1920s, the city was aging, and so was its population. In Penny's mind, It would be the first stop for a serial murderer leaving the state and heading West.

Penny dreamt of catching a serial murderer in her first-ever investigation as she continued to stare at the chalkboard. In that instant, Penny was pulled from her morbid fantasy as the phone on every desk rang. As she reached for the phone on the desk of Jack Riggins, positioned nearest to the chalkboard, it stopped ringing because Frank, sitting at his desk, grabbed it on the second ring. Penny held her breath, hoping it was a detective from one of the five cities on the board. Penny wanted nothing more than to prove her theory right. She believed that Garrison Winter was somehow part of a series of nine murders that spanned forty-nine years, more than two thousand miles, eight cities, and seven states, with two happening less than five miles away in the East Germantown mansion that her great-grandfather built in 1860, FalconClaw.

Penny watched Frank's face as he spoke to the caller, praying that it was the news she'd hoped for. When she saw his eyebrows arch and his eyes go wide, followed by a smile, she knew that her hopes were confirmed. Another piece to the Winter puzzle had fallen into place.

As Penny listened more closely, she heard a different form of good news being conveyed. The FBI was calling.

Frank hung up the phone and said, "Okay, we got the 'go ahead' from the brass over at the Bureau. They've agreed to meet with us tomorrow," said Frank rising from his chair. "We're heading to Virginia tonight."

Penny's smile sagged. While she was happy that she and Frank would be meeting with agents in the emerging *Criminal Profiling Unit* in Quantico, Virginia, she really wanted to get confirmation that her hunch was right. In her heart, she was sure the other missing persons cases would be linked to Garrison Winter, but in her head, she thought it was selfish to wish for more disappearances simply to enhance her value and worth to Ron McClain and the Philadelphia Police Department, but mostly to herself. Detective Penelope Bryce still didn't feel like a bonafide detective, and she was afraid that she never would.

Frank walked over to where Penny was standing and said, "I was just talking to one of the two guys I met last year in Harrisburg at the FBI seminar that dealt with psychological profiling. His name is Douglas Cantrell. This guy's an FBI Profiler that travels the country interviewing serial murderers before the trial phase. Apparently, they're now starting to call Serial Murderers, Serial Killers," Frank paused, writing in his notes. "We should too. We want to come across as knowledgeable and up to speed."

"That's great!" Penny exaggerated her enthusiasm. "You think they'll want to come in on the case?" She feared the Feds would take over the case once they determined that it was an interstate serial murderer that they were looking for.

Frank shook his head. "Not these guys, in particular. They're more on the side of learning how serial killers think. They want to study what makes these lunatics do what they do," explained Frank, "But to be clear, Penny, the FBI would take it over if they determined one guy is behind three or more murders. That's how it works, Rookie."

Penny looked deflated. "That's what I'm afraid of."

"Don't worry, Penny," Frank was supportive. "You and I know that we're on this case because of you," he paused and looked into Penny's eyes and added, "And your instincts!" Frank smiled. "More importantly, the Chief knows that this is your case."

After the two stood quietly staring at the map, Frank, hands in his pockets, said, "Penny, you know how many red pins I see on that map?"

"Eight, Frankie. There are eight cities marked. I see it too," said Penny looking at her partner. She was starting to think the number eight did, in fact, mean something.

Frank snapped from his momentary fog and said, "Listen, it's almost three o'clock. You get out of here. I'll let McClain know we're leaving and that we'll be back tomorrow night. I'll pick you up at seven in front of your house. Tell Joe and the boys I'm sorry for stealing their momma, again."

"Sure you don't want to pick me up at eight instead?" Penny winked.

"Real funny, Bryce! Real funny." Frank pursed his lips and shook his head. "You'll see, I'm right about the eights."

"Alright, Frankie! I'll see you at seven."

After grabbing her coat, Penny walked to the door, pulling it open. Just before she disappeared into the stairwell, Frank yelled out, "Hey Penny!"

"Yeah, Frankie?

"You're a good cop! And an even better detective."

"Yeah, okay, Frank." Penny wasn't convinced.

Later that night, the Buick's horn sounded in front of 2125 Fuller Street. Frank looked up at the house and could see Penny hug Joe and her boys just inside the screen door. As he looked closer, he saw himself hugging Jeanie with his two girls playing in the living room. Frank missed his best girl, and he missed the family they once had. Home wasn't the same, and Frank found himself looking for any excuse he could find not to be there. Sure, he missed his girls when he wasn't home, but Jeanie's ghost haunted his soul, and he lived with the guilt of being a rabid chain-smoker for most of their marriage. Since her cancer diagnosis, Frank hadn't touched one cigarette in the carton of Camels he kept above the refrigerator at home.

Frank was snapped out of his funk by the opening of the passenger door. Penny jumped in and said, "So where we going, Frankie?" Again, Frank looked at Penny and saw Jeanie. Her smile was as big as daybreak, and her hair was the color of sunlight. Blinded by her image, Frank rubbed his eyes, shook his head, and cracked his jaw, trying to get his head right.

"You okay, Frankie Boy?" Penny looked a little judgy. "Every time you pick me up, I get in the car and feel like I just interrupted something." Penny looked into the backseat and said, "You got somebody hiding back there?" She cracked her gum, "So, what's up? You okay?"

"Yeah-yeah, I'm fine. Just thinking about our big day tomorrow. That's all."

Frank was a tortured soul and secretly couldn't wait for it to all be over so that he could be with his Jeanie again in heaven. If there really was such a thing? A question he'd often asked himself since his best girl died on August 26.

"Okay, I got the notepads and number two pencils you told me to bring. I'm feeling pretty excited about tomorrow," Penny was fidgety in her seat. "A little nervous, though. I'm not gonna lie."

Frank smiled to relax his friend. "Remember, just like Lewistown. We're just gonna talk to these guys. We'll give them what we got, and hopefully, they'll take an interest in the case and throw some resources at it."

"What does that mean?" Penny looked curious.

"Penny, if these guys think we're on to something that's interstate and involves a serial killer, they might get field agents to look into the cases without us ever having to step on a plane."

Penny's eyes went wide again. "A plane? Man, that would be exciting! I've never flown before. Did you know I haven't even stayed in a hotel since Joe and I got married and went to Niagara Falls for our honeymoon?"

"When was that, anyway?" Frank was curious.

"1956." Penny stared out the window, smiled, and said, "That was a good year."

"How old are the boys now?"

"Joey Jr. is fourteen, and Tommy's twelve."

"Damn! You guys waited a while to have kids, huh? Why'd you wait so long?"

Penny shook her head. "We tried! But I had some lady issues and just couldn't get pregnant."

Penny's infertility immediately reminded Frank of Jeanie, and at that exact moment, snowflakes showed up in the Buick's headlights.

Penny, looking at the falling snow, didn't notice the sadness in Frank's eyes. Now digging through the glovebox, she said, "So, where we staying tonight?"

In a momentary daze, Frank said, "What?"

"So what motel are we staying in?" Penny repeated herself. "You hard of hearing or something?"

"Oh, it's called the Red Roof Inn or something like that."

"That's the name of the motel? Red Roof Inn?" Penny looked confused. "Whatta you want to bet the place has a red roof?" She laughed wildly at her joke. "So, you got any new music in here, or what?"

"Yeah, um, I don't know." Frank was disinterested. "Just push in the Eagles. It's already in there."

"God, no!" Penny was having none of it. "Enough with the Eagles already." She slammed the glove box closed.

"I guess we could just talk or something?"

Frank rolled his eyes. "Well, that sounds entertaining."

After a few minutes of silence, Penny asked, "So why do they call it a motel anyway?"

Frank was puzzled, "What are you talking about?"

"A motel. What's the difference between a motel and a hotel?" asked Penny.

"Geez, I can't believe you made it all the way up to detective." Frank shook his head and smiled.

"Whatever!" barked back Penny. "You don't even know, do you?"

"Penny, the M-O in motel is short for motor, as in motor-hotel. You know, you pull your car up to the door."

Penny's eyes shot open. "Oh! Geez, I feel stupid now."

"Pretty much!" acknowledged Frank.

"Then what does the HO stand for in hotel?"

Frank paused and slowly turned to look at Penny. "Your mom!" Frank busted out laughing. "I'm gonna piss my pants!" His face was as red as taillights.

Penny shook her head. "Mmm-Hmm, you got jokes, huh, Frankie Boy? Well, I gotta joke for you."

"No Polish jokes, please. I have a newfound respect for Polish people after meeting up with Kowalczyk and the Pittsburgh boys," said Frank, wiping away laughter tears from his earlier joke.

"No, really, I got a good one for you!" Penny swiveled in her seat to face Frank.

"I can't wait to hear this one. Go ahead," Frank motioned with his hand.

"Okay, so an old lady finally decides it's time to get married, so she places an ad in the newspaper. It read, 'Husband wanted.' Must not beat me, can't walk all over me, and has to be good in bed."

"Okay, you got my attention," said Frank, curious to see where the joke was going.

"Well," said Penny, "she got dozens of responses, but after a few weeks, she didn't find anybody suitable. So, she was about to give up when her doorbell rang."

"Okay," Frank nodded his head.

Penny was anxious to get to the punchline, almost bouncing in her seat.

"So, the old lady opened the door and found a man with no arms or legs sitting in a wheelchair on her front stoop."

"So she says, 'Can I help you?' Well, the man smiles and says. 'It's me, your new husband!'" Penny couldn't contain herself. "'You must be joking....' the woman laughed."

"For God's sake! Get to the end already."

"Wait for it, Frankie!" Penny smiled, holding up her finger.

"So the old man said, 'Well, think about it, I have no arms, so I can't beat you. I have no legs, so I can't walk all over you. The woman's eyes narrowed, and she asked, 'Yeah, But are you good in bed?'"

Penny paused before finishing the joke. "Well, the old man leaned back in his wheelchair, smiled, and said, 'I rang the doorbell, didn't I?'" Penny wailed, almost crying in laughter.

"Wait a second!" Frank shook his head. "How'd the guy get the wheelchair up onto the lady's stoop?"

"What?!" said Penny. "Who cares? That's not the important part of the joke."

Frank shook his head, looking unimpressed, and said, "Well, that might be the worst joke of all time."

Still laughing, Penny backhanded Frank's shoulder and said, "Fuck you, Frankie, that was a good one!"

After a few minutes of watching the time and snow fly, Frank said, "We should talk a little bit about how tomorrow's gonna go."

"What do I need to do?" asked Penny, again looking a little nervous about the trip.

"Just be prepared to tell them everything you know about Winter and the disappearances."

"Well, I called Kowalczyk from Pittsburgh yesterday and also got a hold of Jensen in Indiana; they had nothing new to report," she paused. "Damn! I wish we had something from the other cities!" Penny was frustrated. "You think we'll hear back from anyone, Frank?"

"It was a long time ago, Penny. We might not." Frank was pragmatic. "I mean, 1927 is a long time ago. We might need these FBI boys to help us out."

"Frank, do you think I'm just dreaming this whole thing up?" Penny's gaze went to the snow and the darkness that shrouded both the car and her confidence.

"Penny, you didn't dream up the fact that Victor Rogers and the women from Pittsburgh and Indiana went missing."

"No, I mean the connection with my great-grandfather. If I'm wrong about that, then my instincts might not be good enough to be a detective."

"That's ridiculous! This is your first case, and detectives aren't born; they're made. You need experience." Frank tried his best to be supportive of his partner. Looking over at her, he noticed she was getting drowsy as her eyes sagged.

"The answer is in that basement, Frank." Penny yawned as her eyes narrowed.

"FalconClaw?"

"It's down there. I know it!" Penny whispered before dozing off.

Later that night, after driving the one hundred seventy-five miles from Philly to Quantico, the Buick rolled into the parking lot of the Red Roof Inn; it was just before 11 pm. With Penny still asleep, Frank walked in and paid for two rooms. When he got back into the car, the slamming door woke Penny up.

"We here?" Penny was groggy.

"Yeah, we made it, Penny." Frank handed Penny her room key and said, "You won the bet."

"What bet?"

"The place has a red roof!" Frank smiled and pointed up. "That was some good detective work right there, Penny. Your instincts are good."

Penny laughed and then looked down at the red room key in her hand. Opening her hand, she saw the number 10 embossed in white on the red tag. Looking out the window for a moment, she pondered who the tenth victim of Old Man Winter would be and when.

Frank pulled the car down the backside of the motel and parked it in front of Penny's room. Penny got out and grabbed her bag out of the backseat. Leaning in, she said, "Thanks, Frankie. Have a goodnight!"

Before exiting the car, Frank sat and wondered what it all meant. Where would this case lead him and Penny? Who was Old Man Winter? And why did he take his victims? Looking down at his clenched hand, he opened his fingers from around the red key tag. The number that Frank saw staring back at him was the number 8.

Frank looked out at his room door through the snow and the windshield. Looking closer, he'd noticed that the nail holding the top of the room number in place had given way. The number eight had fallen and was now hanging upside down. Looking just above it, he could see the outline of where the number used to be. Frank shook his head and just stared at the two eights that seemed to be staring back at him ominously.

After a few minutes of deep thought and some consternation, Frank finally gained the courage to walk toward the eights instead of running from them.

Chapter 20 – Behavioral Science Unit

After a quick coffee and some Little Debbie powdered donuts from the vending machine in the lobby, Frank and Penny walked out onto the snow-dusted parking lot and got into the Buick.

"Come on, Baby!" Frank bit his tongue as he tried to turn over the engine, frantically pumping the gas while aggressively turning the key. After thirty seconds of hearing the familiar whine of an engine not wanting to wake up, the muffler backfired, and the car roared to life.

"Imagine if we were late for this meeting?" Frank looked relieved.

"Frank, maybe it's time for a new car," suggested Penny.

"Are you crazy?! I'm never getting rid of this Buick. Before you know it, Jessica will be driving it."

"You told me that she's embarrassed to be seen in it," Penny laughed.

"Whatever!"

Frank took a left out of the motel as the windows started to defrost. "Well, here we go! You ready for this?"

"It's freezing in this crate!" Penny rubbed her hands together and ignored Frank's question.

Frank pushed in the 8-Track tape hanging out of the radio, and Witchy Woman blared as he sang along while Penny rolled her eyes.

Fifteen minutes later, the Buick turned left off of University Blvd. and onto Discovery Drive. To their immediate left, they saw a sign that was marked Federal Bureau of Investigation. Frank pulled into the entrance and stopped at a small security gate in front of the sprawling FBI campus in Quantico. As he approached, a guard emerged from a tiny booth. Frank rolled down his window, and when he did, it only came down halfway and was cocked at an angle.

The uniformed man, hands resting on his gun belt, asked Frank for identification while obnoxiously chewing a wad of gum that both he and Penny thought was far too big for his mouth.

"Can I see some I.D.?" asked the stalky black man, wearing a fur-neck collared black coat and a badge. Frank observed the man wearing black nylon slacks with gray stripes running down the outer legs. The man was carrying a .38 in his holster and wore a winter hat with ear flaps. From what Frank could see, the man would rather be somewhere else.

"They got any heat for you inside of that little box?"

The man ignored Frank's question and motioned with his hand, "I.D. please, Sir." The Guard sounded perturbed.

"Yeah, here you go, buddy." Frank handed the guard his detective badge and driver's license.

The man leaned in, handed back Frank's identification, looked over at Penny, and said, "Who's that, your wife?"

Penny snorted and said, "Ha! That'll be the day!" She was more humored than offended.

"That's my partner. We're down from Philly, and we're here to see Douglas Cantrell in the Criminal Profiling Unit."

"Well then, you're at the wrong place. There ain't no Criminal Profiling Unit on this campus. I never even heard of it," said the guard.

Frank looked over to Penny and then back at the guard. "What about the Behavioral Science Unit?"

"Yeah, the BSU," the guard said nonchalantly. "It's right down around the bend. That's where Mr. Cantrell works."

Frank exhaled in frustration. "So, let me get this straight. I just told you that we were here to see Douglas Cantrell, and you jumped to the conclusion that we were in the wrong place because I said he works in the Criminal Profiling Unit? Is that right?"

The guard leaned down again, this time resting his elbow on the top of Frank's door, and said, "You know, your window's all jacked up?"

Frank wanted to kick the guy's ass. "Yeah-yeah! Whatever! Open the gate!"

The guard stood, walked over to the gate, manually lifted it, and yelled, "Follow the signs!"

"Have a great day!" Frank was sarcastic as he waved out his window as they passed the man.

"And get that window fixed!" the guard yelled as Frank drove on.

Penny laughed at Frank as they drove down a long two-laned entrance road that led to a group of buildings in the distance.

"Get that window fixed!" Frank mocked the guard as he attempted to roll up the window. "C'mon, you son of a bitch!" The window seemed to be stuck.

Penny laughed and said, "Now that's some funny shit right there!"

"Keep it up, Bryce, and you'll be walking back to Philly," Frank grunted as he tugged at the window crank.

"I'd tell you to keep it up, but apparently it's 'all jacked up,'" Penny laughed while imitating the security guard.

Up ahead, as Frank squinted to see past the dirty windshield and clapping wiper blades, he saw a fork in the road with signs pointing in two directions. The left arrow was marked *FBI Main Building*, and the arrow pointing right was marked *Behavioral Science Unit*.

Frank took a right and, just moments later, pulled into the parking lot of a small two-story building that looked dated and in need of painting.

"This is it?" Penny didn't look impressed. "Looks like they've got a smaller budget than we do."

"That's what the sign says." Frank pulled the Buick into a parking spot marked *Visitors Only.* "Check that out! We have our own private parking space." he smiled, trying to improve on the meager accommodations.

"You gonna roll up that window, buddy?" Penny smiled as she fought her nerves.

Frank again fought the hand crank and groaned, "The damn thing doesn't want to go up." After another minute of trying, he said, "Fuck it! Let's go!"

"But Frank, it's starting to snow pretty good!"

"What do you want me to do?! We're not walking in there, late!"

"Your call, Frankie Boy!" Penny rolled her eyes and shook her head, reaching for her door handle.

Moments later, the two entered the building and witnessed another security guard sitting at a desk just inside the door to the right. The white male, of average height, stood to greet the two. With a morsel of his breakfast sandwich stuck in his mustache, he requested identification and asked who they were there to see.

Frank said, "We're here to see Douglas Cantrell. We're with the Philadelphia Police Department."

Using his jacket sleeve to wipe his mouth, the guard said, "You guys drove all the way down from Philly this morning?"

"No, we came in last night," responded Frank, staring down at the guard's desk, eyes fixated on the half-eaten bagel with cream cheese oozing out the sides.

"Sign here," said the guard, handing a clipboard to Frank. "Her too," he motioned to Penny. "And I'll need both of your sidearms, too. You can place them in this box."

Frank and Penny emptied their holsters and placed their city-issued .38 Specials in the box provided by the guard. When Penny placed hers in the box, she finally made eye contact with the young man. When she did, she motioned to him, wiping her right index finger across her upper lip, not wanting to say anything to him about the crumb that seemed right at home, dangling from his post-pubescent attempt at manhood.

Frank handed the man the clipboard back, and the guard pointed down the hall and said, "It's the last door on the left."

In 1974, the FBI formed its Behavioral Science Unit to investigate homicide cases and serial rapists and to set up a new Criminal Profiling Assets department. Its first employee was a man named Douglas Cantrell, who'd been with the Bureau since early 1970.

Cantrell was from Brooklyn, New York, and joined the FBI at the young age of twenty-five years old. He was known as a whiz kid to his peers and supervisors because of his multiple degrees, earning a B.S. from New Mexico State University, an M.S. and E.D.s from the University of Illinois, and his Masters, from The Ohio State University.

As Frank and Penny walked through the open door at the end of the hall, they could hear two men talking in the next room.

Franked knocked on the office door, and the talking stopped. After a few moments, a man walked out and greeted the two. Frank thought the man looked to be in his late thirties. He had dark hair with a little gray on each side and looked familiar to Frank, as they'd met the year before.

"There he is! Frank Bruno, right?" asked the man.

"That's me!" said Frank extending his hand to shake. "You must be Agent Cantrell?"

"Not quite. I'm Special Agent Richard Kessler. We met last year in Harrisburg."

"Of course, sorry. Lots of unfamiliar faces that day," Frank was slightly embarrassed. "Hard to remember everyone."

"No problem!" said Kessler. "Come on in! We've been waiting for you guys."

Penny felt slighted by Frank and Kessler, who seem to have forgotten that she was in the room.

"Ahem!" Penny cleared her throat.

Frank stopped, again embarrassed, and said, "Special Agent Kessler, this is my partner, Penelope Bryce."

"Nice to meet you, Detective." Kessler extended his hand to shake.

"And you, Special Agent," Penny reciprocated.

"Please, call me Rick!" said Kessler. "Follow me, guys."

Kessler led the two Philly detectives into what looked like a converted conference room, but the conference table had been replaced with two desks. Penny and Frank surveyed the room and were underwhelmed with its décor. Stained beige carpet, brown paneling, empty nails where pictures once hung, and a solitary clock. The cardboard boxes stacked on the floor gave one the impression that its occupants were moving out and not in.

Rising from his perched position on the corner of a desk to the right was Cantrell.

"Well, if it isn't Cold Case Frank?!" barked Cantrell, dropping a file folder he'd been sifting through onto his desk and standing to meet his guests.

Frank blushed while Penny wore a look of pleasure, happy to have a new nickname to call her partner.

"Special Agent Cantrell! Good to see you again!" Frank extended his hand.

When the two men finished their reciprocal handshake, Frank turned toward his partner and said, "Agent Cantrell, this is my partner, Detective Penny Bryce."

"It's a pleasure to meet you, Detective." Cantrell nodded and said, "Why don't you guys take off your coats and settle in for a minute. Rick and I need to get a few items set up before we get started."

After the two men left the room, Penny looked at Frank and said, "You've got to be shitting me! That kid looks like he just graduated High School!"

"I know," Frank raised his brow. "When I saw him last fall, he looked even younger. That guy is smart, though. Wait until you hear what he has to say." Frank slipped his coat off and hung it on the back of a nearby chair.

"What about the other guy?" asked Penny.

"Well, from what I remember, he's former military." Frank's memory of the seminar from the previous fall was coming back to him now.

"He looks it. Not a fan of the high and tight haircut, but he's a good-looking man."

"I'll be sure to let him know," Frank smiled.

A minute later, the two Special Agents entered the room, pushing a metal cart with a file box, tape recorder, and an overhead projector on it.

"Sorry, we weren't ready for you guys. We just moved into this office, and we're working out of boxes right now."

"No problem," said Frank. "We're thankful that you guys are taking the time to meet with us."

"So, Doug tells me you're working a case and that it could possibly involve multiple victims? Is that right?" asked Rick Kessler.

Special Agent Richard Kessler was an Army veteran, serving from 1957 to 1962, and was a Provost Marshal. After serving for four years in Germany, Kessler was reassigned to the Army's Criminal Investigation Department. After the military, he graduated from Michigan State University with a degree in Police Administration.

"Rick, hold off for a second. I want to record the conversation so that I can play it back later," said Cantrell.

"Sure." Kessler got up and motioned to Frank. "Frank, give me a hand with this folding table, would ya? That way, we can all spread out a little."

Frank helped Kessler as Penny chatted with the younger agent at his desk.

"Excuse me, Special Agent Cantrell, I don't mean to be rude, but can I ask how old you are?"

"Call me Doug," said Cantrell. "And it's not rude at all. I've been asked that same question almost every day since I joined the Bureau. I'm twenty-nine, thirty next month," he smiled modestly. "I'm starting to think I'll always be the youngest person in the room."

"Wow! So accomplished! When I was twenty-nine, I was on my fourth year walking the beat in Philly."

"Wow, to you! I read about your case against the City of Philadelphia. If anyone has earned their detective badge, it would be you."

"Thank you," said Penny. "Yes, it was tough. I didn't think I would ever become a detective, and between you and me," Penny whispered, "I still don't feel like one."

"Now you know how I feel," smiled the baby-faced whiz kid. "You'll feel like one after you solve your first case, I suppose," said Cantrell.

"That's what I've heard. I hope it's my first case that I solve." Penny was hopeful and humble. "That's why we're here."

"Well, if it makes you feel any better, I've never solved a case in my life," confessed Cantrell. "I'm still not sure what I'm doing here. I mean, we're all trying to figure out how to stay busy for an entire day."

"I don't understand," Penny was confused.

"Sorry, let me explain." Doug Cantrell sat on the corner of his desk. "Rick and I interview murderers who have killed multiple victims. We then study their answers and try to determine what led them to do what they did. Our goal is to catalog as many mass murderers as possible and develop a psychological profile of them, their victims, their habits, and their routines. The goal is to find out what makes them tick. If we can do that, we can share that info with police departments worldwide and hopefully head off some of these lunatics before their body count gets too high. The only problem," said Cantrell, "is that there're only so many of them out there to talk to."

"I see what you mean," said Penny. "I mean, how many could there possibly be walking around out there?"

"More than you could imagine, I'm afraid," said Cantrell. "The problem is that almost none of them want to talk to us. They hear FBI and think that their sentence is somehow going to get worse even after butchering a family of five." Cantrell shook his head.

"Geez!" Penny winced.

"You want to hear a secret?" Cantrell looked toward the door making sure his partner wasn't within earshot. "We just locked down an interview with Manson," Cantrell's smile revealed his excitement.

"Charles Manson?!" Penny's chin dropped.

"Helter Skelter, himself!" Cantrell looked around again. "I can't wait to hear what that crazy son of a bitch has to say."

Penny was now more curious about Cantrell's job. "Are you scared to meet him?"

"More curious about his mind than I am scared for my personal safety."

"So, how did you get placed in this department, anyway?" asked Penny.

"Well, I was an instructor. I taught hostage negotiations for two years after working in the field and observing. My advanced degrees precede me wherever I go in the Bureau as many of the Field Agents only have high school diplomas."

Penny raised her hand, "Guilty as charged. I have a high school diploma and fourteen years walking the beat."

Cantrell was impressed, "I wish I had that kind of experience. I was in ninth grade when you were busting perps in the big city. Your experience would come in handy around here. Just saying," Cantrell smiled.

Penny was flattered and wondered if she was being recruited. She was beginning to like the young man and didn't feel inferior in his presence. She felt like an equal and thought that what she had to say would be received sincerely in their meeting. She was all of a sudden at ease and couldn't wait to get started.

At that moment, the two heard laughing as Frank and Rick Kessler walked back into the room after grabbing coffee. Each had a second cup in their hand for their respective partners.

"Okay, you two, break it up over there," said Kessler. "Frank just told me that you guys are heading back tonight, so we need to get cracking. It's ten right now, so that gives us what? About eight hours, Frank?"

Frank heard eight and said, "Yeah, eight hours sounds about right." The number eight started running through his head again, and he hoped the others didn't notice if he zoned out for a minute.

Penny saw the look on Frank's face and knew what he was thinking.

"Okay, so, Penny, tell us about your case?" asked Doug Cantrell.

The request caught penny off guard. She was used to playing second fiddle to Frank and appreciated the mutual respect coming from Cantrell.

"Yeah, sure." Penny sat down along with the others and pulled a file folder from her bag.

Sitting directly across from Penny, Cantrell positioned the tape recorder from the metal cart onto the center of the table, placing a microphone just inches from Penny.

"Penny, I'm going to hit record, and when I do, I just want you to speak naturally. No need to raise your voice at all. Now before I do hit record, I need both of you to agree to be recorded," said Cantrell, looking at Frank and Penny, who were sitting across the table from the two agents.

Penny nodded, and Frank said, "Sure, but tell me again why you're recording our conversation."

Cantrell spoke up, "So what we do is make recordings of our interviews as we do them around the country because contemporaneous notes, while taken at the time, sometimes don't adequately record a person's emotions during the conversation."

Kessler added, "Another reason we record conversations is that things discussed during an interview that might seem unimportant at the time could turn out to be critical later. It's the small things that sometimes can make a big difference."

"Yeah," said Cantrell. "I want to play back what we discuss later so that I might better assist you in the future if called upon."

"And, if this thing turns into a federal prosecution because your guy is killing across multiple states, we can use your initial facts to help our case later." Kessler paused after seeing Penny's facial expression change. "That is if it goes that far."

Frank looked at Penny, and both agreed.

"Listen, guys," said Kessler. "We're here to help and learn. You tell us what you got, and we'll offer our opinions and advice if you'll accept it. Is that fair?"

"Absolutely!" said Frank. "Go ahead and hit record."

Cantrell asked, "Are you ready, Penny?"

Penny nodded and swallowed hard when she heard the click of the button and saw the tape reels begin turning.

She took a deep breath and began, "Okay, so we have no actual proof to support our case, but what we do know has prompted the City of Philadelphia to throw resources our way, which is why we're here today."

"Dating back to 1920, there was a case of a 94-year-old man going missing from a retirement home in Philadelphia, called Heavenly Gates. His name was Samuel Crenshaw. Then, in 1969, another man, named Victor Rogers, aged 95, came up missing from the same retirement home."

Kessler asked, "So, two old guys came up missing from the same place 49 years apart?"

Cantrell interjected, "Rick, wait until you hear the rest. This is fascinating." Doug looked at Frank and said, "I only gave Rick a little idea of what you guys were coming in to talk about because I didn't want him to think it through. I wanted to get his initial reaction in front of you, not before you got here."

"Continue, Penny," said Kessler. "Tell us why you believe the two cases are connected."

"Sure," she nodded. "So, about a month ago, we got a call from our counterparts in Pittsburgh, who told us about a similar case back in '65. In their case, it was a female that came up missing from a retirement community...."

Kessler again stopped Penny. "So, the killer isn't fixated on the sex of his victim. Okay, how old was the victim in Pittsburgh?"

"Her name was Polly Anne Steinman, and she was 94," said Penny.

"Interesting," said Kessler. "Please continue,"

"As it turns out, there was another woman that came up missing in Bloomington, Indiana back in 1957," revealed Penny.

"Let me guess," said Kessler, looking at Cantrell and then back to Penny, "mid-nineties and went missing from an old folk's home."

"That's right," said Frank. "And get this, all of the old folk's homes have religious connotations in their names, like Heavenly Gates, Valhalla Springs, and God's Glory. But it gets even better. You'll love this one," added Frank. "The name of each of the custodians in question have the initials G.O.D. Crazy, right?"

Frank could tell Penny wanted to share her theory with the FBI Agents. "Go ahead, Penny. Tell them."

Penny shot Frank a look of appreciation. Her partner propped her up on equal footing, making it clear to the two Feds across the table that he looked at her as a police detective and not a *female* police detective.

Penny took a deep breath hoping not to be laughed out of the room. "I believe that there are five more victims out there and one more in the future."

"Okay, now wait a second!" Kessler was surprised by the revelation. "How do you go from four that you're not even sure are connected to a total of nine and a possible tenth victim in the future?"

"Tell 'em, Penny." Frank was proud of his partner.

Penny pulled out a chart that she'd made. It resembled the chalkboard back at the 39th.

"I believe that the dates of the disappearances are very relative and tell us a story that isn't finished being written yet." Penny spun her chart around so that the agents could view it more easily.

"The first victim went missing on December 7, and the last three went missing on the 19th, 21st, and 23rd. That leaves all of these odd number dates in between as potential dates for other murders." Penny pointed to question marks and dates.

"Penny, are you just guessing that, or do you have more to go on?" asked Cantrell, who was calm and supportive of her assumption though not convinced it was warranted. Like Kessler, he needed something more to go on.

"Well, at first, it was just my gut talking. I thought that someone who killed in 1920, then '57, '65, and '69, would've surely killed in the thirty-seven years between our first and second victims," offered Penny. "I also theorize that a murderer as sophisticated as our guy wouldn't stop at nine victims. The number ten is an important number in religion, and if there is a tenth, it will happen on a Christmas day in the future."

Kessler liked the way Penny's brain worked but was skeptical. "Yeah, but you don't even know if any of them are connected.

Frank looked at Penny encouraging her to continue.

"That's true, but then something happened." Penny looked at Frank as if looking for his support. "Our main suspect in the case, while being interviewed by us, ended the conversation by providing us with five other cities and told me that," Penny paused, looking nervous about her next admission, and said, "He told me that if I wanted to know what happened to my great-grandfather, then I should first investigate these cities." She then looked to Frank to continue.

"The cities are Youngstown, Barrington, Spokane, Portland, and St. Louis," said Frank.

Kessler stood up in disbelief and walked away from the table. Penny and Frank were taken aback by his reaction.

"Okay, first of all, the supposed first victim is your great-grandfather?" asked Kessler. "Secondly, nobody mentioned to me that you have a prime suspect in the case. And finally, did you say Barrington? As in Barrington, Illinois?"

Cantrell sat back smiling at how animated his partner was with the revelations.

"Yes, to all three of your questions. Although there is a Barrington in New Jersey, it doesn't fit our fact pattern, so we're going with Illinois for now," said Penny. "Again, sorry, I had no idea what you did or didn't know about our case until now."

Kessler exclaimed, "I'm from Barrington!" He was shocked by the revelation. "What are the chances of that!" He shook his head in amazement.

"You knew all this, and you didn't tell me?" Kessler directed his question at Doug Cantrell, who was still smiling.

"Yep!" said Cantrell. "As I said, I wanted to get your initial reaction, and now I have."

Kessler sat back down, highly intrigued. "Please tell me that you've got more? Tell me about our suspect."

Penny looked at Frank, wanting him to jump back into the conversation. He acknowledged her non-verbal request.

"Oh, yeah, there's a lot more." Frank thought Kessler's reaction was promising and that maybe he thought they had a case deemed worthy of possible FBI involvement.

"Tell him, Frank," said Cantrell, looking over to his partner, smiling again.

"Well, I'm obviously the last to know any of this stuff, so by all means, tell me," said a frustrated Rick Kessler. "Start with how old your suspect is because if he snatched the first guy in 1920 and the last one forty-nine years later, he's got to be one old crazy son of a bitch."

Cantrell smiled again and said, "This is the best part of all. Tell him, Frank."

"Our guy is 83, and we think he might be evil," said Frank.

"Well, no shit, he's evil!" said Kessler. "I mean, the guy's snatching up people right before they die. That's some bullshit right there. So if he's 83 now, that means he's been killing since he was 29?" Rick Kessler scribbled the math on his notepad.

Frank looked at Cantrell, who was still smiling. "When I say 'evil,' I mean in the biblical sense. Our guy claims to be 83 today and in '69, '65, '57, and 1920. He says he's always been 83."

"Okay, guys, you lost me here." Kessler stood up again and walked away from the table. "What in holy hell are you talking about?"

"Our guy's either crazy, or he's the devil," said Frank.

"Well, I'm not a believer in any of that," paused Kessler, "so let's go off the assumption that the old guy's crazy. Unless, of course, you're going to tell me next that you found his time machine."

Penny spoke up, "So, in each case that we're sure of, the victims were all last seen with an 83-year-old custodian. In each case, the custodian was well-liked and trusted by everyone who knew him."

"Get this," said Frank. "This S.O.B. tells us that he was on the Titanic and that he 'saved a lot of people that night.' So, I say to him; you mean that you saved some of the 700 that survived the sinking? And you know what he says to us?"

"At this point, I have no idea." Kessler was speechless.

"He said, and I quote, 'I was talking about the 1517 other souls on board.'"

Kessler sat back down. "Okay, so we've got a guy with a god complex on our hands, and either he's lying about the age he was back in 1920, or he's part of a family or cult that has been killing for decades, using the same M.O.," said Kessler.

"Modus Operandi," said Penny.

"Correct," said Cantrell. "I'm impressed you know the term. We travel the country, and many cops and detectives think it stands for 'means of operation.' Isn't that on the detective test that they're given?" Cantrell smiled.

"It was on mine," said Penny. "All three times," she smiled back at Cantrell.

Kessler went on to say, "Someone's M.O. is like their signature or fingerprint. It can help identify a suspect. Like a killer that always kills with a knife, at night, and when it rains. Murderers are predictable because they do things in a fashion that is comfortable to them, and they'll tend to repeat their actions, victim, after victim."

"But what we're finding is that if the killer is psychopathic, then they may be less predictable in the way they operate," explained Cantrell.

"Can you please elaborate? I'm a little lost?" asked Penny.

"Sure," said Doug Cantrell. "It's always been believed that killers were born, but our studies are starting to indicate that they're made and can evolve."

Frank looked confused. "Made?" he asked with a quizzical look.

"Think about a normal kid that fell out of a crib and hit his head when he was just a toddler. Say that kid grows up to be a killer," explained Cantrell. "We can look back and say that he became a killer because he got a screw knocked loose when he was two. Case closed, right?"

"Not so fast," interjected Kessler. "Now say you got a kid that never cracked his head on the floor when he was little, but instead was systematically beaten by his step-mother from the time he could remember anything. Then, at the age of ten, he gets raped by his biological father. The mom then blames the kid and beats him some more. You think that kid's got a reason to be pissed off?" asked Kessler.

"The point we're trying to make here," said Cantrell, "is that not all killers are natural-born killers. Some are made by their circumstances from their childhood or as a young adult."

Kessler added, "We have a psychiatrist joining our team here in the B.S.U., and she tells us that, 'we are who we are,' by the age of thirteen."

"We are who we are?" Penny looked confused.

"Yes, psychologically speaking," explained Kessler. "Who and what we are psychologically by the age of thirteen is who we're likely to be as young adults, middle-aged, and even senior citizens. Meaning, that if you're screwed up as a teenager, then you likely always will be."

"So, what does that mean for our guy?" asked Frank, looking at the agents and then back at Penny.

Rick Kessler weighed in first, "My guess is that a parent or a priest abused him. I'm leaning towards a priest, an old priest. Or maybe a parent who was a pastor or someone in the church," surmised Kessler. "He might be acting out against religion because maybe he thinks that religion is inherently bad and wants to be like his abuser."

"The only problem with that," said Penny, "is that our suspect doesn't put off that vibe. I'm not saying that you're wrong. I'm Just saying that this guy seems far from someone who was abused as a child."

"First of all, don't be fooled, Penny. Psychopaths are good liars. They're very manipulative. Second of all, did you ask him if he was abused as a child?" Kessler raised his brow. "You need to ask him and then observe his reaction to the question. If he hesitates, pauses, swallows hard or doesn't answer the question altogether, that might tell you something."

Cantrell spoke up, "Frank, you said they never found the bodies. Is that right?"

"Hold it right there!" Kessler interrupted his partner. "Frank, there're no bodies?! I'm just finding that out now?"

"That's true. We thought that Doug would have told you before we got here," said Frank looking over at Penny. "Like Penny said earlier, we only just found out what you knew after we got here."

Cantrell threw his hands in the air and said, "Oopsie!"

"So they just went missing? No bodies were ever found?" asked Kessler.

"That could go to M.O., Rick. Hide the bodies or burn or dissolve them in acid," said Doug Cantrell. "Maybe he's keeping them as souvenirs."

Penny winced when thinking of her great-grandfather.

"Sorry, Penny," apologized Cantrell. "Or," he pondered aloud, "what if this is a case of euthanasia?"

"I don't know what that is," said Penny, feeling a bit uneducated.

"It's mercy killing," said Kessler. "You know, you shoot a horse because it breaks its leg, and it was going to die a slow, painful death."

"You mean putting someone out of their misery?" asked Frank, who thought about it. "Except our guy is pure evil!"

"Frank's right," agreed Penny. "This guy wasn't doing anyone a favor by taking them or killing them. Our guy is cunning and conniving. He's off his rocker, no doubt, but he's in total control at all times," added Penny. "These weren't mercy killings. I'll bet anything on that."

Frank switched gears, "Guys, have you ever heard of MK Ultra?"

Doug Cantrell pursed his lips and shook his head, no. Rick Kessler, on the other hand, perked up in his chair.

"You're referring to the brainwashing experiments done at that place in Philly called FalconClaw, right?"

"Oh, yeah! I did hear about that a few years ago when it was all over the news. It used to be called The Allan Institute, right?" remembered Cantrell.

Penny and Frank looked at each other and smiled. They'd just realized that the two FBI Special Agents didn't know that Heavenly Gates, FalconClaw, and The Allan Institute, were all one and the same.

Chapter 21 – Criminal Minds

While Doug Cantrell drove Frank and Penny to McDonald's for lunch, Kessler went in and briefed his boss, Robert Knox, on the case and inquired about FalconClaw and what he knew. Robert Knox was a retired Army Lieutenant Colonel who'd made three tours in Korea and saw action as a Captain. As Frank explained the case, Knox seemed interested until FalconClaw came up.

"I'm not sure that's an avenue you want to pursue," said Knox.

"Why not?" said Kessler, "Pursue Serial Killers is what we do, and this guy may be connected to those exact experiments that happened after you and your boys came home. Doesn't that connection make you the least bit curious?"

"That was a CIA program, not an FBI one," reasoned Knox. "If you think I'm going to go and knock on William Colby's door and ask him to rattle the grave of Allen Dulles, you'd be mistaken, Agent Kessler."

"Well, there you go! Calling me Agent Kessler when we've been on a first-name basis for a year tells me that I struck a nerve," Kessler was agitated. "Just tell me what you know! I don't care what the other guys know. You know what happened over there. Tell me!"

"Okay, here's what I can tell you," said Knox. "During, but mostly after the war ended, hundreds, if not thousands of our boys who were POWs for as many as three years, did not want to repatriate and come home. After they were released and interviewed, our boys seemed to empathize and even side with their captors."

"Many high-ranking officers, not including me," stressed Knox, "just couldn't understand how men who had been tortured for years could come out of captivity somehow singing the praises of the enemy."

"Dozens of Colonels, all the way up to three-star Generals, got in the ear of CIA Director Allen Dulles, who became hellbent on uncovering what he felt was the truth," explained Knox. "More than 7200 of our boys were captured, with more than 2800 dying in captivity. Four thousand four hundred came home, and to the surprise of medical personnel and Army psychiatrists, those returning home were thought to be brainwashed while being held in communist China and North Korea. Dulles needed to know what drugs and techniques were used by Russia and China that could cause our men to turn against us."

"Mind control and brainwashing," thought Kessler aloud.

"That's right, Rick," said a somewhat apologetic Knox. "Once the CIA got involved, it was gloves off. This Cold War stuff has everyone paranoid," said Knox. "Not so much about Russia dropping the big one on our major cities, but more about covert espionage. Like brainwashing somebody high up the military or government food chain and then letting them destroy our country from within. We had to know what they knew. And that son of a bitch, Dulles, spared no expense."

"He needed test subjects for his experiments," said Kessler.

"Yep, and why not use unsuspecting crazy people? No one would be the wiser," said Knox. "If one of them spoke up about their treatment, people would just think they were crazy."

"Except they were," said Rick.

"Eventually, people caught on. But between 1957 and 1965, until the Vietnam War budget exploded, the CIA had money to spend, so they brought in some Canadian quack named Cameron," said Knox. "Once the money dried up, so did the psychiatric experiments on human guinea pigs. Cameron then goes back to his hole in Canada, never to be heard from again."

"He dead?" asked Kessler.

"I think so, but if he's not, he's probably still fucking with people's minds somewhere. I heard that guy was twisted. A mad scientist, that one." Knox looked agitated. "The obvious flaw Dulles and Cameron made was that they were experimenting on people who were broken psychologically, while the Soviets, Chinese, and North Koreans, were experimenting on highly trained, physically fit men who showed no signs of mental defect before being captured."

"That's some sinister shit, right there!" said Rick Kessler. "I'm glad I joined the Army after the war."

"Yeah, good timing," said Knox.

"I'll say."

"Listen, Rick. This is still a touchy subject with the CIA. After everything came out in '70, they've been pretty tight-lipped about the whole thing, and frankly, don't want to take any calls on the subject. So, to be clear. No one from the FBI is picking up the phone and calling anyone at the CIA with regards to this matter," Knox was adamant. "Not me! And most certainly not you! Are we clear, Special Agent Kessler?"

Kessler stood and said, "Yeah, Boss. We're clear."

Knox stood to signal the end of the meeting. "Now, is there anything else I can do for you, Rick?"

"No, but thanks for the history lesson."

"I'd like to say it was my pleasure, but it wasn't. I wanted no part of all of that nonsense. That's one of the reasons I retired in '60," said Knox.

"I got out in '62." Rick Kessler nodded.

"Again, some good timing on your part, huh, Rick?" Knox winked and smiled.

"What can I say?" smiled Kessler. "Fighting overseas just didn't suit me, I guess."

"You would've done just fine!" Knox smiled again.

"Thanks, Boss! I gotta get back."

As Kessler turned to leave, Robert Knox yelled out to him, "Hey, Rick! Whatta you working on that's got you all curious about MK Ultra?"

"Some old nut job up at FalconClaw is snatching up senior citizens, never to be seen again."

"Huh," shrugged Knox. "Wouldn't that be something if that crazy bastard Cameron was still out there messin' with people's minds?"

"That would sure be something, no doubt." Frank turned to leave.

Thirty minutes later, Kessler rejoined the Philly detectives and Doug Cantrell in the BSU building, who were already viewing information on the overhead projector.

"So, the six stages of the profiling process are: profiling inputs, decision process models, and crime assessment..." said Cantrell.

Walking in on the meeting, Kessler chimed in, "Criminal profiling, investigation, and apprehension." Rick smiled and said, "Sorry, I'm late, guys."

En route to the chalkboard, Rick Kessler walked in front of the light from the overhead projector. Squinting his eyes, he encouraged Doug Cantrell to kill the projector for a minute.

Kessler grabbed some chalk, wrote the five Ws on the chalkboard, and said, "These are the questions that need to be asked in every investigation. They are as follows: Who? What? When? Where? and Why?" said Kessler, while writing on the board.

"Who is our victim? What happened to them? When did the crime take place? Where did the crime take place?"

Doug Cantrell walked up and stood next to Kessler and continued the lesson. "Now, if you have a good suspect, the 'Why?' will be likely easier to determine," said Cantrell. "An example would be, a jealous husband finds the 'Who,' his wife, in bed with another man."

Kessler chimed back in, "That's the 'Who' and the 'Where,' we know the 'What,' they're having sex. And now we know the 'Why,' which goes to motive. This example is an easy one to follow," said Kessler. "The husband is likely to be the killer because he has motive. Why else would anyone kill them? Sure, maybe the kid who caught his mom cheating on his dad, but almost always, it will be the husband, and vice versa."

"You guys seem to have a suspect with the means, the opportunity, but what's the motive?" asked Cantrell.

Frank said, "Our guy was a custodian at Heavenly Gates; now he's a resident. Guess who put him in his will and paid for his annual cost of residency until the day he dies?"

"Was it the victim in '69?" Kessler snapped his fingers. "Rogers, was it?"

"Yes, it was," said Penny. "We believe that's the motive in the Rogers case but don't know enough about the other cases yet."

"Well, that is interesting," said Cantrell.

"What we do here in the Behavioral Science Unit is study the psychology of mass murderers," explained Kessler. "We're learning that killers don't always need motive anymore. Hell, some never did. It was always easy to say that they were born sick and killed because of that sickness. But what we're learning with these guys we're interviewing is that some of them kill just for the fun of it."

Cantrell broke back in, "The sorts we're talking to have told us that they see a kid, a woman, an old man," Doug paused and looked at Penny, "and they want to murder, torture, or rape them, for no reason at all. They do it because they want to, and they can. Motive be damned!" said Cantrell.

"I think what Doug's trying to say is that your 83-year-old suspect might not have any motive at all. He might be doing it just for sport and using simply using God as a backstory when it might not have anything to do with God or religion at all," explained Kessler. "What I'm saying is don't get locked into his motive. Find the connection between him and each of the victims first. Then your case gets a lot easier."

Cantrell offered more details about how to interview serial killers. "It's important to know that psychopaths don't feel emotions like normal people. They come across as calm, making them seem like they're in control, giving them the upper hand. They'll manipulate you because you can and will feel human emotion, and they will play on that. They'll say things that will push your buttons and get you off of your game. Stick to the facts in the case. Don't let them steer you down the 'emotion' road."

After Cantrell's comments, Penny and Frank looked at each other, both realizing that the old man did get under their skin. They knew that he controlled them by playing with their emotions. But they also knew that Garrison Winter somehow knew more about them than he should have. More than any other, that fact elicited the raw emotions that resulted in their meetings with the old man.

Kessler added, "Serial Killers are either highly intelligent or overly charismatic. Some can be both. Your guy will likely come across as likable for one very important reason," Kessler paused, "they want you to like them."

"Listen, these guys don't have many friends," added Cantrell. "They will enjoy every second of their time with you because, though loners, in reality, don't want to be alone. Watch for your guy to keep the conversation going, and then, when you're ready to leave, he'll seem disappointed."

"Guys, just be frank with your suspect," advised Doug Cantrell. "Don't patronize him. Be honest, stay calm, act like you're his friend, and just want to learn what he knows. He'll enjoy educating you on what lives in the dark corners of his mind. His inner demons torture him, and for him, it's almost cathartic to talk about it."

Kessler added, "If one line of questioning doesn't work, use another. Just stay the course and keep him talking."

After another two hours of educating the Philly detectives on what the BSU does, It was now 5 pm, and the four wrapped up their meeting by discussing how the FBI might help in the case.

Kessler and Cantrell agreed to assign field agents in each of the five cities mentioned by Garrison Winter. The agents would inquire about cold cases involving missing elderly people between 1927 and 1951.

They requested that Frank and Penny record an interview with their prime suspect and send the recorded conversation to them for analysis.

As the four wrapped up their day, Kessler approached Penny as she was putting her jacket on.

"Hey, Penny. Listen, thanks for coming. I wanted to let you know that I started asking around about the brainwashing stuff at

FalconClaw back in the day, and I ran into a brick wall. If I find out anything at all, I promise to call you directly."

"Do you think we're on to something?" Penny was looking for validation that she and Frank were on to something and not just imagining things. "Be honest with me, Rick."

"Listen, after spending the day with you, I believe your instincts are good. And I can't lie, that whole Barrington thing's got my head spinning," Kessler arched his brows. "With that being said, I do think your confirmed cases are connected, but I think it's a stretch to think it goes back to your great-grandfather," expressed Kessler. "The best piece of advice I can give to you is to not let personal matters influence professional ones."

"I keep hearing that," said Penny. "It must be sound advice."

"When I sit with a mass murderer who's killed little kids, being a father, I would like nothing more than to snap the guy's neck with my bare hands. But I have to leave emotion out of it," said Rick. "That way, I can do my job objectively."

"Thanks for today, Rick." Penny was appreciative. "My eyes have been opened to a whole new world of investigation."

As she buttoned her jacket, she said to Kessler, who was now sitting at his desk, "The answer is in the basement of FalconClaw. When I find out what it is, I'll give you a call." Penny turned to leave.

"And I'll let you know if our field agents dig up anything out west."

Down the hall, standing near the security guard station, Frank was wrapping up with Doug Cantrell. He was letting him know how much he appreciated their input and continued support.

Cantrell spoke softly and said, "Listen, Frank. I want you to go back to Philly and think about maybe joining us down here in Quantico."

Frank was caught off guard. "You're joking, right?"

"No, I'm serious," confessed Cantrell. "When we toured last year, we went to eight cities meeting guys just like you. You stood out among your peer group, though," said Doug.

"Eight cities, huh?" Frank shook his head. "So, that was nothing more than a recruiting seminar," Frank was a little offended as if he'd been taken advantage of.

"No, Frank, you misunderstood me," said Cantrell, waving his hands. "Those seminars were designed to build rapport and relationships with the very detectives that we might eventually have to collaborate with in the field. As cases come to light that required involvement by the FBI, it's helpful to know who we'll be working with and know that those very investigators understand what it is we do. To be clear, though, when you meet high-level, experienced talent like you, you ask the question. That's how you build a great team."

"So what are you asking me then?" asked Frank.

"I'm just asking you to go back and think about it, that's all. What we're building here is special and will likely change the way we handle monsters like the one you're dealing with."

"I got kids, and they need me there," said Frank.

"I get it. Just think about it," said Cantrell. "The pay sucks, but the retirement benefits are great."

"You calling me old?" smiled Frank.

"I'm calling you smart, Detective!" Doug Cantrell launched a sincere smile.

As Penny approached the two men, Frank asked Cantrell, "You think we got something here, Doug?"

"I think your cases are connected," said Cantrell. "And I think Penny's right. There are more unsolved cases out there in those five cities. We'll get our local boys to look into it. The minute I hear something, I'll let you know."

"Great!" said Frank, shaking the hand of Doug Cantrell.

"Frank, you get that old man on tape. I want to hear what he has to say, and I want to hear how he says it. I'll send you a list of questions later today over the telefax. Get me that tape, though."

"Will do," Frank nodded. "Will do."

"Let's talk after Thanksgiving. Monday the 2nd. Sound good?"

"No, later in the week as we probably won't get to Old Man Winter until after the holiday," said Frank.

As Cantrell walked away, Frank yelled, "Hey, Doug!"

Cantrell turned to look back. "Yeah, Frank?!"

"Of the eight cities you went to last year," Frank paused. "Was Harrisburg your last stop?"

"Yeah. How'd you know?"

Frank looked at Penny and back to Cantrell. "Just a hunch. Thanks again!"

"You bet, buddy! Drive safe! I'll teletype the questions to ask the old man later today." Doug Cantrell waved and turned back toward his office.

Penny smiled at Frank. "You doin' the *eight* thing, again?"

"There's no such thing as coincidences, Penny."

"Oh, so now you believe in God again?" Penny laughed. "Let's go home, Frankie Boy!"

Chapter 22 – Goodnight, Jeanie

As Penny and Frank exited the BSU building, Frank could see that the car was covered with several inches of snow. Penny began laughing, but Frank didn't know why. As he walked around the back left bumper to the driver's side, he discovered what Penny found to be so funny. The driver's side window was halfway down, still cocked at an angle.

"Now, Goddammit!" Frank was red-faced, both embarrassed and angry. The driver's side seat had roughly three inches of snow on it.

"Well, what'd you expect Einstein?" Penny took great joy in the situation.

As she opened her door, Penny laughed again. "My side's good!" She looked across the top of the car to her partner and smiled.

Frank tossed his bag into the backseat and then used his hands to clear the snow from his seat.

"Start it up before you get working on that window," said Penny. "It's freezing out here."

"Yeah, no shit!" Frank just shook his head.

After twenty minutes of fighting the window crank, Frank finally got the window to roll back up. After plopping down in his seat, blowing into his hands, Penny blurted out, "Boy, the name really fits you!"

Frank looked perturbed. "What name?!"

"Your nickname, *Cold Case Frank*? It really fits you." Penny laughed at her partner as the snow melted into his salt and pepper hair.

Moments later, the Buick rolled past the security gate as the guard held it open for the departing visitors. When he'd noticed it was the Buick with the bad window, he yelled, "Stay warm and drive safe!"

"Yeah-yeah, asshole!" Frank mumbled under his breath, knowing that the guard couldn't hear him.

After getting back on the highway, Frank looked over to Penny and said, "You know you did good today, don't you?"

"Did I?" Penny's expression indicated that she wasn't sure.

"They liked you. You represented yourself, the City of Philadelphia, and our case, like a true professional."

"Thanks, Frank. That means a lot." Penny was humbled but still unsure that she fit in with him and the Quantico Boys.

Frank stared blankly at the snow illuminated by the Buick's headlights and asked, "Penny, you think the old man really did it?" Frank had a moment of waning confidence.

"Frank, he did it. He's responsible for all of those disappearances." Penny feigned confidence. "He had the means, the motive, and the opportunity, and he was the last person seen with Rogers, that much we know for sure." Penny paused for a moment. "Kessler thinks we're on to something."

Frank nodded in modest agreement. "Yeah, Cantrell thinks we got something, too." He paused and said, "We've got to get the old man to implicate himself."

Penny's eyes narrowed in confused frustration. "What are you talking about? He gave us the other five cities! I'd say that's implicating himself."

Frank looked over at his partner. "Penny, I mean that we've got to get him on tape like Cantrell said. And besides," Frank was pragmatic, "those other cities don't mean shit to our case unless something comes back from those authorities."

"Horseshit!" fumed Penny. "You know as well as I do that we're gonna hear something." Inside, Penny wasn't as confident as her external emotions conveyed. She prayed that they'd hear something soon.

"I agree. I mean, there's no way Winter just randomly threw out those cities to us. I can't see him doing anything without purpose," Frank thought aloud. "That old man is cunning, and he might be hiding more than just bodies."

"He's hiding something, that's for sure." Penny looked off and imagined landing a serial killer in her first-ever case as a detective.

Dozing off just minutes later, she dreamt of being an FBI Agent in the Behavioral Science Unit in Quantico, interviewing psychopaths just like the one living at Heavenly Gates. The one that took her great-grandfather, the man that she was determined to bring to justice.

After an hour of managing the snow, the darkness, and his agony, Frank looked over at his partner and again saw Jeanie sitting there, sleeping. He'd remembered the previous December after the two had been Christmas shopping all day, and Jeanie fell asleep in the car on the way home from the mall. Frank missed his best girl and wasn't sure if he'd be able to Christmas shop for the girls without his Jeanie.

He didn't even know what kind of toys or dolls to get them. He was just getting to know his daughters for the first time in his life. And those girls weren't so little anymore. With every day that passed, he saw his Jeanie in the eyes of Jessica and Maddie. More and more, every day.

Frank worked a lot, but now he had to be both a mother and a father to Jessica and Maddie, and he wasn't sure how he'd do it. He was learning things he'd never known about his baby girls and was getting to know even more about himself.

Two hours later, the Buick carved out fresh tire tracks through the snow on Fuller Street. As Frank pulled over in front of Penny's house, he reached to give Penny a gentle nudge to wake her. Before he did, he recoiled his hand and just stared at her sleeping. He was staring at Jeanie at that moment. He thought that if he didn't wake her, then maybe she would always stay right there, sleeping in the Buick with a trunk full of presents for the last Christmas she'd ever have on Earth.

The porch light came on a moment later from the house marked 2125, and Frank was reluctantly snatched from his fantasy.

Penny woke up at that moment, clearing her eyes; she could see that Frank's eyes were red and teary. "Hey, we made it, huh?"

"Yeah, we're here." Frank was solemn as he looked away from Penny.

"You okay, Partner?"

"Yeah, just tired." Frank rubbed his eyes and said, "Long day, that's all."

"Yeah, long day," Penny replied. "Well, I'll see you tomorrow. Goodnight, Frank."

"Goodnight, Jeanie."

Penny was surprised by Frank's words but said nothing and fought any facial expression that would let Frank know he called her Jeanie. She got out of the car and didn't look back. She wanted Frank to keep thinking that she was Jeanie and not steal that moment from him.

As Penny walked to the door, it opened, and Joe and her boys greeted her. But what Frank saw was Jeanie and the girls greeting him after a long day of work.

An hour later, getting ready for bed, Penny turned off the front porch light. When she did, she looked out the living room window and saw the Buick still idling down on the street. She smiled and was happy that Frank was spending a little time with his memories of Jeanie before heading home to a house where she no longer lived.

Chapter 23 – Saint Louis

The next day was Thursday, and Penny got in a little early. The six detectives in the 39th District would be given off the Friday before, as well as the following Thanksgiving week, and Penny had a lot of work to do before the holiday.

Ron McClain agreed to work through the Wednesday before Thanksgiving, as he had only recently returned from a two-week vacation. He only agreed to give his detective team off if they all agreed to remain on-call and come in should something pressing make it up to the Detective Room.

As Penny walked through the door, the teletype machine was humming, but she was distracted thinking through how Frank and she would convince their boss to allow them to borrow the only tape recorder in the 39th District. In all the years that Penny worked at the 39th, she'd never seen it leave the building.

The other thing on her mind was reviewing the trip to Quantico with her boss. She'd figured that if she and Frank made a compelling case regarding the recommendation of the BSU guys, then McClain might authorize the use of police property outside of the stationhouse.

A few minutes later, Frank, followed by the others, walked in, and hung up their coats. As Tubbs passed by Penny's desk, he wisecracked, "So, how was Quantico, Big Shot?"

"Go screw yourself, Jerry!" Penny fired back. "You're just pissed that Coons and Riggins got the Schuylkill River case, and Frank and me got Heavenly Gates, and you ain't got shit."

"You ain't got shit!" Tubbs mocked Penny as he passed her.

"Easy Penny," said Frank settling in at his desk. "We're all on the same team around here."

"I'm just tired of that prick bustin' my chops every day."

"Don't worry about him. We've got bigger fish to fry. Like getting Old Man Winter on tape."

"So, what's the plan for when McClain comes in?" asked Penny.

"I'll talk to him. He'll let us take the recorder. He hates that old bastard, Winter," said Frank. "If we can get that old man on tape saying that he knew all the victims, that would give us probable cause, and McClain might give us the green light to officially apply for a search warrant."

"A search warrant for what, exactly?" Penny asked.

Frank shook his head. "I'm not sure. Maybe the old records of when he worked at Heavenly Gates back in 1920."

"I'm certain those records still exist," Penny nodded her head with confidence. "They're in that basement, Frank. I know it!"

"Man, you're transfixed with that locked door and that basement." Frank flipped through his notes from Quantico and smiled.

"The answers to every question we have live down there. I'm sure of it." Penny scribbled the name FalconClaw on her notepad.

Thirty minutes later, Ron McClain strolled in, hung up his coat, and unlocked the door to his office, only offering a nod to his team of detectives. A few minutes later, McClain yelled for Frank from his desk. "Bruno, get in here!"

Frank and Penny stood up, and Frank gestured to Penny to stay put. "He yelled for me, not you. Hang back, and I'll call you in if we need you."

"Okay," said Penny with a reluctant nod. Though feeling slighted, she didn't want to hurt their chances of getting McClain's approval to tape the interrogation of Old Man Winter at Heavenly Gates.

"You get Travers on the phone and see if we can get his approval to question Winter on tape tomorrow," instructed Frank before walking into McClain's office.

"Even though we're off?"

"Penny, this is a possible serial murderer we're dealing with. You're never really off when chasing down a killer."

Penny caught Jerry Tubbs out of the corner of her eye smiling because she wasn't asked to go into McClain's office with Frank.

Penny flipped off Tubbs with a dismissive smile and mouthed the words, "Fuck you!"

"Eat me!" said Tubbs.

Penny said, "You wish!" and then looked away.

Now in McClain's office, Frank said, "You want the door closed, Chief?"

"Yeah, Frank. Close it."

Frank sat down patiently and watched as McClain wrapped up, filing some papers away in his lower left desk drawer.

"So, how'd it go down in Quantico?" he asked.

"It went well," Frank nodded.

"How'd Bryce do?"

"Chief, she was a pro!" Frank sat erect in his chair. "She had her shit together, and the guys in the BSU were impressed."

"What's the BSU?" asked McClain.

"Oh, sorry, Chief. It's the Behavioral Science Unit," explained Frank.

"I thought you were going to the Criminal Profiling Unit?"

Frank had a flashback of the security gate guard and said, "Yeah, the CPU is apparently a new department within the BSU."

"It's like alphabet soup down there in Washington," McClain shook his head. "CIA, FBI, BSU, CPU! Whatever! Just tell me what happened."

"It's actually in Quantico, Virginia, Boss."

"Whatever, it's all D.C. down there! Now whatta you got for me?"

"Well, first of all, they think we're on to something. The agents we met with seemed sure that the cases are related."

"Even that nonsense from 1920?" challenged McClain, who wasn't convinced that Penny's great-grandfather was connected to the cases in '69, '65, or '57.

"That one was a toss-up. One guy thought it was, and one guy thought it wasn't."

"And these were the guys you met up with last year in Harrisburg, that right?" asked McClain.

"Yeah, they were great. And they made a strong suggestion for us, and I think we should do what they say." Frank seemed skittish about asking for the use of the tape recorder.

"Yeah. What's that?" McClain knew Frank was going to ask for a favor.

"They think we should get him on tape. They want us to try and draw a connection between him and the victims as well as him and the other cities he told us about."

McClain didn't immediately disagree. "I don't see a problem with that. Just let the boys downstairs know that you'll be bringing him in."

"Um, yeah, that's the thing, Boss...."

Outside of McClain's office, Penny was on the phone with Dean Travers. She called to inquire if she and Frank might be able to stop by and ask Garrison O'Donnell some more questions.

"Hi Director Travers, it's Penny Bryce. How are you today?"

"Ahh, Penelope! So good to hear from you! I trust you've been well since we last saw each other?" Travers was in good spirits. "What's it been, three weeks now?"

"Yes, I believe that's correct. We were there on Halloween."

"Yes, well, I understand from Miss Gruber that you and your male associate have been back since the tour I gave you." Travers almost seemed disappointed that Penny didn't stop by to see him.

"That's true. We came by on Monday the 11th. I'm so sorry I didn't stop by your office. We were in a bit of a hurry, and well, you know me, I could have sat talking with you for hours." Penny hoped flattery would keep her in Travers' good graces.

"I feel just the same, my Dear Penelope, just the same. I, too, have been busy, so perhaps it was a wise move on your part."

"Director Travers...."

"Please, Penelope, do call me Dean. Must I keep reminding you?" Travers made light of Penny's forgetfulness.

"Yes, of course. Sorry to sound so formal, but this call is a matter of police business, I'm afraid."

"Oh, and how can I help the City of Philadelphia today?"

"Well, there are two things: First, I was wondering if my partner and I could possibly get a tour of the basement of Heavenly Gates?"

"Now, Penelope, if you had told me that you wanted a tour of the basement for personal reasons, I may very well have considered it. However, I have no desire for the Philadelphia Police Department to be snooping around in the sub-chambers of this wonderful mansion. It would feel like an invasion. The history of FalconClaw lives down there, and I'm afraid I am the only one with access."

"Oh, I'm sorry to hear that," said Penny. "Perhaps at a later date when I come by for a personal visit?" Penny knew she missed an opportunity by insinuating to Travers that it was for police business. She wouldn't make that mistake again.

"Perhaps Penelope, perhaps." Travers seemed genuine. "Now, what was the other reason for your call?"

"Of course, Dean. The reason for my call is that we would like to visit with Mr. Winter again...."

Travers interrupted her, "Yes, I too heard that you asked poor Mr. Winter to come down to the station to be interviewed there? Is that right, Detective Bryce?"

Penny could tell Travers wasn't happy by his tone and the fact that he'd called her 'Detective Bryce.'

"Yes, our boss wanted to talk to him and was unable to come to Heavenly Gates." Penny scrambled for the right ruse. "You see, his grandmother just passed away in a nursing home, and he was not up to being inside of one, I'm afraid." Penny again thought that her acting skills rivaled those of her partner's.

"Oh, dear! I am so sorry to hear that. Please pass along my condolences to him." Travers fell for the ploy. "What retirement home was it, exactly?"

Penny paused in a moment of panic. "Umm, ah, I'm not sure, but I can certainly find out for you."

"Please do, Penelope. I will have some flowers sent over. As you may not know, there are only four retirement homes in all of North Philadelphia."

Penny bought herself some time but also realized she'd put herself in a jam the next time she spoke to Travers.

"So, it would be okay to come by tomorrow then?" asked Penny, crossing her fingers on both hands.

"That'd be fine. It will have to be tomorrow or the week after next, I'm afraid," said Travers. "I, along with Miss Gruber, will be out all week for the Thanksgiving holiday and would prefer no official business be conducted in our absence."

"Tomorrow would be best," said a relieved Penny. "There is one more item to discuss, though."

"And what would that be, Penelope?"

"Well, to be honest with you...."

Travers interjected. "Figure of speech, I hope, Penelope?"

"Of course, Dean. You'll have to excuse me." Penny felt like her inexperience was handicapping her ability to get things done.

"Very well, then, Penelope. What is it?"

"Well, you see, Dean, when we brought Mr. Winter in for a chat, and even though it was unofficial, I felt bad asking a man at such an advanced age to trek all the way down to our district house just to chat, and I didn't want to impose again."

"Yes, I've already agreed to allow you to see Mr. Winter here tomorrow."

"Yes, of course, the matter I was getting at was that we would like to record the conversation so that we could avoid both bringing him to see us, in addition to having my boss come into an environment that would make him feel uneasy, what with the passing of his grandmother and all."

"Ahh, I see," said Travers.

"Because our boss would need to hear Mr. Winter's responses, we felt it might satisfy both of our concerns if we simply recorded the conversation there." Penny again crossed her fingers.

"Hmmm," Travers pondered. "Well, that would be unconventional," he paused.

Penny held her breath, waiting for Traver's decision.

"But I can see how that might be best for both your grieving employer as well as dear old Mr. Winter," Travers paused again. "Yes, I do believe that would be just fine. Just please, be discreet as we don't want to upset any of the other residents here."

Penny exhaled loudly, covering the phone. "That would be wonderful. Thank you for understanding this delicate matter, Dean."

"Yes, of course, Penelope."

"Oh, and Dean, when might I see you again? You know, just to chat a little off the record?"

"Well, let's see now." Travers thought about it for a moment.

Penny could hear him flipping pages.

"As I consult my personal calendar, it would have to be between December 2 and December 20, as I am on vacation both of the holiday weeks. If that time period does not work for you, it'd have to be after the Christmas holiday, I'm afraid."

"Well then, I will have to find some time, won't I?" Penny feigned sincerity. She knew her next visit would be all business and that that business would include getting a serial murderer to confess and trying to gain access to the bowels of FalconClaw.

"Well, here's hoping we cross paths before then," said Travers.

"Perhaps tomorrow?" said Penny.

"All the best, then, Penelope."

"Thank you, Dean. Have a nice day."

Back in McClain's office, Frank said, "The guys in Quantico thought we should interview the old man in a place where he would be less guarded and more open to our questions...." Frank danced around the issue.

"Frank, just tell me what you want, for Christ's sake!" McClain didn't like when his detectives weren't straightforward.

"We want to record the conversation with him at Heavenly Gates." Frank pursed his lips and held his breath.

"Frank! Do you have any idea what those tape recorders cost?" McClain looked almost offended that Frank asked the question. "We got that one at Radio Shack last month, and it cost like eighty bucks. That recorder cannot leave the station house!"

"Sir, the guys in Quantico wanted to make sure that you could hear the questions and responses from the interview." Frank paused and thought quickly on his feet. "That is unless you would like to join us up at the FalconClaw Mansion?" Frank knew his boss couldn't be bothered making the short trip.

"I think you're full of shit, Bruno." McClain saw through his smokescreen. "I should call your bluff right now and agree to go up there with you, but if that old bastard gets under my skin again, you might have to arrest me for assault and battery of a senior citizen."

Frank could see McClain coming around. His boss was smart and had been around for a long time.

"You can borrow it under two conditions," said McClain. "One, get permission from Captain Wilcox, and two, if you damage that thing, you'll be replacing it out of your paycheck. And I'll make you go down to the mall personally and pick up a new one."

"Sure, Chief! Not a problem!" Frank stood from his chair, elated.

"You have it back here the day after you borrow it, understood?"

"No problem! Thanks, Chief."

As Frank went to leave the tiny office, the savvy McClain said, "Oh, and Frank...."

"Yeah, Boss?" Frank raised his brow.

"I want to listen to that tape before the boys down in Quantico do. Understood?"

Frank was impressed that McClain knew what he was up to.

"Be straight with me next time, Bruno!"

"Will do, Ron! Thanks for this!"

As Frank exited McClain's office, he closed the door and shot Penny a look that relayed the good news.

Penny was just hanging up with Dean Travers and had some good news of her own. "Travers said we could come tomorrow!"

"McClain said we could use the tape recorder!" Frank was excited. "He said if we break it, though, that you have to pay for it out of your paycheck."

"My paycheck?!" Penny only half believed her partner.

"Okay, fine!" Frank conceded with a smile. "We'll have to split the cost."

As the two sat down to plan out the next day, the teletype machine came to life again, and Roger Taylor got up to investigate. Looking over the incoming telefax, Taylor said, "Hey Frank, this one looks like it's for you. It's from the FBI."

"I bet it's the questions Cantrell promised." Penny was excited.

"Yeah, I bet you're right!" Frank rose to retrieved the incoming message.

As Frank looked over the correspondence from Cantrell, he scanned the document and tore off the two pages of questions. As he separated the two pages from the previous incoming message, he saw something that stopped him cold. The earlier incoming message that no one had addressed had the Subject Line: Saint Louis – 1951.

Frank's jaw dropped as he looked over at Penny in stunned silence.

Penny looked back and knew that it was either good news or terrible news. Frank's look of shock did not reveal which one.

Chapter 24 – The Confession

Frank walked over to his desk and sat down, staring blankly. Penny looked at him and said, "Frank, what is it?"

"You were right." Frank looked catatonic, tossing the telefax onto his desk.

Penny got up and walked around to Frank's desk and grabbed the torn, perforated paper. Seeing Saint Louis – 1951 at the top of the page, she gasped. Looking at Frank with no words, she turned and ran to the chalkboard.

Penny had her answer, and her hunch about Youngstown was right. Youngstown, Ohio had to be the second stop for Old Man Winter if St. Louis, 1951 was the last stop before Bloomington in 1957.

Frank joined her at the chalkboard and said, "Penny, my god, you were right the whole time." Frank was still in shock.

Penny was focused. She turned to Frank and said, "Frank, we now know that Youngstown was the second stop for Old Man Winter." She erased several question marks off the board and filled in Youngstown and the year 1927 next to the date December 9. She then erased the question marks that preceded 1957 and added St. Louis.

Frank walked away from Penny and opened McClain's office door without knocking. Once inside, he could barely make out the expletives coming from the mouth of his Chief of Detectives. Frank was adamant while imploring his boss to come out of his office.

Ron McClain joined Frank and Penny at the chalkboard, where Tubbs, Taylor, Riggins, and Coons, had also gravitated with the commotion.

"Chief, we're going to need more help with this one." Frank was humbled by the realization that they were now, without question, looking for a serial killer.

"Whatta ya got, Frank?" asked a slightly bothered-looking McClain.

Frank turned to his boss and said, "You're asking the wrong detective." He then turned his eyes to Penny.

"Right," said McClain. "Penny, whatta we got?"

"Chief, we can now focus our efforts on Youngstown, from 1927. We know the date of the victim's disappearance is likely December 9. What we don't yet know is the victim's name or the name of the retirement home," explained Penny, as she pointed out the updates to the chalkboard.

"Keep going, Penny!" encouraged Frank.

"We also know now that one of our nine victims went missing from St. Louis in 1957. Victim name and retirement home, unknown. The date is likely December 17."

Frank spoke up. "Boss, can we get Tubbs and Taylor on the phones tomorrow with Youngstown and St. Louis authorities? We could use the manpower. Penny and I will be getting a recorded statement from our prime suspect tomorrow afternoon."

"Yeah, sure, Frank. Whatever you need." McClain turned to Tubbs and Taylor and said, "Jerry, Roger, you work for Frank and Penny for the foreseeable future. Whatever they need. Got it?!"

"Sure thing, Chief," said Jerry Tubbs. He then turned to Penny and said, "I got your back, Penny." Tubbs was conciliatory.

"We're here for you, Penny," added Roger Taylor.

Riggins and Coons chimed in and chorused, "What can we do to help, Chief?"

"Nothing! You two stay focused on the Schuylkill River case. I need a name for that kid. We're not going to have another Boy in the Box in the City of Philadelphia!"

The next morning Frank and Penny met up at the Arlington Diner and sat in the back booth like before. There, they discussed a strategy for the recorded interview of Garrison Winter, aka Garrison O'Donnell.

"First of all, let's stick with Winter and stay away from addressing him as O'Donnell," said Frank. "He likes Winter better, and I want to get him as comfortable as possible. The bad guys will divulge more when they like you or when they're relaxed."

"I gotta tell ya, Frank, I'm sick to my stomach," said Penny before the waitress wandered over with a fresh pot of coffee. "No more for me." Penny placed her hand over her coffee cup, denying the young waitress a chance to fill it.

"Fill'er up, please!" Frank was in good spirits as he smiled at the young blonde waitress. "Penny, today's gonna be a good day. We get to lock the old man into his answers. We may very well walk out of there with incriminating evidence that can be used against him in court."

"So, what do we do if he links himself to the other cities or victims?"

"If you mean, are we going to take him out of FalconClaw in cuffs? God no!" said Frank, stirring his coffee. "We have our marching orders from the FBI and Ron McClain. We'll collect our evidence and then share it with the higher-ups. We'll consult and continue to collect evidence," explained Frank. "In my experience, no arrests will be made until we can close the circle on the other cities. While we focus in on Youngstown and St. Louis, hopefully, we'll hear back from one of the other three cities and be able to fill in the chalkboard."

"Well, I'm nervous." Penny was reminded of how the last visit to Heavenly Gates went down. "Frank, he ate our lunch the last time we were there."

"He got the best of me on Halloween, too," Frank remembered that Winter asked about his daughters when he couldn't possibly have known about them. "It's like he knows us or something."

"I feel the same way," nodded Penny. "It's like he's working with someone else, but my gut tells me that he's not. It's unsettling as hell." After a pause, she added, "I had a dream last night that McClain was in on it."

"No shit? Dreaming about McClain, now?" Frank arched his brow.

"Yeah. He was trying to get me to quit," Penny chuckled. "Fat chance of that happening."

Frank leaned forward and interlocked his fingers. "So, listen," he looked Penny straight in the eye. "I want to turn you loose on this guy today. Until now, I've asked you to take a back seat to me, but not anymore. Your instincts are good. You've got a feel for this guy. Go at him a little. Make him think you know more than you do."

"Like what?" Penny leaned in.

"Tell him we've heard from the other cities, but not all of them," encouraged Frank. "Just make him feel like the noose is getting tighter."

"You gonna handle the tape recorder?" asked Penny.

"Yeah, done it a couple hundred times in my career. I've got it under control."

"So, how do we avoid letting him get into our heads?" asked Penny. "That's what I'm worried about the most."

"Let's go in with the assumption that he's gonna talk about our families, where we grew up, what we had for dinner last night, all of it," said Frank. "Don't let him see you flinch!" Frank's eyes went wide.

"That's easier said than done," Penny rolled her eyes and sighed heavily. "That only works up until the point where he does, in fact, tell you what you had for dinner last night."

"Listen, I've seen your acting chops," said Frank. "You're getting pretty good at it. Just act like anything he says is something you've heard ten times before."

"I'll try, but don't you lose your shit either!" said Penny. "If you do, I'll go bat shit crazy."

"I'm gonna try my best to stick to the questions the boys in Quantico gave us."

"You gonna show me that list, by the way?" Palm up, Penny motioned with her fingers for Frank to hand it over.

Pulling it from his inside jacket pocket, Frank gave Penny the tri-folded telefax they'd received the day before.

Penny perused the list and was surprised by some of the questions. "Did you love your parents? Did you have pets when you were a child? When was the first time another person hurt you physically or emotionally? How did that make you feel?" she shook her head. "I sure hope we can add to this list because these questions seem to beat around the bush."

"That's the point, Penny," said Frank. "You have to understand that people are the sum total of every experience they've ever had," he explained. "Lost puppy at the age of eight, parents getting divorced at the age of ten, failed the seventh grade, bullied by kids at school. It all starts when they're young and keeps building momentum until the first crack in their psyche appears. We'll ask all of those questions and more."

"Frank, be honest, did you lose a puppy when you were eight?" Penny joked. "Is that what this 'eight' thing is really all about?"

"No, but I did lose my wife when she was 38. Maybe that's why I keep seeing three eights." Frank threw his napkin and a five-dollar bill on the table, rose to his feet, and said, "Let's go!"

Penny sat there for a minute, feeling mortified. She swallowed hard and needed to compose herself before she could find the courage to walk out the door and get into the same car with Frank. She didn't mean anything by what she said, and she'd never make light of Frank's fascination with numerology and the number eight again.

Penny looked out the window and saw Frank walk through the parking lot and get into his car. A minute later, the engine cranked, and the motor in the '67 Buick revved, indicating her partner's frustration and sorrow. It would be another minute before she would summon the courage to join him.

A half an hour later, Penny and Frank stood at the front door of Heavenly Gates, and as Penny was about to ring the bell, Frank stopped her.

"Penny, I'm sorry I snapped at you back at the diner. You didn't do anything wrong. I just miss her." Frank looked out of sorts. "The 'eight' thing means something. I know it. It's like the Universe is talking to me," said Frank. "The son of a bitch that we're about to take down knows something about the 'eights' too. I can feel it."

"I'm not sure exactly what I did back there. But I'm sorry that I upset you." Penny was apologetic. "Sometimes I say something or say nothing, and you just snap, and I don't know how to come back around to saying anything. The ride over here was awful. Not fun being stuck in a car with someone who's pissed at you and not talking to you either."

"I know, I know," Frank shook his head, looking sad and vulnerable. "I'm sorry, Penny."

"Well, get your shit together because your friend Bernice is about to answer that door." Penny pressed her lips together and gazed at the giant double doors.

"Great!" Frank suddenly felt panicked. "That woman hates me!" He exhaled heavily as his eyes bounced from side to side.

"I'm pretty sure what she feels for you isn't hate, Frankie Boy." Penny smiled and rang the doorbell.

After two minutes, Bernice Gruber answered the door, and after seeing who it was, rolled her eyes and then turned and walked away without words.

Frank grimaced. "I guess that means he's in the solarium."

Penny chuckled and then turned to Frank and said, "Perhaps I was wrong. Maybe she does hate you after all."

Frank was red-faced with embarrassment and said, "Let's go get that son of a bitch to incriminate himself." He pushed past Penny, who stood there for another moment, impressed with her sense of humor.

"Wait up, Frank!" Penny tried to catch up with her partner.

Stopping in his tracks, Frank turned and said, "Penny, what's up with this place?"

"You mean the fact that it's creepy as hell?"

Frank looked around and then back at Penny. "No, I mean every time we come here, we never see any residents other than Garrison Winter. Travers told us that residency was at an all-time high, though I've never seen anyone living here other than Winter."

"I haven't seen many staff members either," Frank shook his head. "I mean, Orderlies, Cooks, Maintenance workers? Where are they all?"

"Now that you mention it, the first time I came, it was a ghost town except for Gruber and Winter. Hmm." Penny thought for a moment and said, "Maybe they didn't want anyone else to be around when we conducted police business. You know, they don't want us upsetting anyone?"

Frank was skeptical and asked, "Was your first visit announced?"

Penny cocked a brow, "No, it wasn't." She started looking around as paranoia began to set in.

"Penny, neither was the second time we came together," Frank seemed suspicious. "Gruber and Travers both seemed surprised with our arrival, even though you called and left a message. Today is the only announced visit in which you actually confirmed with either of them that we were coming."

Frank added, "What time do they end breakfast around here?"

"Jesus Christ! You just ate an omelet an hour ago."

"Penny, we're about to pass through the dining room, which is connected to the kitchen. If breakfast ended an hour or so ago, then we should be able to smell food, hear people cleaning up in the kitchen, or at the very least see crumbs on the floor in the dining room," explained Frank.

Penny nodded her head. "Okay, I'll be on crumb patrol while you get your nose ready to smell what they had for breakfast," she smiled at her partner facetiously.

Frank ignored the joke and pondered for a moment, "Something's up! I'm not feeling good about Travers all of a sudden. They're all hiding something from us. It's starting to feel like a set-up to me."

Penny felt for the sidearm strapped to her chest and said, "Smith and Wesson's got my back."

"I'm pretty sure bullets can't shoot down evil."

"Dammit! I left my bible on the kitchen counter," Penny smiled, hoping humor would mask her fear.

"Just keep your eyes open, Smartass!"

Frank saw no signs of earlier activity, breakfast, or otherwise as the two walked through the massive dining area. "I don't smell anything, do you?"

Penny scanned the floor. "No, and I do not see any crumbs either."

The Philly detectives made their way into the solarium, but Winter wasn't sitting in his chair by the backgammon table. Instead, he was staring out the window with his back to the room. "Isn't it lovely, Detectives?" Winter didn't turn to greet his guests as the snow began to fall.

"How in the hell did he know we were here?" whispered Frank with a puzzled look on his face.

"I'm sure Gruber alerted him to our arrival," rationalized Penny.

"Bullshit! We would have passed her in the hall as she walked out of the dining room."

"Was it supposed to snow today?" Penny stared at the falling snow and looked at Frank with a quizzical look.

"No, it wasn't," Frank shook his head. "Now we know why they call him Old Man Winter."

Penny was brave and took the first step toward the old man. "Thank you for seeing us today, Mr. Winter. I hope we're not a burden."

Winter finally turned to face his guests. "Oh no, I love the company." Garrison Winter smiled and motioned for his guests to sit down. "Always nice talking with friends." Looking over his shoulder, he added, "The falling snow is an added nicety. Wouldn't you agree, Frank?"

Frank sat the tape recorder case down next to the backgammon table and replied, "Always nice to see you, Mr. Winter. I want to apologize for the unprofessional behavior of our supervisor when you came down to our office a week ago this past Tuesday."

"No need to apologize at all, Frank. And please, call me Garrison, for heaven's sake. I don't know how many times I need to encourage you to do so. We're all friends here," said Winter. "Now, please, take off your coats and have a seat."

Now sitting, Winter asked, "So, how is our Chief of Detectives these days?"

"He's always a bit moody," said Frank. "But he's a good man, though."

"Oh, I know he is." Winter acted as if he knew Ron McClain personally. "He's a good man, a family man, I'm sure. He's likely just misunderstood, like me, and so many others."

Frank and Penny looked at each other, their faces drenched in curiosity. Neither could understand who the old man was. The way he spoke and acted caused the two to remain on guard, unsure what baffling utterance would escape the old man's mouth next.

"Can I get either of you a tea or coffee?" offered Winter.

"None for me," said Penny.

Frank, on the other hand, called what he perceived as a bluff by the old man. He thought if the place were abandoned, there'd be no coffee in the kitchen. With a smile, Frank said, "Yes, I do believe I'll take you up on the offer."

"Delightful!" Winter was happy to be hosting his guests.

Penny was surprised, not knowing what her partner was up to.

"Very well then, give me a moment, Frank," Winter was gracious.

As Winter disappeared into the dining room, Penny turned to Frank and said, "What are you thinking?"

"I'm thinking that there's no damn way that old man comes back with a cup of coffee." Frank grinned and nodded, "I just called his bluff."

Penny was impressed. She'd wished she had challenged Winter's deception on an earlier visit when the old man had offered her tea.

Moments later, Garrison Winter returned with a steaming cup of coffee. The fine China cup and matching saucer sat upon a stainless steel serving tray that appeared to Frank to be an antique.

The Philly detectives were shocked, turning to each other in disbelief.

Winter gently sat the tray down and said, "Here you are, Frank. Black with sugar, I'm guessing."

Moments later, the three sat and exchanged pleasantries. Winter's eyes went to what he thought looked like a suitcase sitting on the floor to the left of Frank's armchair. "And what have you there, Frank? A gift of some sort?" Winter smiled; his eyes now locked on Frank's gaze.

Frank looked apprehensively at Penny and then back to Winter and said, "I brought along a tape recorder. Our boss would like to hear what you have to say today without asking you to come down to the station again," Frank paused.

"And...." Penny interjected, "we didn't want to inconvenience you any more than we already have."

"Oh, that's nonsense," exclaimed Winter. "I know that the two of you are simply doing your jobs. Please, feel free to record our conversation."

"Thank you, Garrison," Frank nodded in gratitude, feeling slightly less suspicious of the old man. "It'll take me just a moment to set it up."

Frank unpacked the recorder and placed it on the table next to the backgammon board, extending its cord to a nearby wall outlet. Winter and Penny made small talk while Frank positioned the microphone in the middle of the table, pointing it directly at Old Man Winter.

"Okay, Mr. Winter, I think we're ready if you are."

"I'm ready, Frank. Ask me anything you'd like. Go ahead and take the gloves off." Winter flashed what the detectives felt was a sinister smile. "Isn't that how you say it, Frank?"

Frank was nervous all of a sudden and feigned a smile. "Yeah, sure. Something like that." He turned to Penny and conveyed a look that told her he thought Winter was reading his mind.

In an effort to mask his nerves, Frank reached for the coffee cup. Taking a small sip, he sat the cup down and then flashed a quizzical look. Swishing the last bit of coffee around in his mouth, he swallowed hard. He'd noticed that the coffee had no taste. Confused, he said nothing and just pressed forward with the interview.

Penny played along and shot Winter a phony smile. Both detectives felt like they were in over their heads again.

"Okay, Garrison. For the purposes of this recording, I will address you by your first and last name from time to time," explained Frank. "You just answer every question to the best of your ability, and Penny here will chime in from time to time with a question of her own. Does that sound okay to you?"

"Oh yes, that'd be fine, Frank. Please, go ahead." Winter almost seemed to be excited about the interview.

"Alright, Garrison, now when I push down these two buttons," Frank pointed to the 'Play' button and the red 'Record' button, "the interview will begin."

"Yes-yes, Frank. Please proceed." Winter's enthusiasm was unsettling to Frank and Penny.

Frank pushed the buttons, and the populated reel began to unwind itself onto the empty one. Frank intended to ask simple questions first and then gradually work his way up to questions that might help secure a conviction if a prosecution resulted from the investigation. Penny was also hopeful that Old Man Winter would incriminate himself.

Frank eased into the interview. "My name is Detective Frank Bruno with the Philadelphia Police Department's 39th District. I am sitting here with fellow police detective Penelope Bryce."

"Today is Friday, November 22, 1974. The time is 11:46 am, and I am conducting an interview that will center on the 1969 disappearance of Victor Rogers."

"The questions I'll be asking today will be directed at the prime suspect who is sitting here with me today, Garrison Winter, also known as Garrison O'Donnell." Frank now looked at Winter and began his line of questioning.

"Is your name Garrison Winter?" he asked his suspect. "Or do you prefer that I address you as Mr. O'Donnell?"

"Oh, I do quite prefer Winter, if you wouldn't mind." Garrison was cordial in both his response and demeanor.

"Mr. Winter, earlier this month, Detective Bryce and I learned that the last name on your employment application here at Heavenly Gates is actually O'Donnell. When did you first start going by the name Winter?"

"I believe that would have been January of 1966." Winter thought about it for a moment and said, "Yes, it was 1966."

"And what name did you use before that?" asked Frank.

"Hmm," Winter again collected his thoughts, "From January 1958 to December of 1965, I was known as Gabriel Duncan."

"Did you have a middle name during those years?"

"My full name back then was Gabriel Olen Duncan." Winter, after a moment of reflection, said, "That was my least favorite of all of my names over the years."

"Is that right?" asked Frank, jotting down the initials G.O.D. "And just how many names have you gone by?"

"There have been exactly EIGHT, Frank. Does that number surprise you?" Winter smiled.

Penny swallowed hard, holding her breath for a moment, hoping that Frank didn't overreact to the 'eight' reference.

"Why would that surprise me, Mr. Winter?" Frank remained cool on the outside, but on the inside, his heart began to race.

"Because it's neither seven nor nine, but rather EIGHT." Winter again changed his voice inflection when annunciating the number eight.

"Let's continue with my questions, Mr. Winter. If you wouldn't mind." Frank was trying to avoid letting Winter control the conversation as he had done in each of their previous meetings.

"Not at all, Frank. Please, do continue." Winter smiled as if he were beginning to have fun.

"Were you working here at Heavenly Gates on the morning of December 23, 1969?"

"Yes, I was," replied Winter.

"And, did you know Victor Rogers?" asked Frank as he adjusted the volume control on the tape recorder's microphone.

"Oh yes. Victor and I were very close," said Winter.

"Can you tell me where you worked prior to Heavenly Gates?"

"I worked at God's Glory retirement home from January of 1958 until December of 1965."

Penny suddenly realized that Frank was attempting to take Winter back through his past jobs and get the old man to connect himself to the cities and dates on the chalkboard back at the 39th. She slowly removed her notepad from her jacket and began taking notes.

"And when you worked there, you went by the name Gabriel Olen Duncan. Is that right?"

"Yes, as I already stated moments ago," Winter's demeanor suddenly changed. He no longer seemed to be enjoying himself.

"Frank, we could play games all day while you attempt to get me to associate myself to the other locations, times, and dates. I'd rather you simply ask me what you want to know instead of the silly questions that you intend on asking me."

Frank was impressed with Winter's feisty attitude. "Oh, and what questions would those be, Mr. Winter?" Frank turned toward Penny and shared a look of surprise with his partner.

Penny sat upright and sensed that the interview was about to turn in a twisted fashion. With a look, Frank communicated to Penny that things were about to get strange and that she should keep her cool.

"Frank, you know very well what questions I'm referring to. It's the questions that people above your paygrade told you to ask me," Winter leaned forward in his chair and picked up the dice from the backgammon board and began to rattle them in his hand.

"You know, did I hurt the family dog when I was a young child? Did a priest ever inappropriately touch me? Did my parents ever abuse me? Was I bullied in school?"

Frank looked at the list in his hand, looked back up to Winter, and then over at Penny before saying, "Well, looks like I can sum up my list with just one question, then," Frank paused. "Is the answer 'Yes,' to any of those questions?"

Winter broke out in a smile. "No, Frank. The answer to all of those questions is an unequivocal, no."

Frank rose to his feet and said, "Well then, I guess we're done here." He then acted as if he was about to turn off the tape recorder before Penny quickly interjected.

"Garrison, what was the name of the retirement home you worked at in St. Louis back in 1951?"

Frank sat back down and thought to himself, *"That's my girl!"*

"Ah, my dearest Penny, thank you for taking my time here today seriously. I am so happy you finally spoke up."

Penny felt as if she was in complete control. "Please answer the question, Garrison. We don't want to waste any more of your time."

"Elysian Fields," said Winter.

"I'm sorry?" said Frank.

"I was speaking to your partner, Detective Bruno." Winter was polite, smiling as he looked over at Penny. He'd hoped she'd continue with her line of questioning. "*Elysian Fields* is the name of the retirement home in St. Louis."

Penny wasn't surprised. She took to heart what Cantrell and Kessler told her and Frank, and she changed up the line of questioning and kept Winter talking. Penny knew that was precisely what he wanted to do. She could feel a confession coming on.

Penny glanced down at her notes. "Garrison, did a friend of yours go missing from Elysian Fields back on December 17, 1951?"

"Well," paused Winter. "Missing is not the word that I would use, Penny."

"What word would you use then, Garrison?"

"I would say that he went to a better place," offered Winter.

Frank sat back and got out of Penny's way. He was shocked by her instincts and tenacity. He kept his eye on the recorder, hoping that it captured every word.

"Did you hurt your friend, Garrison?" Penny spoke softly.

"Hurt my friend?" Garrison seemed surprised by the insinuation. "I helped poor old Calvin Johnson."

"How old was Calvin?" asked Penny as Frank sat back in shock and awe.

"Calvin was 93 years old. It was time for him to move on." Winter stared into blank space as if fondly remembering his old friend.

"Did Calvin agree that it was time to move on?"

Winter replied, "Not at first, no. It took some convincing, but after a wonderful game of backgammon, we talked for a while, and he agreed to go with me."

"Go with you?" asked Penny, who was now getting anxious thinking that Winter was about to confess to killing Calvin Johnson.

"You know," Winter said as if Penny and Frank knew what happened to his friend, "for a walk." Winter was matter of fact.

Frank saw an opening and asked, "Did the two of you go on that walk, Garrison?"

"Oh yes," Winter regaled in his memory. "It was just lovely." Winter's smile revolted Penny and Frank.

"What name did you go by back then?" asked Penny.

Winter seemed genteel in his answer, "George Donovan."

"Did you have a middle name too, Mr. Winter?" asked Frank.

"Orwell is the name that you're looking for, Frank."

"Garrison, with regards to your walk with Mr. Johnson, where did your walk end? Where did you go?" asked Penny.

Winter looked up, cradling his chin in his right hand, and said, "You know, I can't remember. I only recall that we did, in fact, take a walk."

"What about Youngstown?" Penny asked after consulting her notes again. "It was December 9, 1927."

"Oh, yes," Garrison Winter smiled when he thought back to the date. "Such a lovely woman she was," his face overflowing with joy.

Frank glanced at Penny as Winter looked off again. His look encouraged his partner to keep it up.

"What was her name, Garrison?"

"Helen was such a joy to be around. Taking her for that walk was one of my greatest joys." Garrison flashed a warm smile.

Penny and Frank were sickened by the 'taking' reference but fought hard not to show it to their suspect.

"And what name did you go by back in 1927?" asked Frank.

"The name I used was Gael Olsen Devlin," Winter smiled at Frank.

Frank again wrote the acronym G.O.D. on his notepad. Sitting behind Frank and to his right, Penny could see the letters as Frank circled them several times.

Frank and Penny were nauseous seeing the joy in their suspect's eyes as he recounted murdering innocent people.

"How old was Mrs. ???" Penny paused, trying to elicit the victim's last name.

"Folgers," said Old Man Winter. "It was Helen Folgers."

Frank calmly asked Winter, "Garrison, where did the two of you walk to?"

Winter tried to recall. "Oh, yes. It was quite a lovely walk that we had, but I can't be sure where it ended, I'm afraid. A beautiful morning, though. Snow was everywhere. So white and so pure. Oh, and how Helen loved to walk and talk," Winter reflected. "And the snow, it was so deep."

"And what was the name of that retirement community, Garrison?" Penny readied her pencil.

"It was simply called, *Our Creator.*"

Frank and Penny were astonished by the information that Garrison Winter revealed to them. Over the next two hours, Winter would provide the names of the remaining victims but would not admit to hurting any of them. Penny's hand-written notes included John Walker Tate, 94 years old from Portland, Oregon, missing since December 15, 1945. Before Tate, David Westerfield, 95, of Spokane, Washington, went missing on December 13, 1937. And finally, John Cook, 97, of Barrington, Illinois, missing since December 11, 1931.

Garrison Winter also revealed all of the aliases that he had previously used; for Frank and Penny, it'd confirmed their suspicion that their suspect had a god complex. The other aliases were George O'Doyle, Gerald O'Day, Gavin Obed Dunn, and Gordan Oliver Daniels.

The circle was complete, and Penny now had enough information to remove every single question mark on her chalkboard. Of the remaining questions, the most important was who would be the tenth and final victim and when?

After packing up the tape recorder and saying goodbye to Garrison Winter, Penny visited the lavatory in the hallway near the door to the Admin Ward. As Frank waited for his partner, he could hear her vomiting and crying. At that moment, his back found the wall just outside the door, and he slid down the wall and buried his face into his hands. Neither he nor Penny could have imagined that Garrison Winter, O'Donnell, or whatever else he called himself, could be so callous as to take the lives of elderly people who'd befriended him in their final years. Frank knew that Winter was as evil as they come and that there would be a reckoning waiting for him. Wiping his tears away, he suddenly felt the urge to visit his priest, Father Brian Maloney.

That Saturday, Penny would spend her afternoon in The Philadelphia Public Library looking through old newspaper articles on microfiche.

The next day, the Sunday before Thanksgiving. Frank found himself in the Confessional Box at St. Ambrose Catholic Church. Frank cried to his priest that day, and Father Brian Maloney cried with him.

Chapter 25 – For Christ's Sake

It was Monday of Thanksgiving week, and Frank and Penny were supposed to be off. Instead, they met at the Arlington Diner in the morning before heading into the office.

Though on vacation, Frank had notified Ron McClain on Friday that he and Penny had secured enough probable cause to apply for a search warrant, with Frank telling his boss that what Garrison Winter had to say was just short of a confession.

Sitting in their favorite back booth, the two laid out their contemporaneous notes from the interview and still couldn't believe everything they'd heard.

"It was too easy, Penny," said Frank. "After thinking about it for the whole weekend, it just doesn't make sense."

"I know, I know." Penny seemed to agree. "I went to the library on Saturday and couldn't find anything regarding missing persons from any of the cities Winter copped to. Nothing!" she shook her head.

"Don't misunderstand me, Penny. I think he incriminated himself. I believe everything he said, but the question I have is, why?" Frank couldn't wrap his head around the way Winter offered up the names and dates so easily. "Why did he tell us anything? Why's he even talking to us at all?"

"It's so surreal. It's like this is one big prank, except for the fact that Rogers, Tipton, and Steinman are missing." Penny stared into her coffee cup. "Maybe it's like the Quantico boys said, these psychopaths like to talk about what they did."

"We need the other cities to confirm all the names and dates that Winter gave us," said Frank. "Then we'll have something."

"What time is McClain gonna get there?" asked Penny.

"He said noon." Frank drowned his coffee with sugar.

"I guess he was gonna take it easy this week with all of us out, huh?" Penny sorted through her notes, looking up for a moment to notice the volume of sugar going into Frank's cup. "You okay there with the sugar, buddy?"

"Oh. Yeah." Frank caught himself. "Well, we're one step closer to a search warrant. If McClain hears enough on the tape, he might go see Judge Corbin himself."

"But what does that really get us?" asked Penny.

"Well, it will allow us to search his private quarters at Heavenly Gates, and it'll cover his employment records, too," said Frank. "It's unlikely it will cover access to the basement, though. Unless we can show probable cause that Victor Rogers is buried down there." Frank stirred his coffee.

"So, the search warrant won't cover all of FalconClaw?" Penny was bummed.

"The company that owns FalconClaw is not under investigation," explained Frank. "The Fourth Amendment protects citizens and corporations against broad searches, so the specific search warrant we get will be narrow and likely only include his personal resident information, past employment file, and his private room."

"Well, that sucks!" Penny's eyes flashed her agitation. "Because what I'm looking for is in that basement. You mark my words, Frank." Penny snapped her fingers. "Wait! Winter told us he worked there back in 1920! That means there must be employment records from way back then. Maybe that information can get the basement added to the warrant. Old employee files are likely stored down there."

"Maybe, but we have no actual proof that he did work there back in '20. Just the ramblings of an old man," said Frank. "I'd be curious to see what's down there after what we learned about MK Ultra, though," said Frank.

Like Penny, Frank believed the psychological experiments conducted at FalconClaw between 1957 and 1965 must have something to do with some of the disappearances.

"Yeah, but isn't that enough?" Penny was puzzled.

Frank ignored the question, lost in thought for a moment. "Penny, what if they've been conducting experiments the whole time?"

"The government?" clarified Penny.

"I don't know," Frank was unconvinced. "I just wonder if crazy shit's been happening around the country to old people like Rogers and Steinman for all of these years? I mean, maybe your great-grandfather stumbled across some shit, and they offed him."

"That, I don't buy," said Penny. "I think Winter's either evil, crazy, or both. I think he did all the killing on his own. But what I don't believe is his age, then or now." She looked through her notes and reconciled the dates of the disappearances. "Frank, let's just say Winter really was born in 1888, that means he would have been 32 in 1920, and then 39, 43, 49, 57, 63, 69, 77, and 81, for all the other disappearances. You can commit murder at any of those ages."

"You did your math, I see." Frank busted Penny's chops. "I see it differently than you do, though. Winter keeps saying he's 83," he paused, "and that he was also born in 1888." Frank scribbled on a piece of paper and held it up to show Penny. What he'd scribbled was 8-8-8.

"Frank, I get it! You keep seeing three eights. But he's neither the devil nor an angel." Penny was adamant. "He's a man who's killed nine people and is searching for a tenth."

"Penny, I'm going to show you another number, and I want you to tell me what it means." Frank did some more math and then held up the number 510. "What does that mean to you?"

"I don't know, Frank," said Penny. "My guess is that it means absolutely nothing. That's what!" Penny no longer wanted to humor Frank and his eights.

"510 is all of the ages that you just gave me added together," said Frank. "And you're right; they don't mean anything." He slapped the paper face down on the table. "But one thing is undeniable, though," he paused. "Eights are turning up everywhere!"

"You know, you're really starting to worry me." Penny began gathering her notes to place back in her bag.

After looking at the numbers again, Frank exclaimed, "Holy Shit!"

"What?!" Penny thought maybe Frank stumbled upon something significant.

"When I add up only the second number in each of the victim's ages, it comes up to...." Frank flashed Penny the sum he'd scribbled on his notes. The number he held up was 48.

"Four eights! Really?" Penny rolled her eyes. "You need help, Frank. After doing the calculation in her head, she said, "Plus, your math is off."

Frank was perplexed, studying his math.

"Can we get the check, please?" Penny yelled to the waitress.

"We're both crazy," Frank laughed. "You've got your basement, and I've got my eights."

"Yeah, but you know what else we've got?" asked Penny, smiling.

"What's that?" asked Frank.

"We've got a tape!" Her eyes went big. "Now, let's go play it for McClain."

Thirty minutes later, Frank and Penny walked into the Detective Room and saw McClain standing at the teletype machine holding several pages of telefaxes. The look on McClain's face told the two detectives that what he was holding had everything to do with the Winter case.

"You're not gonna believe this," McClain was surprised but stoic.

Penny and Frank quickly peeled off their coats and hung them on the backs of their chairs. Penny shot over to where McClain was standing, and Frank joined them after setting the tape recorder case down next to his desk.

McClain stepped aside, handing the pages to Penny, not yet torn away from the teletype machine. When she saw what was written in the text, her jaw dropped. The first heading was titled YOUNGSTOWN - 1927. Frank now by her side, Penny did a cursory search of the other pages, and two of them said SPOKANE, then BARRINGTON.

"There's still a missing city," said McClain, "But we've got everything we need to get a search warrant providing you guys have that son of a bitch on tape linking himself to the disappearances."

Penny scrolled through the list and said, "We're still missing...."

McClain finished her sentence, "Portland."

"Frank! We got it, Frank!" Penny smiled, fighting her tears, not wanting to look weak in front of her boss.

Frank hugged his partner as McClain stood by, indifferent to their celebration.

"Yeah, Chief, we got him on tape admitting to working in each of the cities, and he even provided us with the names of the victims."

Penny scanned the printout in her hand, feverishly looking for a name she recognized as one Winter provided them with. "It's here, Frank! John Cook, Barrington. Missing, 1931. It's here, Frank! It's all here!"

"Alright, listen, Frank," said McClain. "Get the recorder set up. I've got to run downstairs to see Captain Wilcox. When I talk to him, I'll let him know you'll return the recorder later today. Have that thing set up by the time I get back."

"10-4, Chief!" said Frank.

After McClain walked out the door, Penny was almost giddy. "Holy shit, Frank. We're gonna get this guy! He did it! He really did it!"

Frank was happy, too, but was also pragmatic. "Penny, listen, murder investigations take time. We need to get all of our evidence together, and then we'll bring Winter in for a formal interrogation downstairs."

"So what? We need like the murder weapon or something?" asked a now deflated Penny. "So, you're telling me that the only chance we have is an actual confession with Winter saying how he did it and where the bodies are? We're never getting that!"

Frank cautioned Penny, "In lieu of having a murder weapon or an eyewitness, yeah, we'll need a confession. So far, he's only indicated that he knows about the disappearances, not that he's the reason for them," Frank reminded his rookie partner. "That's why we've been taking it slow. All we need is to get enough information out of him to establish probable cause. After that, we get the warrants. If more evidence is found, then that will allow us to put more pressure on him. More pressure could coax a confession."

Frank walked to his desk, lifted the recorder case up onto it, and opened it. Removing the recorder, he placed the box back down onto the floor and plugged in the machine.

"So, did you listen to it over the weekend?" Seeing the recorder on the table restored Penny's excitement.

Penny Bryce knew that when Ron McClain heard what they'd elicited from their prime suspect, that he'd have to finally admit that she was worthy of her promotion to detective.

The top of Frank's nose wrinkled as he lowered his brow. "No, I didn't listen to it! I didn't even rewind the thing yet. I don't get my rocks off by listening to serial killers talk when I'm sitting back on my recliner at home. Plus, I got two little girls running around, and they don't need to hear some lunatic talking about putting people out of their misery."

"No shit?!" Penny was surprised. "I would have been playing that to my family, friends, and neighbors."

"Don't celebrate a victory until we actually have one to celebrate," said Frank. "We have a lot of good detective work that still needs to be done."

"Pragmatic Frank. That's your new nickname." The smile ran from Penny's face.

Frank hit the rewind button, and the reels began to spin clockwise. "You know, Penny, I've always said that the secret to life is the successful management of people's expectations. That starts with your own. Just slow it down. We need to talk to the detectives in the other cities first. We might be months away, still."

The tape stopped, and Frank made sure it was ready for his boss. He hit play and heard himself on the tape saying, *"My name is Detective Frank Bruno with the Philadelphia Police Department's 39th District...."* Frank then stopped the tape.

Penny looked at him and said, "What are you doing?! Play the tape!"

"Cool it, Penny!" said Frank. "McClain will be back soon, and I don't want to be halfway through it when he walks through the door."

"Fine!"

At that moment, Ron McClain walked in and saw Frank and Penny crowded around the tape recorder. "You guys ready for me?"

"Yeah, Chief, it's all set." Frank nodded.

McClain pulled up a chair and said, "This better be good."

Penny's face lit up. This was her big moment. One that would solidify her standing in her boss's eye.

Frank rewound the tape to the very beginning and then pushed 'Play.' The reels began turning and the three detectives, all sitting down, inched closer to the recorder perched on Frank's desk as the sound began to play. The smile that Penny wore was impossible to hide, so she didn't bother trying. Frank gave her a look that reminded her about managing expectations, and McClain only wanted to hear one thing, the old psychopath placing himself at the scene of each crime on the dates in question.

Suddenly Frank's voice came through the scratchy recording. *"My name is Detective Frank Bruno with the Philadelphia Police Department's 39th District. I am sitting here with fellow Police Detective Penelope Bryce."*

"Today is Friday, November 22, 1974. The time is 11:46 am, and I am conducting an interview that will center on the disappearance of Victor Rogers in 1969."

"The questions that I will be asking today will be directed at the prime suspect who is sitting here with me today, Garrison Winter, also known as Garrison O'Donnell."

"Is your name Garrison Winter? Or do you prefer that I address you as Mr. O'Donnell?"

The recording went silent for several seconds even though the reels were still turning. Hearing the silence caused Frank and Penny to perk up in their chairs. McClain just listened intently.

The sound of Frank's voice came back on the recorder. *"Mr. Winter, earlier this month, Detective Bryce and I learned that the last name on your employment application here at Heavenly Gates is actually O'Donnell. When did you first start going by the name Winter?"*

Only silence could be heard in place of Winter's response.

"And what name did you use before that?"

Penny and Frank were puzzled and leaned in to listen more closely. The recorder again went silent for several more seconds before Frank's voice came back on.

"Did you have a middle name during those years?"

Again the sound disappeared with no responses being picked up on the tape.

"What in the hell is going on here?" Frank said as he reached for the 'Stop' button.

"What's going on, Frank?" asked McClain.

"I don't know," Frank looked panicked as he rewound the tape.

Frank pushed 'Play' again, and the three leaned in.

"Is your name Garrison Winter? Or do you prefer that I address you as Mr. O'Donnell?"

Again, there were no audio responses from Old Man Winter. Frank and Penny were visibly agitated, unable to understand why Garrison Winter's voice was not picked up on the tape.

"Frank, what did you do?" asked McClain, still unsure of what was happening. "Do you even know how to work this thing?"

"Of course I know how to use it!" Frank snapped back at his boss.

Penny said, "Fast forward it a little and see what happens."

Frank fast-forwarded the tape and then pushed 'Play' again.

"Why would that surprise me, Mr. Winter?"

Silence replaced Winter's voice as Frank's face went white. He was both shocked and embarrassed. Penny slumped back in her chair, looking utterly defeated as the tape rolled.

"Let's continue with my questions, Mr. Winter. If you wouldn't mind?"

Again silence. Frank reached for the fast-forward button and sped up the tape. The whining sound of voices and blank tape could be heard as it wound itself forward.

"And when you worked there, you went by the name Gabriel Olen Duncan. Is that right?"

More silence came from the speakers.

McClain stood up and said, "For Christ's sake, Frank! You pointed the microphone in the wrong direction."

"No!" Frank raised his voice. "I've recorded dozens of suspects on this thing. I know what I'm doing!"

"That was on the old tape recorder! This one's new!" McClain was both angry and disappointed in his best detective. "Total waste of time!" exclaimed McClain. "This is ridiculous! The two of you ask me to help you out, and you can't even get this right!"

McClain walked into his office and slammed the door. Penny's face displayed panic as she looked over to Frank, whose face was sacked by humiliation. "What happened, Frank?"

"I don't know!" said Frank as he wrestled with the recorder, rewinding, and fast-forwarding the tape incessantly, somehow hoping for a different outcome. "This thing is fucked up or something. You were there, Penny. You heard everything!"

"I know, I know," Penny was flustered. "You had the mic in the middle of the table pointing right at Winter."

Frank stood and said, "Let me take it downstairs and have Wilcox's guys take a look at it. You stay put!"

The door to the stairwell closed, leaving Penny alone in the Detective Room with McClain, who was still in his office.

After several minutes, Penny summoned the courage to knock on her boss's door. Thinking that it was Frank, McClain yelled, "Come in!"

The door opened, and Penny stepped inside. Not immediately looking up, McClain said, "What do you want, Bruno?"

As McClain looked up and saw Penny, he said, "Oh, it's you!"

Penny said, "Chief, we took contemporaneous notes. Two detectives from the Philadelphia Police Department witnessed their prime suspect confess to being at the crime scene at the time of each disappearance. That must account for something." Penny was humble. "That microphone was pointed right at Garrison Winter."

McClain was still hot. "That tape was the reason I was going to seek a search warrant for our suspect, and you guys fucked it up!"

"So, a witness implicated himself to all or part of a crime, and it means nothing because there's no recording of it?"

"Yeah!" That's what it means!" said McClain. "Now get out!"

"That's not what it says in the Police Officer or Detective Training Manual." Penny was defiant. "Look it up, Chief. If I'm not mistaken, it's on page 167 of the Detective Training Manual, Section 2, Article 7. It's there. Look it up." Penny smiled, turned, and closed the door.

McClain was furious. He got up, walked over to his door, opened it, and then slammed it shut just to make a point, causing the crack in the glass to become bigger. He knew that Penny was correct, but he was in no mood to tell her she was right.

Minutes later, Frank walked back in, and Penny's hopes were buoyed. "Well?" she asked.

Frank's face said it all. He said nothing. He just walked over to his chair and plopped down in it, placing the reel of tape from his hand up onto his desk. Frank was dumbfounded and didn't know what to do next.

"Send the tape to the boys in Quantico, Frank," said Penny. "Have the Bureau analyze it."

Chapter 26 – Loose Ends

Two weeks later, Frank and Penny were still tying up loose ends. They'd heard from all but one city and had sent off the defective tape reel to their friends in Quantico for analysis.

Sitting in the Arlington Diner, the two had their case notes and victim summaries spread across the table. It was now Monday, December 9, and Penny was hoping for a Christmas miracle. She'd hoped to find out the true identity of Garrison Winter before the holiday break.

"Okay, so we're still missing confirmation on John Walker Tate from Portland, but all the others named by Winter check out," said Frank.

"Okay, let's go over what we have so far and see if we can determine some kind of pattern or connection between the victims, the cities, and the dates. Something must be here that will tell us a story," said Penny.

"Well then," said Frank, "let's start at the beginning with your great-grandfather. You go first."

"Okay, Samuel Crenshaw, born December 7, 1826, went missing on his birthday 1920?" Penny double-checked the information she had on her great-grandfather. "Damn, what a shitty birthday present he got."

"What else you got on him?" Frank organized his files.

"He was born in Philadelphia and was an only child. Married and had three sons, the youngest being my grandfather, Ernest. Appears to have devoted his life to helping build up Philadelphia and the country. Civil servant under the Lincoln Administration." Penny sorted through her files. "Not much more to add. You know about him donating FalconClaw to the city and, of course, his time with Garrison O'Donnell."

"Well, next we got Helen Folgers from Youngstown, Ohio. She was 92, so she was born in 1835, birthdate was December 9."

Penny perked up. "Did you say December 9?"

"Yeah," Frank nodded. After looking more closely at the case notes, he said, "Holy shit!"

"Yeah! Holy Shit is right!" Penny echoed Frank's reaction. "Went missing on her birthday?! That can't be a coincidence." Sorting through her paperwork, she pulled the file for John Cook of Barrington, Illinois. "Frank, John Cook went missing on his birthday too! He was born on December 11, 1834, went missing on the same date in 1931!"

"How the fuck did we miss this?!" Frank rifled through his files. "I'll be damned! David Westerfield from Spokane went missing on December 13, 1937, and was born on December 13, 1832!" Frank sank back into his seat. "How in the hell did we not make this connection earlier?"

"My God, Frank!" Penny pulled another file. "Calvin Johnson, born December 17, 1844, went missing on his birthday in 1951!" Penny was in shock. She shook her head several times and then double-checked her facts. "Do you have Barbara Jo Tipton's file?"

Frank looked pale and said, "Disappeared on her birthday in 1957!" Shaking his head, he said, "What kind of sick mother fucker kills people on their birthday!"

Penny, looking at more files, said, "Steinman and Rogers too! Son of a bitch! So we have a psychopath who may have targeted his victims because they were born in the month of December and then killed them on their birthday. That means he knew when their birthdays were."

"Meaning he knew them relatively well," said Frank. "That backs up Winter's story that he was close to all of the victims."

"Well, we may be waiting on Portland authorities to get back to us on a missing person from 1945, but we can safely assume that John Walker Tate was born on the day he disappeared, December 15," said Penny.

Frank doing the quick math in his head, said, "Based off of what Winter told us about Tate, he was 94 years old. That would put his birth year in 1839." Frank jotted that information down. "Let's get that info to the guys in Portland. It might help them track down information on Tate's disappearance."

"Got it!" said Penny. "I'll make the call when we get in."

Over the next hour, Frank and Penny concluded that the missing victims were all born in the 1800s, went missing on their birthdays, last seen with a custodian, led away from a retirement community with a religious name, two sets of footprints walking away from the home and no footprints coming back. Their list included six men and three women, Calvin Johnson being the only black man and Polly Anne Steinman being Jewish.

"You know, Penny, I'm still stuck on the ages," said Frank.

"Here we go!" said Penny, preparing for Frank's bad math and fixation on the number eight.

"When I add up the ages, they come out to 848."

"Meaning what?" Penny busted her partner's balls.

"I don't know?" Frank was visibly racking his brain. "The eights on the ends and the four in the middle...." Frank couldn't figure it out.

"Frankie Boy, you're reaching," challenged Penny. "You can't get to 888 no matter how hard you try."

"Maybe I don't need to," Frank paused. "Maybe it's like one of those things that are spelled the same backward and forwards," he struggled to put his finger on the term.

"Hey, Cindy! Come over here!" Penny yelled to the waitress.

The young blonde grabbed a fresh pot of coffee and made her way over to the back booth. "You guys ready for the check?"

"Cindy, you go to college, right?" asked Penny.

"Yeah, why?" The question caught the waitress off guard.

"Cindy, what's a word called that's spelled the same backward or forwards?" asked Frank.

"Let's see," Cindy thought about it. "Mom, Dad, Radar, civic, refer, madam....hmmm?" She squinted her blue eyes. "It's called a palindrome!" she said with a smile. "So, you guys ready for the check, or what?"

"No to the check," said Frank. "But are you sure it's called that?"

"Yes, it's a palindrome," said the waitress. "That was like in seventh grade that they taught us that."

Penny smiled and launched her brows, looking impressed and insulted at the same time. "Thanks, Cindy!"

"Sure. So you guys need a refill?" said Cindy, still holding the pot of coffee.

"No, we're good," said Frank. "Thanks!"

Frank pressed his lips together, nodded his head, and said, "Smart girl!" He paused, "Cute too!" he smiled at Penny.

Penny rolled her eyes. "First of all, she's like twenty, and second of all, she said she learned that in the seventh grade! So, what's your point, Frankie Boy?"

Frank shrugged. "I'm just saying that she's smart and she's cute, that's all!"

"I mean about the palindrome, dumbass!" Penny shook her head and smiled.

"Oh, yeah, sorry." Frank refocused. "I'm saying that the eights are prominent in the number 848. Then when I see two eights, I take the number two and multiply it by the four and get eight. Or I can divide one of the eights by two and get four. You see what I'm saying?"

"No, I don't." Penny cut her partner off. "Frank, I love you, buddy, but you are really reaching, man!"

"Penny, I'm saying that maybe the four means something. In the bible, the number four means creation, the four seasons, and the four creative elements: earth, air, water, and fire."

Penny shook her head and began gathering up the files strewn across the table. "Sounds like you've seen Father Maloney recently."

"Maybe I have, wiseass!" Frank got defensive. "Say whatever you want, Penny. It's all going to mean something in the end."

Thirty minutes later, the two walked into the Detective Room, and Roger Taylor yelled out, "Penny! Something came in for you from Portland. I put it on your desk, over there." Taylor pointed.

Penny quickly hung her coat and looked down at her desk. Reading over the telefax, she saw that it was regarding John Walker Tate and then panned down and saw his birthdate, December 15, 1839.

Frank looked on and said, "Well, what's it say?"

"This is it, Frank. It's Portland. Tate went missing on his birthday!"

Frank said, "No shit!" shaking his head. "I think we need to go see birthday boy, Old Man Winter!"

"I agree!" Penny reached for her coat.

"Let me get with Ron and tell him what's up. I'll meet you downstairs in ten."

"Okay, Frank!" Penny grabbed her bag and headed downstairs.

Ten minutes later, Frank emerged from McClain's office, and Riggins and Coons called him over to their desk area.

"Yeah, what's up, fellas?"

"Yo, Frankie, we just wanted to say that we think Penny's alright," said Jack Riggins.

"Yeah, Frank. Listen, I give her a hard time, but she's okay by me," added Doug Coons.

Overhearing the conversation, both Jerry Tubbs and Roger Taylor spoke up.

"Frank, she's a tough broad!" said Tubbs. "She belongs here in the 39th! But don't tell her I said so. Capiche?"

"Yeah, I understand. But let me tell you boys somethin'. That 'broad' worked these streets for fourteen years. That's longer than any of ya!" said Frank, pointing his finger at all four of the other guys. "She's a good detective, and sometimes it'd be good if she heard it from any one of ya. Show some respect for her. She's one of us now!"

"You got it, Frankie!" said Coons as the others chimed in agreement.

As the conversation between Frank and the guys ended, Ron McClain walked out and said, "What the hell you guys doin' wasting taxpayer dollars? Break it up and get back to work."

As the men went back to their desks, Riggins yelled out to his boss. "Us guys was just sayin' that Bryce is okay by us."

"Well, isn't that just lovely!" McClain was sarcastic. "So, whatta you think we should do, put some flowers on her desk or something?"

Coons spoke up, "We're just sayin' Chief, that broad's alright with us."

"Coons, you're getting me all choked up over here," McClain was facetious. "You got an I.D. on the Schuylkill kid yet?"

"Not yet, Boss," Coons looked down at his desk, shuffling papers.

"Then get back to work before I hand the case over to Frank and the broad!"

"Easy, Boss," said Frank.

"Don't 'easy Boss' me, Bruno. You need to bring that old son of a bitch in one of these days, and he better be wearing bracelets the next time I see him! What in the hell's taking you two so long, anyway?"

"We'll get 'em, Boss. You don't worry about that." Frank threw his coat on and said, "Be back in a few hours. Heading up to Heavenly Gates now."

"Yeah-yeah-yeah!" McClain said before walking back into his office and closing the door.

Before disappearing into the stairwell, Frank said, "I'll see you, boys, later!"

Chapter 27 – The Elevator

It was approaching noon, and Penny and Frank sat inside the Buick on Bedford Street in front of Heavenly Gates.

"Heavenly Gates, my ass!" said Frank, looking up at the mansion on the hill through the passenger side windshield. "There ain't nothing heavenly about it!"

"So, what's the plan when we get in there?" asked Penny.

"First of all, they don't know we're coming, right?"

"Right."

"I mean, you didn't call Travers while you waited for me and McClain to finish up, right?"

"Right. I just told you that."

"Well then, we're gonna see how many people and staff are walking those halls in the middle of the day." Frank looked determined.

"It's creepy, ain't it?" Penny stared up at FalconClaw. "It's like it's staring down at us."

"I don't know about all that," responded Frank. "The old man that lives there is evil; that's all I know."

"Well, that old man's got a name, and I bet you that it's not Winter or O'Donnell or any of the other aliases that he's been peddling." Penny shook her head. "Like I said, everything we want is locked away in that basement."

"What I want to know is who's the psycho sitting in that solarium?" Frank paused. "He's probably looking down at us right now."

"I'll tell you what else I want to know; who owns this place?" Frank wondered aloud, scratching his chin. "I want to talk to the owner about Travers and the only resident I've seen so far."

Penny turned to look at Frank. "Maybe I can find out while we're in there."

"Whatta ya got in mind?" Frank was up for anything.

"How about when we're done speaking to Winter, we drop in on old Dean Travers?"

"I got a better idea." Frank arched his brow.

"What's that?" asked Penny.

"How about you drop in on Travers, and I take a look around?"

"Now we're talking, Detective Bruno," Penny launched a sly grin. "What if you get caught, though?"

"Whatta they gonna do? Call the police?" Frank kept a straight face as he turned off the engine and said, "Let's go!"

At the top of the hill, Frank said, "I'll ring the bell this time. I want to see if the old Frankie charm works on Gruber."

"You're not that charming, Frank." Penny laughed.

"Well, I bought some new soap. Maybe the scent will win her over."

"I did notice you didn't smell like an old pair of shoes earlier." Penny smiled and asked, "What's it called? I like it."

"Easy, Penny," Frank tried not to smile. "Let's keep it professional."

"No, really, what's it called? I'll pick up a bar for Joe."

"Irish Spring, or something."

"Yeah, I think I saw a commercial for that last night after The Walton's finished up," remembered Penny. "Well, it's better than the Italian Hell you've been wearing the last couple of months."

"Yeah, well, no need to shower every day when you sleep alone." Frank pursed his lips and looked resigned.

"Well, don't forget, you still got kids."

"Alright, already. I told you I got some new soap and took a bath last night."

"It does smell good," smiled Penny. "Get over here and let me take a whiff." Penny leaned in close to Frank's neck.

"Hot damn! Mizz Gruber's not gonna know what hit her."

Frank shooed Penny away with his forearm. "Come on, Smartass. Let's get in there!"

Frank walked up the steps, looked up at the steel doors and the arched window above, and admired the beauty that FalconClaw once was. "This place has seen better days."

Penny agreed with a nod. "Yeah, from the outside, it looks abandoned."

"From the inside too." Frank squinted his eyes and nodded before ringing the bell.

Two minutes later, the deadbolt turned, and the massive door swung open with a squeal.

"Well, surprise-surprise!" Gruber didn't look happy to see the visitors standing in front of her.

"Bernice!" Frank feigned excitement. "It's so good to see you! I was wondering if we could talk for a moment before we visit Mr. Winter?"

Gruber rolled her eyes, turned, and walked away without another word.

Frank looked at Penny and then down at himself. He lifted his arm to smell his armpit and said, "Geez, I'm not sure what happened there."

Penny laughed and said, "Maybe you can get a refund on that soap, Frankie Boy." She then pushed him forward through the door.

"Okay, Detective Bryce, follow my lead when we get in there."

"Sir, yes, sir!" Penny saluted the 39th District's senior-most detective.

"Knock it off and follow me, Rookie."

Walking down the long foyer and peeking inside the small sitting rooms along the way, Frank said, "You see what I mean? There's no one around. I can't even hear people above us walking around." He paused, "It's like a ghost town."

"Creepy as hell. That's for sure," Penny agreed, peeking her head into empty rooms that seemed long void of attention or occupancy.

The two took a left at the end of the hall and walked into the formal dining room. As they passed by the nook where food would be served, Frank pointed out, with the raising of his chin, that no one seemed to be back in the kitchen preparing lunch.

"Nothing," Frank whispered. "Not a sound coming out of there." Frank stared at the double swinging doors on the back wall of the serving area.

"No crumbs from this morning either, Frankie Boy." Penny squinted and scanned the massive room's wall to wall, Tavolato Venetian Italian wood tiles, inspecting every square foot.

"It feels like death in here." Frank wrenched his neck, and Penny could hear the popping of tiny fluid sacks. It sounded to Penny like someone cracking their knuckles.

"You okay there, buddy?" Penny looked up at her partner.

"Yep. Just a little good versus evil about to go down here in a minute," Frank whispered.

"Why are we whispering?" asked Penny.

"Because I want to catch that son of a bitch off guard. That's why."

From fifty feet away, the two detectives could see the left arm of Old Man Winter sitting in his chair at the backgammon table. Their eyes fixed on the back of the old man's chair and his familiar flannel shirt.

"Ahh, Detectives! I was expecting you!" came the words from the man sitting with his back to the approaching visitors.

"How in the hell did he know we were here?" Frank asked under his breath.

Garrison Winter rose from his chair and turned to meet his guests. "Detectives, what took you so long?" Winter smiled and bowed his head slightly.

Frank and Penny stopped in their tracks, turned toward the other, and found it impossible to conceal their shared look of surprise and confusion.

"You were expecting us?" Frank questioned the old man.

"Yes, the first of many questions I'm sure that you have for me today, Detective Bruno. What with the recording fiasco, and all."

Frank played dumb with the 'recording fiasco' comment and had hoped Penny would too. "And exactly how is it that you were expecting us today, Mr. Winter?"

Winter paused for a moment as if to formulate his response. "Yes, of course. Well, as you know. I love to look out of these massive windows and take in the serenity of the landscape. I believe I saw your car parked down on Bedford Street. I recognized it from one of your other previous visits." Winter motioned to two of the three chairs sitting around the backgammon table. "Please do sit down, won't you?"

"Is that a Buick, Detective Bruno?" asked Winter. "A '67 if I'm not mistaken. I wasn't sure if you two were ever going to get out of that car."

"Yes, a 1967 Buick, Mr. Winter," Frank answered the old man's question. "Mr. Winter...."

"Garrison, please."

"Yes, of course, Garrison." Frank smiled insincerely. "Garrison, you mentioned something a moment ago about a recording fiasco. What exactly did you mean by that?"

"Oh, I was referring to your visit in general," smiled Winter. "I wasn't feeling well that day, and I believe that I may have given you incomplete or inaccurate information."

Frank looked at Penny and wasn't convinced that the old man was truthful.

Frank turned back to Winter with a quizzical look on his face and said, "And you characterized that as a 'fiasco,' is that right?"

"Poor choice of words, perhaps," shrugged Winter. "Again, please sit down. Let's talk." The old man smiled.

"Garrison, we have some follow-up questions for you. I hope you'll take the time to answer them today."

"Of course, Penny, my dear. Please go ahead with any questions that you might have. Winter then turned to Frank, smiled, and winked, "I promise that I'll be truthful."

The hair on the back of Frank's neck stood on end as he interjected bluntly and said, "Where in the hell are all of the people?"

Winter looked confused. "Why, whatever do you mean, Frank?"

"The residents? The staff?" Frank nearly shouted his questions in frustration. "Where are all of the people that live and work here?"

"Why Frank, they're everywhere." Winter dawned a sinister smile.

"What in the hell does that mean?" Frank looked heated.

Penny spoke up. "Garrison, we haven't seen anyone walking about. Where are the residents and staff this time of day?" Penny spoke softly, hoping that Frank would calm down.

"They're everywhere, Frank. Can't you see them?" Winter looked over Frank's shoulder, lifted his chin, and motioned with his eyes for Frank to turn and look into the far corner of the solarium near the dining room.

Frank turned tentatively, followed by Penny, and saw no one. "Enough with the games, Mr. Winter," Frank looked pissed. "We're not buying the whole crazy act!"

"Garrison, please. Answer the question," implored Penny.

Garrison Winter shook his head as if to come to his senses. "Residents only come down here during meal-times and for holiday celebrations. Outside of those times, they remain on the upper levels," explained Winter. "As far as staff, they are typically where the residents are. This time of day that would be upstairs."

"So, why are you down here, Mr. Winter?" asked Frank.

"Why, I love it down here." Winter beamed. "All the natural sunlight does wonders for my eczema."

Frank and Penny glanced down at Winter's hands as his arms were covered in the same long-sleeved flannel shirt that he always seemed to be wearing each time they'd visited him. Studying Winter's hands more closely, they saw no signs of a skin condition. Looking even closer, they noticed that his hands didn't seem to match his age. They both thought they looked like the hands of a much younger man.

"It appears the sunlight has done wonders for your skin, Mr. Winter, as I don't even see a freckle on your hands." Frank tried to sound skeptical.

Winter held up his hands and smiled as if to display them for the detectives. "Yes, the sun shining down from above is quite a miracle, isn't it?"

Frank and Penny sat down and pulled their notepads from their pockets.

"What, no tape recorder today, Frank?" Winter smiled.

"Nope, just good old-fashioned pencil and paper," said Frank.

"Yes, I do find it more reliable than technology," said Winter staring blankly. "Sometimes technology can malfunction." The old man winked and smiled in Frank's direction.

Frank looked at Penny with suspicion and then back to Winter. "Yes, it sometimes can." Frank was rattled by the old man.

"So, what brings the two of you here today, Detectives?" Winter looked at both Frank and Penny.

"Mr. Winter," said Penny. "Do you remember if there was anything special about the day your friends went missing?"

"Well, yes, I do!" Winter perked up. "It was their birthday!" The old man smiled with joy.

"Mr. Winter, why do you think they went missing on their birthdays?"

"I think that everyone should leave this world on their birthday. A birthday is a celebration of a person's very existence. What better day to move onto the next life than on the very day you celebrate your own?"

Penny gasped, "Mr. Winter! Did you just say that you took the lives of your friends?!" Penny's face was distorted by anger and surprise.

"Good Heaven's, no, Penny! As I stated on the tape recorder, I never hurt my friends. Listen to the recording later today. You'll hear it."

"Then what are you saying, Mr. Winter?"

"I'm sorry, can you repeat the question?"

"Did you hurt your friends?!" Frank showed contempt for the old man sitting in front of him.

"As I have stated clearly to you on multiple occasions, no, I did not hurt or cause harm to my dear friends."

Frank and Penny looked at each other. Neither had a plan for what to ask after their suspect adamantly stated that he'd hurt no one.

"Detectives, why did you come to see me today? Surely you have more to ask me than what you already have? Surely you did not come all this way to ask me the very questions that I've answered time and time again?" Winter was in complete control of the conversation.

Penny stood up and said, "We're actually here to see Dean Travers, Mr. Winter. We only had the one question about the birthdays for you. We neglected to ask you during our previous visit."

Frank played along, impressed by his partner's quick thinking and deception skills. "Yes, Mr. Winter, thank you for your time today. You can rest assured that we'll be back to see you very soon."

"Oh, I would like that very much, Frank!" Winter stood from his chair and smiled. "My hope is that you both have a very good day."

Frank and Penny summoned only modest smiles, desperately attempting to conceal their disdain for the psychopath.

"Good day, Mr. Winter," said Frank.

"I will be back to see you soon," Penny smiled.

"Oh, I know you will, young Penny," smiled Winter.

The statement sent chills up Penny's spine.

As the two detectives turned to leave, Old Man Winter had one more question. "Penny, before leaving today, would you entertain me by engaging in a friendly game of Backgammon?" Winter smiled.

Penny turned and politely declined. "Mr. Winter, as I have told you, I don't know how to play the game."

"Don't you worry, Penny. Before you leave this place, I will teach you. A simple rolling of the dice will get things started." Winter's eerie words frightened both Penny and Frank.

"Yes, I'm sure you will," Penny smiled uncomfortably as she and Frank again turned to leave.

Moments later, standing in the foyer, Frank said, "God! I just want to take him in right now! I'm so pissed!" Frank balled up his fists. "We have nothing on him, though. He's crazy! And everything he says is nuts, but we have nothing on the old man!"

"He's been so careful not to admit committing even a small crime," said Penny. "He's smart."

"Yeah? Well, we're gonna get that old fucker!" said Frank. "Penny, I think that you're right! The answer to this whole charade is in the basement. It's down there."

Penny was excited that Frank finally agreed with her suspicions.

"C'mon! Let's go see Travers," said Frank. "Work your magic and get him to agree to let us down there."

"Okay, I'll do my best!" Penny took a deep breath and said, "Let's go!"

She and Frank passed the lavatories, made a left into the Admin Ward, and then stopped in front of the locked door leading to the basement.

"Okay, Penny, here's where we separate."

"What's the plan, Frank?"

Frank looked left, then right, then back at Penny and whispered, "You go down there and chat him up. Try to find out who owns this place and when you can get access to the basement."

"Got it," Penny whispered. "And what are you going to be doing?"

"I'm gonna try to get upstairs," Frank flashed a mischievous grin.

Penny's eyes went wide. "Holy shit!" she said. "Let me know who you run into up there. I'd be curious to know."

Frank smiled and said, "I got money that I don't see anyone up there. This place is a sham!"

"Good luck, Frankie. Be careful, though."

"Find out who owns this place, would ya?"

"Here goes!" Penny took a deep breath, closed her eyes, and exhaled. When she opened her eyes again, Frank was gone.

She crept slowly down the hall, dreading walking into Travers' office unannounced, not knowing how she'd be received. She passed by Gruber's office first and saw no one in it. She stopped and looked around, and then down at her watch and said to herself, *"Where in the hell is everybody?"* Continuing the next several feet before reaching the massive arched doorway. Penny whispered aloud, "Frank might be right; this place does feel deserted."

Now at the door of Dean Travers, Penny looked up in awe, staring at the marble sculpture of the gold-encrusted Falcon with its talons extended. This time, however, Penny felt like its prey.

Penny knocked on the door in angst but was relieved when she heard Travers' voice.

"Yes, come in," Travers said loudly.

Penny stepped through the door and said, "Hello, Dean."

"Oh, my word!" Travers sprung from his chair. "Well, if it isn't Detective Penelope Bryce!" Travers had a big smile for his new friend. "How long has it been?"

Penny smiled, "I'm sorry to say that it was Halloween."

"No? That long?" Travers looked shocked. "Why in heaven did you wait so long to come back and see me?"

Penny's eyes got big. "We've been so busy. Including a trip to Virginia."

"Well, you're here now," said Travers. "So, is today business or pleasure, my dear Penelope?" Travers looked hopeful that she'd say pleasure.

"I'm afraid it's business again today, Dean."

Travers looked deflated. "Well, one day, very soon, hopefully by Christmas, we can do lunch and just talk about whatever comes to mind."

"That would be nice." Penny smiled graciously.

"Please, Penelope, do have a seat, won't you?"

"Oh!" As Travers took his seat, he snapped his fingers. "That reminds me. Did you find out the name of the retirement home?"

Now seated, Penny was confused. "I'm sorry...." she looked lost at that moment. "Retirement home? I don't understand, Dean."

"Penelope, the home where your boss's grandmother passed away?" Travers was puzzled by Penny's reaction.

"Oh! Yes, of course! My boss's grandmother?" Penny blushed, caught in a lie.

"Well, did you get the name of the home?" asked Travers.

"No, I'm afraid that I didn't. It's been so hectic lately," said Penny. "And apparently, he had his mother cremated."

"Oh, so he's not Catholic, then?"

Penny needed to change the subject as her original lie was spinning into several more.

"Dean, the reason for my visit today is to ask who owns Heavenly Gates?" Penny sat back and pulled her notepad from her pocket. "We need to contact the owners to inquire about non-related items like liability and licensing information."

Travers seemed put off by the question. "Well, I'm not sure that I'm at liberty to discuss any of that as it's a private trust that holds a majority share in the estate. Getting you the answers that you need is not as straightforward as one might think."

"Well, I'm sure you understand that we can find out through legal avenues, but I thought I would just ask you first."

"Well, the company's not public, and while I'm sure you can go through legal channels to find out, I'd prefer that you give me some time to contact them and discuss the matter."

Penny slid to the front of her chair, detecting an opening. "Might you inquire with them my desire to tour the basement?" asked Penny, attempting to look like a child wanting ice cream on a hot summer day.

"Yes, I will bring it up to them, Penelope."

"When might that be, Dean?" Penny was persistent.

"Well, it wouldn't be until the Monday after Christmas, I'm afraid. They are taking an extended holiday, and I, too, am on vacation beginning December 20, not due back until the 30."

Penny tried to look disappointed. "Yes, I recall you telling me that during our last call."

"I can see that you're disappointed, Penelope. I'll tell you what, though," said Travers enthusiastically. "If anything changes, I will call you and let you know. How's that?"

"That would be fine, Dean."

Thirty minutes earlier, Frank exited the Admin hallway and began checking door handles for one that was unlocked. Door after door was locked, except for the lavatory and a library with mounted boar's heads on the wall.

Frank inspected and then exited the library and made his way to what appeared to be an elevator. Examining the buttons and levers, he believed that the elevator would not only lead to the upper floors but perhaps even down to the basement.

Grunting, Frank brute-forced his way through the non-functioning doors and into the modest-sized elevator. After several minutes of pushing buttons and turning handles, he was unable to get it to function. As he tried to exit, he found the doors to be stuck, locking him inside the dimly lit elevator car. Muscling the doors, he could only get them open slightly, just enough to get one arm through. Then, Frank saw what appeared to be an old man pass quickly in front of the elevator doors and was startled, thinking no one was in the hallway. Spooked for a moment, he yelled out, "Mr. Winter? Hello! Is anyone there?"

He tried in vain to pry the doors apart and then heard the sound of footsteps approaching. Listening closely, Frank determined that the person in the hallway was walking away from his location rather than toward it. Sticking his face through the crease, he yelled, "Is anyone there? I'm stuck!" Suddenly, and without warning, the smiling face of an old man appeared through the six-inch gap in the doors, terrifying Frank. As he recoiled in fear, the weight of the elevator car shifted, causing him to fall backward and down onto one knee, tearing his pant leg on a rusted metal panel. Clutching his left leg in pain, Frank pulled his hand away and saw blood. Inspecting his leg further, the dim lighting in the elevator car revealed a deep gash in his knee.

As he climbed back to his feet, he heard a woman's voice outside of the elevator. Frank said, "Hello! Is anyone there?"

"Frankie, is that you?" It was Jeanie's voice.

Recognizing the voice, Frank stood frozen in fear. Unable to breathe with heartbreak bleeding through his eyes, he was paralyzed. Finally finding his breath, he yelled through his tears, "Jeanie! Jeanie!"

"Frank, is that you?" Jeanie's voice tore through Frank's heart. "Frankie, I'm stuck! I can't get out of here. Save me, Frankie!" I want to come home! I miss you and the girls."

Frank could hear Jeanie crying. Hitting his knees, Frank cried with her. "I'm coming, Jeanie! Don't leave! Wait for me!" Frank wailed as he clapped his hands on the elevator doors. "I'll save you, Honey!"

"Frankie, I can't leave! I'm stuck in here! Please help me. I'm bleeding, Frankie!" cried Jeanie.

"Jeanie!" Frank screamed. "I'm coming, Jeanie!" Frank stood up and used all of his remaining strength to pry the door open. "Wait for me, Jeanie! I'm coming!" Frank sobbed as he wrestled with the door.

"I won't leave you, Frankie!" cried Jeanie. "I'll wait for you, Baby."

"Jeanie!" He screamed again. "I'm coming, Honey!" Frank cried out but could no longer hear his wife crying for help.

Using his final bit of strength, Frank finally pried the elevator doors open. Falling to the floor, he laid on his back, crying. "Jeanie!" he sobbed. "Jeanie!" But she was gone.

A short while later, Penny emerged from the front doors of Heavenly Gates, looking for her partner. Staring down the steep hill looking over Bedford Street, Penny saw the Buick spitting its exhaust into the air. The headlights were on, and the wiper blades were shooing away snowflakes as if they were insects. As she made her way down the hill, through the front gates, and onto the street, she'd realized that it was dark out and wondered how that could be. She and Frank had only been there for an hour, and it was noon when they'd arrived.

Now at street level, she could make out a silhouette in the driver's seat. Penny could see the burning coal at the end of a cigarette grow brighter as it pulled in the oxygen around it, followed by a large, exhaled cloud that seemed to fill the car's cabin. This confused Penny because Frank had quit smoking after Jeanie's death. Opening the door, allowing the cigarette exhaust to clear, Penny saw Old Man Winter sitting behind the wheel and, with Frank's voice, said, "C'mon Jeanie, get in! It's cold outside." Penny's breath was taken from her as she stood there, frozen by her fear and the frigid mid-December air that consumed North Philly on that day.

Old Man Winter smiled, tapping the passenger seat; he said, "Hurry up! Get in!" again in Frank's voice.

Penny finally caught her breath, closed her eyes, and screamed.

Overcoming her fear and terrified of what she might see, Penny opened her eyes and saw her reflection in the bathroom mirror in the lavatory outside of the Admin Ward. She turned around in terror, not understanding what'd just happened, then fell to the floor, panting and sobbing.

Several minutes later, Penny composed herself and walked out of the lavatory. Exiting the long hallway and into the foyer, she could see Frank down the hall, leaning against the wall, his face ravaged by loss. As she approached him, she could see his ripped pant leg and bloody knee.

"Frankie, are you okay?!"

"Yeah, Jeanie, I'm fine. I cut my knee inside the elevator," he said. "I might need a little help getting down the hill."

Penny took a deep breath, not daring to correct her partner. Instead, saying nothing, she put his arm over her shoulder and helped him through the door and down the steps.

As the two exited FalconClaw, the sun had evaporated into the grey clouds, and snow was just beginning to fall.

The two didn't speak on the car ride home that day, and they would never speak of what they'd experienced inside the relic that stood, looking down over Bedford Street, in judgment.

Chapter 28 – Christmas Eve, 1974

It was Christmas Eve, and Penny and Frank ended their day at the Arlington Diner, their favorite place to decompress, before heading home after a long day of work. They first came to the diner the day before Penny met Garrison Winter.

It hadn't even been two months since then, but for Frank and Penny, a lot had happened. Frank was learning to be a single dad, and Penny was still learning to be a detective. But mainly, the two had connected nine cold cases spanning more than five decades, and they both felt that they were on the precipice of solving the case of who or what Garrison O'Donnell was.

Penny and Frank each ordered a coffee, then pulled out their files to chat about the case before it would resume on Monday. It was only Tuesday, but Christmas was the next day, and McClain gave the two of them off the rest of the week to celebrate the holiday. A reward for the job they'd done on the Winter case, though he'd never admit how proud he was of the two or how happy he was with Penny's performance. The Chief still didn't like having a woman in his midst, but quietly he was happy that Penny was one of the boys in the Detective Room at the 39th District. Like Frank, he was learning to trust her instincts more and more.

"Okay, so where are we?" Penny said to Frank as she flipped through her case notes.

"I'm still pissed about the tape!" said Frank. "Cantrell said their guys are still analyzing it."

"When will they know something?"

Frank shrugged, "Not until after the New Year, unfortunately. Cantrell said nearly the whole department is off until after the first."

"What do you think happened to that tape, Frank?" asked Penny. "I still don't like the way Winter mentioned it back on the 9th. What was it that he called it?"

"The word he used was 'fiasco,'" said Frank. "It did feel like he knew something, right?"

"Oh, yeah!" Penny's eyes went wide. "That was a strange day, wasn't it?"

Frank didn't want to relive that day or his experience inside the elevator, so he changed the subject instead. "You heard McClain. He thinks it was the way the microphone was positioned," said Frank. "I could've sworn I pointed it towards Winter, but because it only picked up our voices, McClain might have a point."

"I saw that microphone pointing directly at Winter, Frank. It wasn't the microphone!" Penny was adamant.

After a moment of silence, Frank asked, "What else do we know?"

"We know the names, the cities, and the dates," said Penny. "We know that our prime suspect has a god complex and murdered these people on their birthday. But what we don't know is when another old man or woman is going to disappear." Penny stirred her coffee and added, "Or, his real name."

"There's no way his real name is O'Donnell," Frank agreed. "It's just another alias. G.O.D. my ass!"

"It's the basement, Frank," said Penny. "That basement holds the key to the identity of the person who killed my great-grandfather. If we can find out the true identity of Garrison O'Donnell, then we'll discover the truth about everything."

"I'm with you, Penny. I agree," Frank nodded. "So, Travers is back on Monday?"

"Yep." Penny kept stirring her coffee.

"What in the hell are you stirring?" Frank busted Penny's chops. "That's a black coffee."

"Just thinking, that's all." Penny's thoughts were scattered.

"Are you sure you can convince him to let us down there this time?"

"Us?" Penny scoffed. "You mean me?! He's not letting you down there, Frank. You stiffed his personal assistant," Penny winked and smiled. "If she doesn't like you, then HE doesn't like you."

"You see the way she looks at me every time we go there?" Frank exhaled fully while shaking his head.

"She's got it bad for you, Frankie Boy!" Penny chuckled. "What did you do to that poor woman?"

"We just kissed, that's it! I swear, Penny!"

"I don't know, Frank," Penny shook her head with skepticism.

"Penny," Frank raised his right hand. "On a stack of bibles!"

"What can you say? You're like *Luden's Wild Cherry Cough Drops*. You can't eat just one."

"That's a pretty weird thing to say." Frank rolled his eyes. "I don't even know what that means."

"It's like you got *Luden's* written across your neck or something," Penny laughed.

"Alright! Alright! That's enough!" Frank blushed.

"You should see your face right now, Frankie! You look like a giant cherry cough drop!" Penny had a good time at Frank's expense.

"So, Monday then? What time is Travers expecting your call?"

"Don't know. I'm just gonna call him in the morning and roll the dice. I just hope he agrees to let me down there. He said he'd ask the owners."

"Yeah," Frank exhaled suspiciously. "I can't wait to find out who owns that place. I got ten bucks it's still owned by the federal government."

"I'm thinking that too." Penny arched a brow. "More and more every time we go there," she paused. "Every time we go, it just gets weirder and weirder."

Frank again stayed away from Penny's comment. He was trying hard to forget what he'd experienced back on the 9th.

"So, you think the employment records from sixty-some years ago are still down there after all this time?"

"That and a lot more, I bet." Penny was convinced.

"Be careful you don't step on a landmine down there!" Frank chuckled. "You remember what Travers told you, don't you? They were making H- Bombs down there."

"It was bullets, not bombs, you dumbass!" laughed Penny as she threw a balled-up sugar wrapper into Frank's coffee.

"What in the hell's wrong with you? You're always throwing shit at me when we sit down at a table," said Frank, fishing the wrapper out of his coffee with a spoon. "That's like your thing, now."

The laughing subsided, and the two looked over each other's notes, thinking that a different set of eyes might spot something overlooked by the other.

Penny could hardly believe how many times the number eight appeared in the pages of Frank's notes. Every page had it written out in word form or the actual number. She knew he was fixated on the number but thought that his notes revealed more of an obsession. She was getting more and more worried about her partner, a man that she'd gotten very close to and cared for very much.

"Penny, what's your obsession with the number ten? I mean, Jesus, you've got the number ten penciled in on every page. You're a lunatic, and I'm starting to worry about you." Frank grinned at his partner.

"Me?! You're the crazy son of a bitch with all of your eights!" Penny shot another balled-up napkin at Frank's coffee but missed.

"Frank, I'm telling you right now," Penny defended herself. "there will be a tenth victim! One more completes the circle of ten." Penny was sure of it.

"Whatever that means?" Frank shrugged. "Yeah, well, while I believe you're great-grandfather was the first victim," he paused, "for all we know, he could've been the fifteenth or the fiftieth. That would shoot your theory right out the window."

"Yeah, well, looking at your math here, the 888 thing doesn't add up either," Penny quipped. "You can't get to 888 when adding the victim's ages together. It's nothing but old people coming up missing unless the old man changes his M.O. The first nine add up to 848. Looks like your theory went right out the window along with mine, Frankie Boy."

"Palindrome, Penny! Remember that! That's what you'll see when the shit hits the fan," said Frank. "Be prepared to ask for forgiveness, Little Penny Bryce."

"Frank, let me ask you something," Penny was serious now.

"Go ahead," Frank sipped his coffee.

"You said Jeanie passed in August, right?" Penny paused, looking down into her coffee cup.

"Yeah?" Frank could see that his partner was apprehensive with her question. "Go ahead, Penny."

"What day was it again?"

"It was a Monday. Why?" Frank didn't know why Penny was asking.

"No, I mean the date. What was the date that she died?"

"The twenty-sixth." Frank was puzzled. "What are you getting at?" He almost looked irked.

"Think for a second, Frank," said Penny, walking on eggshells. "The month? The numbers in the actual date. What do you see?"

"August is the eighth month, and two plus six equals eight." Frank shook his head. "No, that can't be! That can't be why I'm seeing eights! It can't be!"

Frank's reaction was visceral as his face went white. Penny could see the wheels spinning in Frank's head. At that moment, she wanted to be somewhere else. But she knew she had to bring it up as her partner seemed to be going down a path that was unhealthy for him and everyone around him.

Frank got up without words and stormed off into the men's restroom. There, he paced frantically back and forth, finally stopping and looking in the mirror. Clutching the sides of the filthy sink with both hands, he stared into his own eyes and said, "It can't be!"

Frank desperately wanted the eights to mean something to the case, and the evil he believed lived in FalconClaw. The number eight had to be associated with Old Man Winter. If it didn't, it meant that he was going mad. If he saw the eights because of Jeanie's death and mental anguish, he knew he was going crazy. He stared in that mirror, and he cried. Frank cried for his Jeanie, and he cried for his sanity.

Minutes later, Frank emerged from the restroom and rejoined Penny, his eyes consumed by his pain.

Penny, who'd been staring out the window, turned and said, "Hey, Frankie, sorry about that, I had no right to...."

Frank cut Penny off. "It's okay, Penny. Maybe I'm crazy. Maybe I'm not, but...."

"Frank, no. I'm not saying that...."

"I got it, Penny. Don't worry about it." Frank wanted the subject over with.

After a few uncomfortable minutes of silence, Penny said, "Well, we can at least agree that Winter hates God and that he's injecting religion into these disappearances."

"I agree, but what if he's just a psychopath, and none of it's meant to be tied together? What if it's all random?" asked Frank. "Maybe it's just some bat shit crazy family that likes killing old people?"

"Or, putting them out of their misery, like Kessler said." Penny cocked a brow.

A minute later, she conceded, "But then again, there's no way in hell that this is random when you factor in the birthday thing."

"I see what you did there with the little 'hell' comment," smiled Frank. "That was good. And yeah, you've got a point with the birthdays. There's definitely purpose there." Frank was back in detective mode.

At that moment, their waitress, Cindy, walked over and said, "Hey guys, someone's on the payphone upfront asking for a 'Detective

Penelope Bryce.' You told me your name was Penny once, so I figured that was you."

"Yeah, that's me." Penny had a look of concern on her face. She looked at Frank and sat up straight in her seat.

"Yeah, it's some guy. He sounds smart. He was talking really formal-like."

Penny looked at Frank and said, "Well, that can't be Joe." She wondered who it could be.

"You want me to tell him something?" asked Cindy.

"Just go answer it!" Frank motioned with his head. "Go!"

Penny looked strangely nervous. "Did he give a name?"

"Um, I thought he said something like Tavares? Something like that," Cindy shrugged.

"What?!" Penny looked at Frank. "Why in the world would Dean Travers be calling me here?"

"Well, go talk to him and find out," said Frank.

Penny pulled her napkin from her lap and threw it up on the table. "I'll be right back!" She quickly slid out of the booth as the waitress stepped aside.

Several minutes later, Penny returned to the booth and looked thunderstruck.

"So, was it him?" Frank was anxious to know. "What did he want?"

"Holy shit!" Penny was shocked, plopping down into her side of the booth. Shaking her head, she said, "Apparently, he came back early from his trip and wanted to tell me that I could come to look for the files whenever I wanted. He said the owners approved my access to the basement because I was a descendant of the person who built the place." Penny had a blank look on her face. "He thought I'd be happy with the news, and he didn't want to wait until after the holiday to tell me."

"So, what're you going to do?" asked Frank. "We're off until Monday."

"I'm not waiting!" Penny shook her head. "Frank, are you crazy? This could break the case wide open!"

"So, Thursday morning, then?" asked Frank. "I'll go with you!"

Frank quickly regretted volunteering to accompany Penny back to FalconClaw. He knew that he'd have to walk by the elevator to get to the basement door in the Admin hallway. The thought of it terrified him.

Frank saw a peculiar look in Penny's eyes. He was trying to read her mind before he'd realized what she was thinking. "Penny! No! You can't go tonight. It's Christmas Eve, for God's sake. Are you crazy?"

"Frank, I'll only be there for an hour or so. If I can't find the records, I'll head home, and we can look again on Thursday."

"Wait!" Frank shook his head in disbelief. "How in the hell could Travers possibly have known that we were here?"

"He said he tried me at the office and at home and that he'd remembered I once mentioned this place to him." Penny thought it was plausible.

"Well, the office is closed. Did you call Joe and ask if Travers called there?"

"I tried, but all the lines are busy. It's Christmas Eve, after all," rationalized Penny. "Everybody's on the phone calling family and making plans. I'll call him when I get to Heavenly Gates."

"Something's not right, Penny. This is all too strange." Frank wore a look that was intended to convey that his gut was talking to him. "I'm going with you, then," Frank said reluctantly.

"Frank, this is the girl's first Christmas without their mother," said Penny. "You need to be home with them. Plus, Jeanie's sister needs to get home to her kids, too."

"I don't know, Penny. I mean, it's Christmas Eve. What in the hell is Travers doing there, anyway?"

Penny had one more thing to reveal from her conversation with Travers. "Frankie, get this. He said there's a big shindig going on there tonight for Christmas Eve. He said the place is packed with residents and their family members."

Frank sat up in his chair and said, "Bullshit! I ain't buying that!"

"That's one of the reasons I want to go tonight. I want to see if for myself," said Penny, adding, "There'll be plenty of people there if he's telling the truth about the party. Plenty of staff, too," reasoned Penny aloud. "It's not like I'll be alone in the place with just Travers."

"You will be when you're in that basement with him!" Frank cautioned his partner. "Either way, you know very well there's no party going on in that place tonight, or any other night, for that matter." Frank paused. "I don't think it's a good idea, Penny."

"How about this," said Penny. "If the place is dark and it looks like he's lying about the party, then I'll just say hello to him, and you can drive me home?"

Frank thought about it for a moment. "Maybe," he said.

"I trust Travers, Frank," Penny appealed to her partner. "He's a good man," she said, with a look that told Frank she'd be okay. "Frank, remember, you're supposed to start trusting my instincts more."

"Fine! But if that place looks dark and empty, I'm driving you home immediately," insisted Frank. "I won't let you out of the car. Got it?"

"Well, I hope you wouldn't just leave me standing there on Bedford Street. What am I, a hooker or something?" Penny looked outside. "Plus, it's starting to snow, you know."

Penny smiled at her partner. "Travers said the front gate would be open due to the number of visitors coming and going."

Frank sat and thought to himself that there was no way a party was going on at Heavenly Gates. He shook his head in doubt as he stared at the falling snow through the diner's window.

Thirty minutes later, the Buick turned left on Bedford Street and rolled up to Heavenly Gates. Like Dean Travers had promised, the front gate was left wide open, and there appeared to be activity at the top of the hill with several cars parked near the front entrance. Frank was shocked.

"Travers wasn't lying. The place looks pretty busy," Frank shook his head as he leaned forward to get a better look up the hill. "Well, I'll be damned." He was starting to doubt whether they were chasing a phantom or if the old man really was guilty.

"Every floor is lit up. Looks like we were wrong all along, Partner," said Penny.

"My instincts are all jacked up, then." Frank shook his head, still surprised that there was activity at Heavenly Gates when there appeared to be little to none on each of their previous visits.

Staring up at the mansion on the hill, Frank said, "Hmm, that's weird!" His eyes focused on the mansion's tower.

"What is?" asked Penny, now looking in the same direction as Frank.

"It looks like someone's standing up there in the tower," said Frank, pointing.

"Oh, yeah, that is weird. Whoever that is looks kind of creepy."

"Kind of creepy?" Frank thought Penny's characterization was an understatement.

Frank and Penny could see the defined silhouette standing motionless. Though the snow began falling harder, they could clearly see that it was a man.

Frank muttered under his breath, "Is that Winter?"

"What'd you say?" asked Penny.

"Nothing," said Frank, just staring at the tower, squinting his eyes.

Sitting back now, Penny said, "It looks like a white Christmas for the kids, huh?"

Frank was lost in thought, just staring at the shadowy figure who appeared to be looking down over their arrival.

"What? Yeah. That's awesome!" Frank snapped out of his trance. "The girls are gonna love it!" Now admiring the snowfall himself,

Frank added, "Look at the size of those snowflakes! It reminds me of our drive back home from Lewistown."

Penny could see that her partner was in better spirits seeing the snowfall. She knew that a white Christmas would be a welcome distraction for him and the girls.

Seconds later, the Buick came to a stop in front of the mansion. Seconds after that, the door opened. Travers stepped just out of the door and waved to both Frank and Penny.

"You sure about this, Penny?" Frank looked concerned. "We can always come back during the daytime on Thursday."

"I'm sure, Frankie." Penny touched his hand.

"You want me to hang around out here to give you a lift home?"

"No," said Penny. "Get home to your girls. And besides, Travers said he would arrange a ride for me. If not, I'll just call a cab."

Frank grabbed Penny's arm as she opened the passenger door and said, "Penny, listen," he paused, "I'm thankful for you this year. I don't have my Jeanie, but at least I got my second best girl." Frank's smile was warm. He hoped Penny knew how much she'd meant to him.

"Thanks, Frankie! You're the best partner a girl could have," Penny said before stepping out of the car.

As the passenger door opened, Frank and Penny heard the unmistakable sound of muffled music and people laughing coming from inside of FalconClaw. Frank looked further down the front of the house and observed shadowy light coming from the solarium, illuminating the snow that now blanketed the ground.

Before shutting the door, Penny stuck her head back in and said, "This is going to be a big night, Frankie Boy. I can feel it in my bones."

"Roger that, Penny," Frank smiled. "Call me if you need a lift home. Merry Christmas, Partner!"

"You too, Frank! Drive safe!" Penny looked to the sky, squinting her eyes, and said, "Boy, it's really coming down out here!"

"Be careful down there!" yelled Frank, but Penny couldn't hear him over the sound of the slamming door and the party going on inside.

Frank watched as Penny ran up the stairs to meet Travers. Slipping on the stairs but avoiding a fall, Penny turned embarrassingly and looked in Frank's direction, giving him a thumbs-up and a smile. She waved goodbye just as Travers welcomed her into Heavenly Gates. Before closing the door, Dean Travers stepped back outside and gave Frank a wave and a smile.

Frank waved back at him and mumbled under his breath, "You better make sure nothing happens to her, Creep!"

Frank's gut was talking to him again, but he gave Penny's instincts the benefit of the doubt.

As Frank navigated the parked cars in front of the mansion, he glanced over at the solarium windows and saw what appeared to be party-goers watching him through the window, with one raising their glass in his direction. Frank suddenly felt a cold chill run through his body.

Frank exited the front gates at the bottom of the hill and took a left onto Bedford Street. He turned on the radio to listen to some music that would calm him down on the ride home. FM 98.7 was on a commercial break, and Frank heard the DJ commenting on the sudden snowstorm and the fact that there was no snow in the forecast.

A minute later, the Eagles came on. Frank turned up the volume and cranked up the heat, then leaned back heavily into his seat. Don Henley started singing, 'Raven hair and ruby lips....' Frank sang along as the snow fell even harder.

Chapter 29 – The Basement

Now inside the mansion, Penny shook off the snow from her favorite gray jacket and laid it across her arm. "Director Travers, thank you so much for allowing me to come by tonight," said Penny with a look of gratitude. "I promise not to keep you long."

"Not to worry, Penelope. I have as long as you need. And as promised, I'll make sure you get home afterward. Here, let me hang your jacket for you."

Dean Travers opened the coatroom door to the left of the main entrance and stepped in to hang Penny's coat. When he did, Penny leaned slightly forward to glance into the tiny room. When she did, she noticed that the room seemed oddly empty despite the number of visitors to the home that night.

Travers turned, and Penny recoiled and said, "Wow, it sounds like they're really whooping it up in there!" Penny wore a look of surprise. "I've never seen it this busy around here."

Penny looked around and spotted activity at the end of the hall leading away from the foyer. She thought she saw people walking into the massive dining room from the long hallway that led down to the Admin Ward.

"Well, Penny, you've never been here before on a holiday. Most of our residents cannot leave for more than a day or so, so their families usually come here to visit for special occasions, and tonight," Travers paused, "is the most special occasion of all." Travers smiled, motioning for Penny to follow him. "Follow me, my dear Penelope."

Penny thought Travers seemed a little off tonight. She began to feel slightly uncomfortable in his presence but chalked it up to never being around him at night. She'd noticed that he went back and forth from calling her Penelope and Penny.

"Dean, are you sure I'm not taking you away from your guests?" Penny suddenly felt guilty for the imposition she must have been on her friend.

"Not at all, Penny. Tonight is your night. It's all about you," he turned and smiled. "You are my only guest tonight. I'm just so happy that you're here," said Travers, still smiling.

Penny wasn't quite sure what to make of his comment but didn't question it. She felt excited that she'd finally get the chance to see the basement and hopefully get the answer to the question that had plagued her and Frank for months. Who was Old Man Winter?

"Please excuse all of the noise, Penelope," Travers spoke loudly as the two approached the dining room where the festivities were being held.

Following just behind Travers, Penny said, "Yes, it does sound like quite a party." Getting closer to the end of the hall, she could hear both men and women laughing and celebrating the occasion.

Now at the end of the hall, and before taking a right turn into the long hallway that led down to the Admin Ward, Penny peeked to her left to get a glimpse into the grand dining room and the party that was happening there.

Looking in, she saw dozens of people dressed up for the holiday, all laughing and carrying on. In the crowd, she spotted Garrison Winter standing in the middle of the room with nine other people. From what she could see, he appeared to be the center of their attention. Before she turned the corner, Garrison Winter abruptly turned his head in her direction, somehow spotting her through the large crowd. Tilting his head, he held up his glass and saluted her with a smile. When he did, the others in the circle, six men and three women, all turned to look at Penny and raised their glasses in recognition of her. The look on his face suddenly made Penny feel apprehensive about her visit. And without getting a good look at the others, she felt as if she knew them.

Without breaking stride, she followed closely behind Travers as they passed the bathroom and library. Looking at the now-familiar décor surrounding her, Penny felt calm again. She had now been to Heavenly Gates several times and was starting to feel like she belonged there.

As the noise became more and more subdued, the further away they got from the dining area, Travers said, "I just need to grab some flashlights, and then we can make our way down to the basement."

"Flashlights? You mean there's no working lights down there?" Penny wore both a look of surprise and concern.

"Oh, no," Travers said reassuringly. "The power is working just fine in the basement. At least it was the last time I was down there. It's been some time, you know. Surely some lightbulbs will have burned out after all of these years. I'll grab two, just in case."

Penny followed Travers to a storage closet nestled between two offices in the Admin Ward. The same hall as Travers' and Gruber's offices were located. As she and Travers passed the locked door to their immediate right, with a sign denoting *Authorized Personnel Only*, she studied it closely and took a deep breath as if fearing what was behind it.

The hallway looked much darker in the evening than it had during the day, and Penny felt a little spooked. She could barely hear the party going on and was beginning to feel alone in the mansion even though she stood next to a man she'd trusted.

"The Admin Ward is a lot darker in the evening than it is during the day," Penny wore a nervous smile. She reasoned that the old mansion wasn't equipped with good lighting amenities due to its age.

"Yes, without the sun from the western sky coming through that door," Travers pointed to the back door at the end of the Admin hallway, some fifteen feet past his office door, "the place is quite dreary, I'm afraid."

Travers stopped at the supply room door, situated on the opposite side of the hallway as he and Gruber's offices. "Ah, here we are," he said. Reaching into his pocket, he removed a small ring of keys. Keys that Penny had heard rattling around in Travers' pocket as they navigated the dimly lit halls en route to the Admin Ward.

Travers rummaged through the closet and found what he was looking for, two silver flashlights, each roughly one foot in length.

"Here you are, Penelope." Travers handed her a flashlight. "One for you and one for me." Travers looked down to inspect the flashlight in his hand, pointing it upward; he turned it on and momentarily blinded himself. "Oh! Goodness!" He quickly pointed the flashlight to the ground and rubbed his eyes with his left hand. "That was silly of me. Please do forgive me, Penelope."

Penny looked on and suddenly found Travers to be somewhat clumsy and inept. Now examining her flashlight, she found the button on the side, turned it on to test it, and then turned it back off again. She'd wait until it was necessary to turn it on again, not wanting to drain its batteries.

Travers also turned his off, smiled at Penny, and said, "Hopefully, we won't need these silly things down there." He then turned toward the locked door at the beginning of the hall and said, "Shall we?"

He led his guest to the door and, using the same keyring, tried a key in the lock that didn't seem to work. After several more keys and failed attempts, he was finally successful. Travers' struggles indicated to Penny that he'd rarely accessed the door, easing her consternation about entering the basement and what the two might find there.

As the door opened, the hinge let out an eerie squeal, causing Penny's heart to race, but only until Travers' hand found the old light switch to the left of the door frame and clicked it on. The click was loud, and as Penny followed Travers down the stairs, she studied the porcelain switch, noticing how old it looked, and her confidence waned even further. She feared the lights in the basement would be unreliable and possibly not remain on the entire time she was down there.

Stepping down onto the first stair, Penny was immediately hit by the musty smell of mold and mildew and an odor that she assumed must've been the gun powder that Travers had referred to during her tour of the mansion. To ease her anxiety, she thought of Frank and his earlier comment about H-Bombs. At that moment, she wished that her friend and partner were there with her.

As she navigated the poorly lit, creaky stairs, following closely behind Travers, she noticed the air had become increasingly humid and thick, more and more with each step. When the two reached the bottom of the stairs, she'd heard the basement door slam shut at the top of the stairs behind her. She was startled by the sound and suddenly felt like it was only her and Travers alone in the mansion. The comforting sound of the holiday party on the main floor was now gone, and along with it, her comfort level of being alone with a man she hoped could be trusted. She turned on her flashlight, hoping to ease her nerves. Unfortunately for Penny, it didn't help.

Turning on his flashlight, Travers turned to Penny and instructed her to stay put as he would have to walk down a hallway adjacent to the stairs in order to find the breaker box. Penny listened closely and was sure she could hear the unsettling sound of scurrying mice, rats, and other vermin in the distance, which caused the hair on the back of her neck to stand up.

"Just a moment, Penelope, the breaker is just over here." The sound of Travers' voice got harder to hear the further he walked away from Penny.

A moment later, Penny heard the loud crank of a breaker box switch being forced up into the 'On' position. Then, a second later, the basement seemed to be only partially illuminated by a strange orange glow. She observed white two-inch tiles lining the floor and covering the first four feet up the walls on both sides. To Penny, the basement looked more like a hospital ward. Caged light fixtures hung from the ceiling while patient gurneys, with dangling leather straps, littered the halls as far down as she could see. The tiles were filthy and appeared to have rat droppings all over them. Her eyes squinted as her nose filled with the smell of ammonia. Penny likened the smell to a forgotten litter box in a home with far too many cats.

Travers re-emerged from the electrical closet some fifteen feet away and said, "Now, that's better. We likely won't need these things anymore," he said while turning his flashlight off.

Penny followed suit, turning hers off to save the batteries, and said, "Man, this is one creepy place." She'd reconsidered her earlier notion that her grandfather and his siblings ran around in the basement as small children. It was scary, she thought, even for an adult. She could only imagine how frightening it would be for a small child.

"Penny, I do believe the archives room is this way." Travers led his guest, who followed behind but not too closely.

As they passed rooms with signage stating *Medical Personnel Only*, Penny could almost hear the screams of patients as doctors and nurses wrestled them into comatose states, plunging needles dripping with insulin into their arms and covering their airways with chloroform masks. She envisioned the mentally ill struggling for their freedom while desperately grasping at their sanity as it was torn from their desperate grasps.

"Boy, it's really quiet down here," Penny looked nervously at her surroundings. "I would think we could still hear the party going on upstairs."

"Yes, FalconClaw is a solid structure," said Travers proudly. "Sadly, they don't make them like this anymore."

Penny Bryce felt safe with a gun strapped to her chest during the day and above ground, but not in FalconClaw's basement at night. She didn't feel like a gun would help her fight off the tortured souls that lived there if they'd come calling for her. "Creepy as hell, down here," she mumbled, but Travers couldn't hear Penny's trepidation as he walked some ten feet ahead of her.

Penny's fear grew with each step. She kept looking back at the stairwell and the growing distance between her and her only chance of escape, should she need to flee. Then, she saw what appeared to be old elevator doors to her right and immediately found her bearings. She'd remembered seeing the elevator entrance on the first and second floors of the upper levels and remembered precisely where they were with regards to the mansion's floorplan.

"Is that the elevator, Director Travers?"

"That would be the one," he turned and smiled. "The only one in the entire home," said Travers. "It runs directly up through the middle of the house. An equal distance from the North and South sides of the home," he explained.

"Yes, I remember seeing it in the main halls on the first and second floors." Penny breathed a little easier, seeing a second possible exit from what felt to her like a mausoleum.

The two walked a little further when Travers yelled out, "Ah, here we are, the Archives Room. No telling how much history lives in this room and its contents." Travers took a left and walked through a tiny door that was unlocked.

Penny walked into a cavernous room that seemed to be filled with hundreds of boxes, crates, and what appeared to be several old classroom-style tablet-arm desks, the kind with the table bolted to the chair. The smell of old mildewed paper began to intoxicate her senses. Shaking her head and shielding her nose with her forearm, Penny said, "Oh my, goodness!" Penny covered her nose and mouth. "The smell in here is awful!"

Travers appeared to be unaffected by the noxious odor. "Yes, the smell is quite strong, isn't it?" said Travers. "Like rotten eggs."

Though the room was likely only half full, it would take a small army of people many days to sift through every box. Penny knew immediately that she'd need Frank's help on Thursday and likely Friday if only Travers would grant him access.

"There are far more boxes down here than I had anticipated," she said.

"Yes, but you're in luck, my dear," Travers smiled. "The oldest boxes appear to be positioned closest to the front of the room. The more and more items they stored down here, the deeper they'd have to go."

Travers pointed his flashlight toward the back of the room, which was dark and without functioning lights. When he did, several rats, with glowing red eyes, ran in front of the flashlight's beam, startling Penny, who audibly gasped.

"Fear not, my dear Penelope. We're all God's creatures sharing one Earth. No need to be frightened by what lurks in the darkness." Travers tried to reassure his guest. "Well, I'll leave you to it then."

"Wait. What?" Penny was taken aback. "You're leaving me here, alone?"

"Oh, heaven's no. I'm just going back down the hall to fiddle with the elevator. It's been a few years since we last operated it," said

Travers. "There's no need to worry. I promise to remain close at all times."

"Please do," said Penny as her eyes searched the dark corners of the basement.

"Penelope," said Travers looking her straight in the eye, "I have a feeling that you're going to find precisely what you're looking for here in this room."

With his eyes and flashlight beam, Travers directed Penny to a stack of boxes just feet away from where the two were standing. Each was labeled with the year 1920 through 1929.

"It looks like they stacked them by decade. Please let me know when you're all finished up in here, would you?" Travers smiled and walked away.

Penny got nervous and excited all at once. Her fear and apprehension regarding the basement, along with the odor, all but evaporated when she saw the stack labeled with each year of the 1920s.

She almost immediately found a box marked 1920. Before lifting it to prop up on a nearby stack of boxes, she blew off the dust and brushed away the cobwebs. When lifting the box, her fingers became entangled in the thick webs running down the side of it. The texture of the cobwebs made her pull away instantly, causing the box to fall to the floor spilling its contents. Penny immediately looked up and listened for Travers, hoping that he didn't hear.

"Everything okay in there, Penny?" a voice echoed from down the hall.

His words seemed muffled to Penny, though, as if the cold, dank, and humid air was just thick enough to deaden the sound of his voice. She immediately thought of the mentally ill who were likely tortured in the basement, and the thought of no one hearing their screams terrified her.

"I'm fine, Dean," Penny yelled. "I just tripped over a box, that's all!"

"Do be careful and call me if you need me," The Director yelled out to his guest.

Penny reached for the contents and found hand-written letters and forms, along with old black and white photos of staff working in and outside the home. The photos included many black men and white and black women who seemed to be dressed in staff uniforms. The women wore long gray dresses and white aprons, while the men wore long-sleeve white shirts buttoned to the top and what looked to be gray wool pants.

As Penny continued picking up the contents, she came across a series of photographs that appeared to be of the home's residents. She'd determined this by how they were dressed. The old men wore three-piece suits while the gray-haired women were almost all wearing what appeared to Penny as ball gowns, with many wearing bonnets and ribbons in their hair.

As Penny grabbed another stack of photos, she saw an old man that looked like her great-grandfather, Samuel Crenshaw. She shined her flashlight on the image and though grainy and in bad condition, thought that she might have stumbled across the first image of her distant relative that wasn't an oil painting. While she couldn't be sure, she set the photograph aside and looked for more.

In the next stack, she saw more images that appeared to be her great-grandfather. In the photos, he seemed to be surrounded by other residents who looked like they enjoyed his company. They seemed to flock around him as if he owned the place, concluded Penny, laughing out loud with her pun.

Then Penny noticed a man she thought closely resembled Samuel Crenshaw, sitting at a backgammon table. He appeared to be playing with another man whose face was obscured by the side of the tall chair he was sitting in, but his shirt sleeve was visible and appeared to be flannel and dark in color. Penny became unsettled when looking more closely at the shirt sleeve as it looked oddly familiar to her. She wondered if that was the man who was last seen with her great-grandfather. She quickly shuffled through the series of photos that all appeared to be taken on the same day. She'd surmised, as all of the people in the pictures were wearing the same clothes in each photograph.

Penny picked up another photo that revealed the man playing backgammon with her great-grandfather. As her eyes focused in on the man, terror took over her expression and stole her breath. Tears began to well in her eyes as she whispered, "No, no, no," while shaking her head frantically from side to side, covering her mouth with her left hand. Her trembling right hand, unable to grip the picture any longer, dropped it as she stumbled backward as if trying to escape the man shown in the photo. Paralyzed by fear, Penny found herself on the ground, hyperventilating. Recoiling in horror, she tried to yell for Dean Travers but found that she couldn't speak, almost unable to breathe.

Screaming on the inside, with tears streaming from her eyes, Penny was unable to make a sound. She began stomping her feet and thrashing about, banging on the stacked boxes positioned to both her left and right, hoping to make enough noise for Travers to hear. When her strangled moans and flailing limbs failed to get his attention, she began banging her flashlight on the ground.

Crying and overcome by fear, the image of the man seemed to be burned on the inside of Penny's eyelids like a flashbulb burns a negative onto film. The gray-haired man that Penny saw in the picture with her great-grandfather was the man she'd first met just two months prior. Old Man Winter, Garrison O'Donnell. And he was wearing the same gray flannel shirt that he'd worn each time she'd visited him at Heavenly Gates.

Chapter 30 – A Friendly Game of Backgammon

Frank finally arrived home. It had taken him ninety minutes to drive the eight miles that he lived from Heavenly Gates. The weather had gotten so bad that traffic signals were out, and the streets were nearly all snow and iced over. Even the plows were having trouble navigating the roads, with fender-benders blocking nearly every intersection. Frank couldn't comprehend how much snow had fallen in such a short time.

After walking through his front door, he immediately picked up the phone and dialed Penny's house, worried that she might get snowed in at Heavenly Gates overnight.

"Joe, it's Frank. Have you heard from Penny?"

"No, she hasn't called, and we're all pretty worried about her, what with the weather and all. She said she was with you, Frank."

"Yeah, she was, but I dropped her off at Heavenly Gates more than an hour ago...."

Joe interrupted. "What in the hell is she doing there on Christmas Eve? For Christ's sake!"

"Did she not call you when she arrived there? She told me that she would."

"The phone hasn't rung. You're the first person to call tonight. Frank, what in the hell's going on?"

"Joe, did you say no one's called there?"

"Not since earlier when Penny called to say you two were grabbing a coffee." The sound of concern was growing in Joe's voice.

"So, you didn't hear from Dean Travers today?" Frank was bewildered.

"Travers? Why would he be calling me? Frank, where in the hell is Penny? We have a birthday cake here for her and dinner's on the table."

"Birthday cake? Whatta you mean?"

"Penny's birthday is on Christmas day. We always celebrate it on Christmas Eve so that it doesn't take away from the kids' Christmas," said Joe.

"Joe, listen to me. I need you to tell me how old Penny is going to be tomorrow?" Frank held his breath and closed his eyes. He knew the answer but desperately hoped he was wrong.

"She turns forty tonight at midnight. Frank, what's going on?!" Joe sounded desperate.

Frank dropped the phone in horror and raced out the front door into the driving snow to get his notepad from the car.

Joe's voice could be heard blaring through the receiver, which was now laying on the living room floor. "Hello! Hello! Frank, you there?!"

Snow blanketed the Buick, and several inches were already on the ground. Frank, now sitting behind the wheel, frantically thumbed through his notes, trying to catch his breath. Turning the page that listed the ages of all of the victims, he re-calculated the sum total of all of them. Frank's face turned as white as the falling snow when he'd realized that his math was correct. Turning the page, he saw the number 848 taking up the entire page and circled a dozen times. Frank circled it every time he looked at it, knowing it had to mean something. Penny was turning 40 in just a few hours.

Frank didn't need to do the simple math. He knew what it all meant. Now trembling uncontrollably, he screamed, "EIGHT-EIGHT-EIGHT!" at the top of his lungs.

He tried to start the car, but the engine wouldn't turn over. "Come on, you son of a bitch!" he growled as he desperately pumped the peddle while frantically turning the ignition key. "Come on! Come on! Start already!"

The engine finally roared to life, but Frank didn't take the time to brush the snow from the rear window. He revved the engine and threw it into reverse. Tires spinning down the driveway, Frank

Michael Cook

backed out into the road, slamming into a nearby car parked on the street.

Jeanie's sister heard the sound of metal crunching and came downstairs to see the front door wide open and the phone off the hook and laying in the middle of the floor.

She hung up the receiver and picked it back up again, and rapidly pushed the plungers knowing that it would automatically call the last number dialed. The phone rang, and a man frantically answered and said, "Frank, is that you?!"

"No, this is Frank's sister-in-law, Judy. Frank just ran out of here like a bat out of hell. I'm not sure what just happened?"

"Judy, this is Joe Bryce, Penny Bryce's husband. If Frank calls or comes back, you tell him that I'm heading to Heavenly Gates!"

Frank recklessly sped down the street and nearly lost control when making a left out of his street. Now on Chastain, he swerved to avoid two cars that had just been involved in an accident. Up ahead, Frank saw a red light, and with few tire tracks running through the intersection, he decided to gun it. A police car, coming from the opposite direction, witnessed the Buick run the signal and immediately turned on their sirens. After Frank passed them, they did a fish-tailed U-turn, nearly crashing, and attempted to catch up to him. Frank was undeterred by the police car closing the distance behind him. He floored the Buick and would stop at nothing to get to Penny.

Frank could care less about the police car that was now in hot pursuit. Speeding through another intersection, Frank had hoped they'd follow him just in case he needed backup after arriving at Heavenly Gates.

Frank saw that the light was green at the next intersection but noticed that the car approaching the intersection from his right couldn't make the stop. Instead, it slid into the intersection and into his path. Frank was unable to avoid the car, smashing into its back left quarter panel, causing it to spin 360°. Frank lost control of the Buick, and he plowed into several parking meters, launching coins high into the air. The Buick finally came to a rest on the sidewalk in front of Sal's Liquor Store on the corner of Prospect and Main. With steam coming from the radiator, the car had stalled.

The squad car pulled up next to the Buick, and a uniformed officer jumped from the car with his service revolver drawn. Frank continued his struggle to get the car started again as the officer screamed, "Let me see some hands!" pointing his gun at Frank.

Frank rolled down the driver's side window and raised his detective shield. He yelled to the officer, "Get me some cars up to Heavenly Gates. We've got a possible 2901 in progress!" Just then, he got the engine to turn over and shouted, "Follow me!" to the patrol car.

The officer's face went white, and he quickly jumped back in the black and white and yelled to his partner, "Follow that Buick! There's a possible 2901 in progress!"

The officer driving the squad car said, "What in the hell's that?"

"I have no idea, but that guy's a detective, and he needs our help!"

Frank could see in his rearview mirror that his backup was right behind him.

Back in the basement of Heavenly Gates, Penny banged the flashlight violently on the floor until it shattered, sending pieces flying in every direction. Regaining her ability to speak, she screamed for Travers. "Dean! Dean! Travers!" she wailed, but nothing came back! Then, between her pleas for help, she heard footsteps in the distance. Then she'd heard the dreaded clap of the breaker box switch going off, plunging her into complete darkness.

Hearing only her breath being inhaled and exhaled, Penny felt her heart beating out of her chest. Frozen in fear, she again picked up the sound of footsteps. She could only feel the storage boxes around her and hid behind the ones to her immediate left. The footsteps seemed to be getting closer as they became louder and louder with each step taken. Dred befell her, and she immediately thought it was the end. She now believed that she would meet the same fate as her great-grandfather and the other eight souls that came after him. She sobbed loudly, thinking of her boys and her Joey, and hoped that Frank would get there in time to save her.

Suddenly, like an ice pick through her brain, she heard the elevator roar to life. The sound of squeaking belts and gears rattled her senses. It was too loud, she thought. Then, coming from behind her, she heard the sound of rapid strobe lights zapping as if she were right next to them. Next, Penny could hear the sound of struggling patients and their muffled screams, trying desperately to escape their captors, but were unable.

Suddenly, she'd heard the sound of Dean Travers' calming voice. "Penelope, I'm coming for you. It'll be alright. You're safe now," announced Travers. The sound of footsteps continued as Penny desperately sought light. She'd wondered how and why Travers was navigating through the dark.

The elevators roared, and the sound of Travers' voice got louder and closer. "Penny, I got the elevator working. I know how you hate the locked basement door." His subtle voice no longer calmed her as she struggled to focus her eyes on the darkness.

Again paralyzed by fear, Penny climbed to her feet, searching for any ray of light or hope. Feeling the boxes around her, she could see nothing. She felt her way around what she perceived was the back of the stack, hoping it might shield her from whoever or whatever was about to walk through the door.

Suddenly, a beam of light illuminated the hallway outside of the room Penny was hiding in. The light swayed from side to side and back and forth as it got closer to the door. "Penelope, it will all be okay. I'm here to save you," said the voice of Dean Travers, continuing to switch back and forth between Penny and Penelope.

Penny was no longer sure that it was Travers coming for her. She continued to hear the screams of mentally ill patients, fighting off their white-clad assailants, who were disguised as doctors, nurses, and orderlies.

Then, as the beam of light turned into the archives room, Penny felt a warm wet fear running down her gray pressed slacks, pooling at her feet. She could barely muster a whimper when the source of the light stood directly in front of her, blinding her and her tears.

"Penny, I've come for you." It was as if Travers was standing right beside her. His voice was deafening, and his message even louder. The beam of light slowly began to point upward, gradually revealing the face of the man standing in the doorway.

"Penelope, it's okay," the light now hitting the chin of the man holding it. Penny screamed when she heard Travers' voice coming from the face of Old Man Winter. The next thing that Penny heard was the unloading of her .38 caliber service revolver into the man's chest. Six explosions followed by the sound of a flashlight hitting the floor. As it rolled to a stop, it illuminated the dark, gray-colored long sleeve of the shirt that Penny saw in the old photograph. The same flannel shirt that Garrison Winter had always worn.

As Penny fled the room, trying to navigate the body lying in the narrow doorway, she grabbed the flashlight and ran. As she headed for the stairs, some eighty feet away, she heard the elevator doors crank open and the words, "It's okay, Penny. I'm here to take you home, my child."

Penny ran past the rumbling elevator and up the stairs and closed the door behind her. Running through the dark halls, illuminated only by the flashlight, she saw a different Heavenly Gates than she had on her other visits to the mansion. The place she saw now was covered in dust and cobwebs. There were no working lights, and much of the furniture and portraits hanging on the walls were covered with canvas tarps. The floor was dusty yet had no footprints or signs that they had been walked on in years.

As she walked by the bathroom, the door flew open, but no one was there. From inside, she could hear the sound of a woman crying. The voice that Penny heard was her own. She continued down the long hall, which led to the foyer, and in the distance, she could see a man lying on the floor just outside the elevator. As she got closer, she could see that it was Frank. She screamed for him, but no sound came from her lips. The only thing she could hear was Frank crying for his Jeanie. As she got closer, she could see his ripped pants and bleeding knee and then heard the elevator door as it began to open.

Penny knew that she would have to get by the elevator and whoever was in it if she was going to make it to the foyer and out the front doors of Heavenly Gates. Her gun was out of bullets, but she refused to slow down. As her flashlight danced on the walls and floor, it captured a gray, long-sleeved flannel shirt coming through the slowly opening elevator doors. The next jump of her flashlight beam would reveal a smiling face of an old man named Garrison Winter.

Outside, the Buick turned left onto Bedford Street, and Frank hauled ass to the front gates, which were now closed and locked. Picking up speed in the blizzard conditions, Frank closed his eyes and rammed the front gates. The Buick hit the gates and the large brick pillar to the left of the double wrought iron fencing, launching Frank halfway through the windshield. Now unconscious, his hips and legs lying across the steering wheel and dashboard, while his torso, head, and arms laid limp across the hood, as a broken windshield wiper rod stood pierced up through his jacket. In the dead of night, the sound of the Eagles' *Witchy Woman* blared down Bedford Street as a single police car rolled up behind the stalled Buick.

Back inside Heavenly Gates, Penny sat with Garrison O'Donnell in the well-lit solarium. "I hope you don't mind, Penny, but I kept the backgammon table and board out here despite the snow. One of my favorite things is to watch it fall freely from the night sky. I hope it's not too cold in here for you," Garrison Winter smiled at his friend.

"It feels wonderful," smiled Penny.

"So Garrison, can you please tell me why I'm here? Why me?"

"Well, first of all, Penny, it's your birthday. Happy Birthday to you!" smiled Old Man Winter. "Secondly, it's time," he explained.

"What do you mean, it's time?" Penny was stoic and understanding but sat, a little confused. "The others all lived long lives, but I'm less than half of their age, so again, why me?"

"Penny, age has nothing to do with it. It comes down to if you're ready for the next journey or if you need more time," explained Winter. "And let me tell you, my dear Penelope, you're ready."

"But what about Joe and my boys?" asked an unafraid and relaxed Penny.

"They'll be just fine," reassured Winter. "You'll be seeing them soon enough. Until then, you'll be able to watch them all grow older and do wonderful things in the very short time they'll have on Earth. I promise you, Penny, they'll be fine."

"Short time?" Penny looked confused.

"Ahh yes, I have so much to tell you, my sweet Penny," said Winter.

"Penny, the time that we have on Earth is a mere blink of an eye," the old man explained. "Time is not measured in Heaven by days, months, or years, but rather by the light of one's existence. Some shine bright and come home soon, while others take just a little longer to shine through."

Winter smiled and said, "What if I told you that in all of the time since my friend, and your great-grandfather, Samuel Crenshaw, passed over, he has not even made it all the way to Heaven yet?"

Penny looked surprised. "But it's been so long." She shook her head.

"Again, time on Earth is nothing but the whisper of a child, the beating of a heart, or the sound of the wind blowing. Your Joey and your boys will live a long and happy life but will join you in just a short while," Winter smiled.

"Happy life?" Penny was calm and at peace, but her questions persisted. "You're taking their mother and wife from them. How can they be happy, never knowing what became of me?" Penny shook her head. "They will be devastated. What kind of God would do that to a family?"

"They will know what happened to you, and they will be pleased," Winter's smile was warm and calming. "Penny, you've often said that God doesn't take but rather welcomes. You must understand that one's existence is filled with trials and tribulations. From time to time, every being will suffer loss in one form or another after coming into existence. It is that very loss that will come to define the spirit that makes up their soul."

"Some are challenged more than others because their paths require it," explained Winter. "In your current bodily form, here in this world, it will be impossible for you to understand."

Penny sat and pondered the old man's words.

"Trust me, Penelope. Those three souls will be strong and embrace the heartbreak and loss once they come to accept it. They will be stronger because of it," Old man Winter reassured Penny, placing his hand on hers'. "You will understand everything in a very short while, I promise."

"What about Frank? He's lost without his Jeanie."

Garrison Winter smiled, "Oh, I do like Frank. But he's not quite ready just yet. His life will be long and fruitful while on Earth, but he, too, will join us very soon as we complete our journey to Heaven."

"So, what should I call you, then? Old Man Winter? Garrison Winter? Garrison O'Donnell? You have so many names."

"Penny, you can just call me, Friend," said the old man.

"So, why me?" Penny asked again. "Why now?"

"Penny, you completed the circle," said Winter. "And it's your birthday.....," he smiled.

Penny nodded her head and also smiled. "Good old Frank and his eights, he was right!" She felt nothing but love and affection for her partner.

Winter smiled, "Frank is such a good detective! He will go on to do great things in his career. He will bring peace and closure to many lost and broken souls."

"Yeah?" Penny's eyes went wide.

"Yes," nodded Winter, smiling warmly. "He's such a good person."

"Penny, would you like to play a friendly game of backgammon? I can teach you how to play if you want," said the old man.

"I would love to," said Penny. "But only if I can ask you some more questions, first?"

"Of course, you can."

"All of that stuff in the basement. Why?" Penny was perplexed.

"Penny, you saw and heard what you wanted to see down there. That wasn't my doing. You wanted so much to believe what you experienced was real, but it was only in your mind," revealed Winter.

"Penny, do you remember the first time you came to visit Heavenly Gates?"

"I do. I remember feeling unwelcomed."

"Yes, I recall," said Winter. "In fact, you almost turned to leave. Do you remember that, too?"

Penny thought back to that moment where she'd stood at the door, reconsidering her visit. "I do," she said. "When no one came to the door, I doubted my reasons for being there and turned to go."

"Well," Winter smiled. "Just before you turned to leave, I gave you a sign, a little nudge, if you will. Do you remember what that was?"

Penny's eyes opened with enlightenment. "The thunder, and the gust of wind? That was you?"

"It was indeed," smiled Old Man Winter.

"Like that day I helped you through the doors of this heavenly estate, I led you here tonight, too."

"Why?" Penny knew the answer but wanted to hear it from Winter.

"Yes, well, before I welcomed you into Heaven, I needed to ensure that you solved your first and only case as a detective."

Penny was surprised and pleased. "So, God does work in mysterious ways, then?"

"If you mean do I have a sense of adventure? You bet," smiled Winter.

"So, that wasn't Travers down there?" Penny almost looked disappointed. "I thought that for a moment. He kept calling me Penny instead of Penelope."

Winter pursed his lips, raised his brow, and threw up his hands. "Yes, that was me, I'm afraid. You see, Penny, Dean Travers only ever lived in the shadows of your mind."

"Frank's mind, too?" asked Penny.

"Frank's too," smiled Winter.

"But, if Travers never existed, then neither did the intern."

"I'm afraid that your fascination with the basement, along with your wonderful imagination, concocted her too."

"But what about Bernice Gruber?" Penny was confused.

Winter smiled, almost blushing, and said, "I'm afraid that she was never really there. Frank was testing himself. He felt that he needed Gruber to test his love for his Jeanie." Winter paused and smiled. "He passed that test, didn't he?"

Penny was confused. "But, he went to her house."

"No, I'm afraid not," said Winter. "He went to a house, but never had the courage to get out of the car and walk up to the door."

Penny shook her head and smiled, "But what if he had?"

Winter threw up his hands again, returning Penny's smile. "Oh, I don't know. I'm sure I would have thought of something."

"So, it was necessary for me to see her too, then?"

"Yes, I'm afraid so."

"And the tape?"

Winter smiled and shook his head. "You can't record something that isn't really there, now, can you?"

"So, the others? My great-grandfather? Why take them?" asked Penny.

"They were all saints, too," said Winter. "And I didn't take them. They were ready to come home."

"Why on their birthday, though? Why do that to their families?"

"As I told you before," offered Winter, "It was a celebration of the day they left Heaven and the day that they'd journey home," Winter was solemn. "As I explained to you earlier, all of your questions will be answered once you complete your heavenly journey."

"Garrison, the others you were standing with in the dining room as I passed with Travers, were they who I think they were?" Penny waited for confirmation of what she knew in her heart to be true.

"Did you not notice your great-grandfather standing to my left? Or the priest standing to my right?" Winter asked.

Penny gasped and was speechless for a moment. "I would give anything to see their faces again. To meet my great-grandfather."

"Oh, you will, Penny. You will indeed."

Penny looked off for a moment and tried to take in what was happening to her. She felt sad but happy. A feeling of serenity came over her, and she was at peace.

After another moment of reflection, something had occurred to her. It was something Old Man Winter had said moments earlier. "Wait a second! A moment ago, you said the word 'too,' when referring to the saints. What did you mean by that?" Penny was confused.

"Penelope Denise Crenshaw Bryce, you are a saint."

"A saint?" Penny laughed modestly. "I'm no saint. You'll have to explain that one to me."

"Penny, do you remember when you were in the third grade, and some older girls were bullying Becky Lynne Schuster during recess, and you stepped in to save her?"

"I do. I always wondered whatever became of her." Penny pondered for a second.

"And she often wonders about you too, nearly every single day," smiled Winter. "Anyway, you decided to skip school the rest of the day and walk her home because you were concerned for her well-being, and she was going to walk home with or without you."

Penny nodded with the recollection.

"What you might not remember, Penny, is that a middle-aged man, driving a black 1930 Buick Roadster, was parked just across the street from the playground. That man watched Becky crawl through the hole in that fence, and then started his engine."

Penny sat up in her chair and paid close attention to what Old Man Winter said next, almost trembling.

"Penny, that man was going to offer Becky a ride, and she was going to accept it," explained Winter. "Without your selfless intervention, that little girl would not have made it home that day or any day after that."

Penny swallowed hard, and her eyes began to fill.

"Becky Lynne Shuster is now Dr. Becky Lynne Shuster McBride. She is a pediatric surgeon in the Children's Hospital in Baltimore, Maryland. To date, she has saved more than eight hundred little boys and girls from unnecessary pain and suffering, not to mention the torture their parents would have suffered through if they had joined me in heaven prematurely," smiled Winter. "Before your friend, Becky Lynne, joins you in Heaven, she will save a thousand more."

Penny was crying now, with tears crossing over her smiling lips. "But," she paused, "I never saw the man in the car."

"I know, Penny," Winter nodded his head and smiled. "And you walked her home anyway."

"I don't think that makes me a saint, though," Penny looked confused.

"I'm not finished telling your story yet, Penny," Garrison Winter smiled.

"Oh?"

"Do you remember when you fought so hard to be a detective, taking on the City of Philadelphia?"

"Yes, of course, I do," said Penny.

"Penny, that hard-fought victory will go on to inspire women around the country for decades. In less than forty years from now, this city will elect its first female mayor. Many little girls born in the coming years will be named after you. You are, and will be, an inspiration for many years to come."

"But that doesn't make me a saint, either." Penny was still confused.

Winter leaned in close to Penny and took her hands into his. "Penny, two weeks after your promotion to detective, Frank Bruno, in a moment of unbearable heartbreak and insufferable pain, was going to drive his 1967 Buick off of the Walt Whitman Bridge and into the Delaware River, killing himself along with his little angels, nine-year-old Jessica, and seven-year-old Madeline."

Penny gasped. Covering her mouth and holding her heart, she began to cry.

"I didn't put you through that four-year ordeal to inspire women, Penny. I did it so that you would become a detective and save Frank and the girls. You could have understandably quit your legal battle, but you didn't. Frank needed a strong woman in his life after Jeanie died, if only for a short while, to inspire his girls with the stories he will tell them about you until the day he dies."

Garrison Winter rolled the dice and then took Penny's hand again and squeezed it. "You are now *Saint Penelope*. People will be talking about you and following your example for many decades to come. I have ten more stories just like that and thousands more that will come from those you touched in your life, people you saved. You will meet all of them one day very soon, and they will thank you themselves."

"So, now what?" asked Penny.

"Roll the dice, Penny."

Penny rolled snake eyes and, looking at the dice, said, "That's me and you, isn't it?" Looking again at the dots on the dice.

"Yes," Old Man Winter smiled, "that's you and me, surrounded by beautiful, pure white snow. Can you see it, Penny?"

"I can," smiled Penny. "I can see it."

"Come on, let's walk for a while," said Old Man Winter.

"Can I take my favorite jacket with me?" asked Penny.

Winter smiled. "Oh, my dearest Penelope, you won't need your jacket where we're going." He leaned in and touched her arm.

As the two walked out the front doors of Heavenly Gates, Penny said, "It's not as cold as I thought it would be."

"It's beautiful, isn't it?"

"It really is," said Penny.

Walking into the snow, they heard a crash at the bottom of the hill and saw headlights and smoke coming from the main gates.

"Is that Frank coming to get me?" asked Penny with a smile.

"Oh, yes, how he did try to get here," smiled Winter. "He's such a good man. He deserved to have you in his life. You saved him, Penny."

"And I was lucky to have him," Penny whispered. "Will he be okay?"

"Who, Frank?" Winter looked at Penny. "You bet he will."

"What about the Buick? He loves that car, you know?"

"Oh yes, I'm well aware," Winter nodded and smiled. "He'll have it until 1984, and then he'll give it to Madeline. She'll have it for a year, and then Frank will retire it to his garage."

"Jessica didn't want it?" Penny's brows went up.

"No, she's not a fan of that car, I'm afraid. Frank, on the other hand, will never give it up. After the girls grow up and leave, Frank will go out into that garage every Saturday morning and play Witchy Woman. He'll look over and see his Jeanie sitting there, and he'll smile."

"Good old Frank, he loved that woman," said Penny.

"You mean 'loves,' that woman."

Penny nodded. "And Joe and the boys? You sure they're going to be okay?" asked Penny again.

Winter nodded, "I promise."

"One more question," said Penny. McClain? Will they ever solve the Schuylkill River case?"

"Oh, yes, and many others, too."

Penelope Denise Crenshaw Bryce walked into the snow holding the hand of God. She disappeared into the woods just off the south lawn of the FalconClaw estate that night. She would never be seen again, and neither would she be forgotten.

As Frank ran bleeding to the top of the hill, he screamed for Penny after being assisted by the two officers down on Bedford Street. Running into the house, he saw Penny's gray jacket laying on the floor just inside the double doors. He picked it up and ran back outside into the snow, screaming again for his friend. Looking for any sign of Penny, he spotted two sets of footprints in the snow and followed them as far as he could before finally collapsing.

The two officers chasing closely behind Frank helped him from the snow, with one officer saying to the other, "What's he even doing here? Didn't this place close down early last year?"

Chapter 31 – Detective Frank Bruno

It was January 3, 1976, and it had been just over a year since Penny disappeared without a trace. Reluctantly, and at the direction of his boss, Ron McClain, Frank boxed up the files from Penny's case and labeled it 'Cold Case,' and then placed it into storage in the tiny closet with the other unsolved crimes and disappearances.

As Frank exited the closet, his eyes went back to Penny's old desk. It was just the way she'd left it. Frank made sure it stayed that way as he always believed she'd again one day walk into the Detective Room on the second floor of the 39th District and get started on the next case. Most of the time, Frank sat at his desk working. He'd stared at Penny's desk and wished that she was sitting behind it. He missed their ride-alongs and pizza at Tony's, but mostly, he missed her enthusiasm for the job. Nothing was the same anymore, and neither was Frank.

Frank Bruno never understood what went down at FalconClaw. At first, he thought he was going crazy, but he knew something beyond his understanding was at work.

After that night, Christmas Eve, 1974, Frank learned that Heavenly Gates had closed down in the Spring of 1973. So then, who were Dean Travers, Bernice Gruber, and Garrison Winter? He'd wondered as he packed up his desk.

It took Frank Bruno months before he finally accepted that he wasn't crazy. Someone took Penny, and if not for her disappearance and the two sets of footprints leaving the front door of Heavenly Gates, his boss might've thought he was crazy too.

Frank then gathered his things, walked over to Ron McClain's office, and tapped on the half-opened door. "Got a minute?" he asked his boss.

"Sure, Frank, always got time for my best man." McClain motioned him in.

"Ron, I just want to tell you that I quit." Frank looked as timid as a kid who'd been bullied his entire life.

"Frank, listen, I know how you're feeling. We all miss her, but it's time to move on from the case."

"Ron, you don't miss her. You're happy that she's gone."

"Frank, shut the door and take a seat."

Frank turned to close the door, and as he did, he could see the others sneaking a peek into the tiny office, curious as to what was about to happen. They understood the fragile state he was in and feared that he might indeed walk away from his career.

After closing the door, Frank took a seat and stared at the helmet above Ron's desk, trying not to make eye contact with his boss.

"Frank, listen. Penny was a good cop and an even better detective. I was hard on her. I know it. And I was wrong for it." McClain was sincere. "What happened to her and the whole mess up at Heavenly Gates is a mystery. But she deserved better than what she got, and she deserved better than me, that's for sure."

"Ron, whatever, I'm still quitting. There's no talking me out of it." Frank pressed his lips together and shook his head defiantly. He wore a look of benign resignation. He was defeated and had nothing left to give to the department or society. He was finished.

"Frank, don't do it."

"I'm done, Chief. Take care."

Frank got up and walked out of McClain's office. He said nothing to the others as he packed up his desk. They, in return, said nothing to him, each of them avoiding eye contact. Frank was the most tenured detective in the unit, and none of the guys knew how things would go if he left.

As Frank packed his things into the backseat of the Buick, parked back on Yelland, Ron McClain came jogging toward him.

"Frank, I'm glad I caught you!" McClain was out of breath.

"Chief, I told you, I'm done."

"Frank. I accept your resignation, but I need a quick favor."

"What is it, Ron?"

"I need to know which one of the guys you think I should promote to run the 'Penny Bryce Cold Case Unit.' It's a full-time job," said McClain. "There's no pay increase, but they'll have the autonomy to pick and choose which cases they feel are the most solvable."

Frank was caught off guard. "Umm, I'm, umm, not sure. Can I sleep on it and let you know tomorrow?"

"You bet Frank, take your time." Ron placed his hand on Frank's shoulder and said, "It's been my honor to work alongside of you these last five-plus years. I'm gonna miss you, Frank."

"You too, Ron. Maybe we'll talk tomorrow or something."

"Sure, Frank. You bet." McClain shook Frank's hand and walked away. He didn't look back, but Frank wished that he had.

The next day Ron McClain walked into the office, and there was a buzz in the Detective Room. He didn't understand why everyone looked so energetic. As he gave a 'what gives?' look to his team of four detectives, they motioned for their boss to look in the 'Cold Case' closet.

McClain crept slowly toward the closet and heard rustling around inside like someone was re-organizing it or something. As he leaned to look in, Frank walked out with a file box in his hands, nearly running into McClain.

"Oh, sorry, Chief. Just getting the place in order."

"Oh, okay, Frank." Ron was confused and relieved.

"Oh, and Ron. I figured I'd take the job of running the cold case unit, seeing as I invented it."

"Of course, Frank. I think you'd be the best man for the job." Ron was matter of fact. "But remember, there's no pay increase, right?"

"Don't need one. I'm good, Boss."

"Okay, so, we're all good, then?" Ron sounded a little unsure of himself.

"Yep, we're all good, Chief."

An hour later, Frank tapped on McClain's door. "Hey Boss, got a second?"

"You bet, Frank. Come on in."

"Listen, I'm heading out. I'll be back in a few weeks."

McClain was confused. "Um, okay. Sure, take some time off...as much as you need."

"No, I'm not taking time off. I'm heading out to work a case."

"Oh, which one?" asked a curious-looking McClain.

"I'm heading up to Burlington. Those parents need to know what happened to their daughter. I'm gonna work with their detectives. It's out of our jurisdiction, but they said they'd appreciate the help if the Philly P.D. can spare me."

"Of course, Frank. I'll get it approved by the brass downtown. Just a formality, I'm sure they'll say yes."

"Thanks, Chief! I'll stay in touch."

"Sure thing, Frank."

As Frank was leaving, he turned and stuck his head back into McClain's office. "Oh, and Ron. When I get done up in Jersey, I'm gonna need your help with another case."

McClain cocked a brow. "Ah, Frank. I don't work cases anymore. You know that."

"Well, your help will be needed. I left the file on my desk. Look it over and be ready to go when I get back."

"Frank, listen, like I said...."

Frank Bruno walked off in the middle of his boss's sentence.

McClain got up to catch Frank to make sure he understood that he didn't directly investigate cases anymore and hadn't for years.

As he walked out of his office to catch him, the door to the stairwell closed. Ron McClain stopped himself from yelling out to Frank as he was gone. Before McClain returned to his office, his eyes went to the file on Frank's desk. He walked over for a closer look, and his face turned white. Ron said aloud, "Well, I'll be damned!" The file sitting on Frank's desk read, 'The Boy in the Box.'

McClain picked it up, took it into his office, and closed the door behind him.

Frank Bruno retired from the Philadelphia Police Force in 1991. During his time as the head of the *Penelope Bryce Cold Case Unit,* Frank, and his team, working closely with the BSU in Quantico, solved thirty-six cold cases in total, including the Schuylkill River Case. He, Douglas Cantrell, and Rick Kessler became good friends over the years, but Frank never did join them in Virginia. He would never leave the home where Jeanie once lived.

Because of the Cold Case team's success in the 39th District, more than twenty other police districts in Philadelphia created similar cold case divisions. As a result, more than two hundred cases were reopened and eventually solved.

Cantrell and Kessler brought Frank along when they interviewed the likes of John Wayne Gacy, Ted Bundy, Randall Woodfield, Ed Kemper, Rodney Alcala, and Richard Speck.

Frank Bruno's biggest cold cases solved were Margaret Ellen Fox's disappearance and the death of Benjamin Watts, the 'Boy in the Box.'

Margaret Ellen Fox – Born February 4, 1960 – Missing since June 24, 1974.

Twenty-seven months after Frank began assisting the Burlington Police Department in the search for the fourteen-year-old Fox girl, there was a break in the case. The 5' 3" 105 lb. Margaret Fox ran an ad in the Burlington and Mt. Holly newspapers, offering her services as a babysitter. According to her younger brother, Joe, only one person ever responded to the ad. A man, who called himself John Marshall, answered the ad on June 19 and agreed to hire the Fox girl. The two had agreed to meet in Mt. Holly at a bus stop near the

Mill & High Streets' intersection. After canceling on three separate occasions, a date and time was set for June 24, 1974.

According to the younger brother of Margaret Fox, the man instructed Fox to purchase a red balloon from a small candy shop in Mt. Holly so that he could identify her in the crowd. The man told the girl he would meet her in his red Beetle, and he'd give her a ride to his home to meet the child that needed baby-sitting.

According to the younger brother of Margaret Fox, the man gave his phone number to Margaret. The younger sibling turned over the number to the police. The telephone number was traced to a grocery store in Lumberton Township, New Jersey, just south of Mt. Holly. Frank Bruno joined detectives from both Burlington and Mt. Holly and interviewed every employee of the store. When doing so, a man admitted to knowing someone with a red Volkswagen and provided authorities with the person's name and address. The man was interviewed and denied ever knowing Margaret Fox but permitted authorities to search his red Beetle. When the police searched the car, they found a deflated red balloon under the passenger seat that'd been popped. The balloon had Margaret Fox's fingerprints on it.

The man, twenty-four-year-old John Riley Martin, confessed to killing Fox during a thirteen-hour long interrogation. Though he confessed to the crime, he did not reveal his motivations or how he killed the girl. He also refused to lead detectives to her body. John Riley Martin was arrested and convicted of killing the girl but admitted to having an accomplice he'd refused to identify. The police closed the case and never searched for any other suspects believing Martin was the sole perpetrator in the abduction and murder.

The Boy in the Box – Age 4-6 years old – Found dead on February 25, 1957.

In 1987, Frank Bruno and Chief Detective Ron McClain finally solved the 'Boy in the Box' case. In following the original hunch that McClain had back in 1957 – 1958, that the boy was likely connected to a foster home just 1.5 miles from the location where the boy was found naked and stuffed in a box that once held a baby's bassinet. The two detectives re-interviewed the owner of the foster home and his then step-daughter. Upon interviewing the two some thirty years after the child was found dead, it was discovered the step-daughter had married her step-father, and the two had a son. While the two refused to give a blood sample, their son, twenty-year-old John Michael Watkins, fully cooperated and provided Bruno and McClain with a sample of his DNA.

Bruno and McClain theorized that the step-father impregnated his step-daughter and killed the boy before he could reach school-age in an effort to conceal the inappropriate relationship between the two. During their investigation, Bruno and McClain attended an estate sale at the house in 1986, after the bank had foreclosed on it. There, they purchased a bassinette that appeared to be the same type, size, and brand that the local J.C. Penny store sold back in the 1950s. When breaking down the bassinette, it fit perfectly into the box in which the boy was found, thirty years earlier. The box had been perfectly preserved while in police custody.

Then, in 1987, the body of 'America's Unknown Child' was exhumed from Potter's Field Cemetery, located in the Parkwood Manor area of North Philly. DNA was extracted from the enamel from one of the child's teeth. After tests were completed, it was determined that the DNA was a close match to John Michael Watkins, sharing characteristics of both of his parents. When confronted with the evidence, the step-daughter, Alice Marie Watkins, confessed that the young boy, named Benjamin, was, in fact, her son, but claimed the boy died accidentally after falling down the basement stairs and hitting his head in the foster home that she once lived in. The step-father, John Thomas Watkins, denied his involvement and was never charged. The mother was also never formally charged as there was no proof that a homicide was committed as the cause of death was ruled undetermined. Additionally, the statute of limitations for desecration of a corpse had expired.

Frank Bruno spent the last several years of his time on the force looking for his friend and partner, Penelope Denise Bryce. After retiring in 1991, he continued to investigate her disappearance in an unofficial capacity. Frank would regularly flash his detective badge in an effort to get through a door when his foot wouldn't do the trick. Frank had always hoped Penny was out there, still alive, but in his gut, he knew he'd probably never find her. He knew, though, that if he ever did, he would also find Old Man Winter. He spent more than ten years of his retirement looking for her until his health deteriorated, making it impossible for him to get around town.

People who knew Frank best weren't sure what drove him to keep busy looking for Penny long after he'd retired. Some said he feared going to his grave, never solving the coldest case he'd ever worked on, while some believed that he was afraid to go home and be forced to spend his days morning the loss of the love of his life and 'best girl,' Janine Louise Bruno.

Epilogue – Room for One More

Hospital room of Frank Bruno – Christmas Day, 2016 – 1:14 am.

The Nurse's stations were all quiet in Nazareth Catholic Hospital. Available bed capacity was high due to the holiday. Only the very sick or dying remained. Hospital staff was minimal, and nurses were scarce, and at each nurse's station sat those R.N.s with the least seniority, stuck there at night and on Christmas.

No one noticed the old man walking through the halls, creeping along as if he was invisible. Frank lay sleeping, dreaming of those three eights as he did most nights. The heart rate monitor showed a slow but steady heartbeat coming from the dying man. Soon, it would go flat, but not yet.

The old man wandered into Frank's room undetected. His daughters, Jessica, and Madeline, had paid a little extra so that their father could have a private room. They wanted him to die in peace. And they desperately hoped they'd be there when he eventually passed.

As Frank rambled in his sleep about FalconClaw, Heavenly Gates, Penny, and Old Man Winter, something stirred in his soul, and he was awakened. Was it the Nurse coming to check his catheter or his intravenous drip? His tired eyes took a moment to focus. A silhouette stood between him and the window. The curtains were opened wide, and Frank saw a shadow next to him framed by the backdrop of snow falling from the sky. Ignoring the person at his bedside for a moment, Frank couldn't stop thinking that they were the biggest snowflakes he'd ever seen.

Back at the nurse's station, the thirty-year-old, second-year nurse was on the phone with her husband, and they were quietly arguing about something, likely the fact that she wouldn't be there in the morning when their kids opened their presents. Though distracted, she was keenly aware of the heart rates she was tasked with monitoring for the eight patients in her care that early morning. Everything was normal, nothing that would distract her from her phone call, though she'd hoped for an excuse to hang up on the guilt trip that chirped loudly through her phone.

Back in room thirty-eight, Frank's eyes grew accustomed to the room's darkness, and his heart began racing, but the machine monitoring all of his vitals didn't show it, though. Frank's breathing seized for a moment. The old man standing next to him wore a familiar face. It was Old Man Winter who'd come calling for him.

"Hello, old friend," said Garrison Winter in a warm, calming voice.

Frank's eyes were filled with terror as his body shook. Unable to speak, he managed to mouth the words, "NO!" Frank desperately tried to cross himself, but his tired arms, bruised by the I.V., lacked the strength needed to lift them. A solitary tear ran from his right eye as his lips quivered and his hands trembled. The nurse back at the station had ended her call and was now playing solitaire on her phone. Glancing at the monitors for each room, from time to time, she could see they were all normal. Everyone seemed to be having a peaceful night, according to the station monitors.

However, back in room thirty-eight, the body that Frank now wore would do little to protect him from his unwelcome guest. The former police detective was once a strong man that protected the citizens of the rugged City of Philadelphia but was now reduced to someone that couldn't defend himself.

"But how?" Frank softly whined. "How is it possible? You haven't aged. What do you want from me, you son of a bitch?!" Frank tried to act tough, just as he had back in 1974, but now he was a frightened old man. He was paralyzed, his eyes teeming with fear. Like his friend, Penny, Old Man Winter had come to take him, too.

"Frank, don't be frightened," Garrison tried to calm him.

Now openly sobbing, Frank spewed saliva as he managed to say, "Is that what you said to the others, too?"

"It's not what you think, Frank." Garrison's voice was soft. "I'm not here to hurt you. I'm your friend. Just have faith in me."

Frank couldn't contain his horror, and the sound of urine filling his catheter bag could be heard amongst the silence in room thirty-eight on Nazareth Hospital's eighth ward, the acute care unit.

"Just do it, you bastard! Take me!" Frank sobbed. His voice was gaining strength but not enough to alert Katie O'Connell and her fourth game of solitaire.

Garrison Winter then took Frank by the hand, and a jolt suddenly ran through his withered body, thrusting his chest skyward, his eyes tightly closed. Once his body came to rest again, his eyes opened slowly. His tears were gone, and the color in his face turned to that of a younger man.

"What happened?" said a surprised and curious Frank, not yet aware of his transformation.

"Frank, I want you to get up out of bed and stand with me. We're going for a walk." Winter stepped back, giving Frank room.

"I can't get up. My body won't allow it."

"You can do it, Frank," encouraged Old Man Winter as he leaned in and pushed aside the bed trapeze floating above Frank's head.

Frank lifted his arms and then wiggled his toes, surprised by the revelation that he could. Just moments earlier, both gravity and a fragile body fought the gray-haired, ninety-year-old man.

"You can do it, Frank. I believe in you," said Winter. "Stand up, Son."

Frank sat up in bed and easily swung his once tired feet over the side, now dangling. Frank looked at Old Man Winter and smiled.

Winter returned Frank's smile and said, 'Go ahead, Son, stand up."

Frank challenged his uncertainty and was determined to do what he'd been unable to do for weeks.

Frank looked down at his brittle, crusty feet and stepped down off of the bed. Looking as surprised as he was proud, Frank looked at Winter and smiled again. There was no fear left in the man who had lived with it since 1974.

"Frank, I want you to look down at your feet again." Garrison Winter's smile was reassuring to Frank.

Frank looked down and saw the feet he once wore when he was just forty-eight years old. In both shock and amazement, he looked at Winter and then his left and then right hands. They were no longer used up and wrinkled. They looked strong and vibrant. He again looked at Winter in disbelief and joy. His hair went from silver to raven black, with only gray threads running through it, and the wrinkles that once framed his tired eyes were now gone.

"I want to take you for a walk, Frank."

"Where are we going?" Frank looked like a curious but fearless child.

"I think you know the answer to that," smiled Winter.

"But wait, I want to know your real name?"

Old Man Winter placed his hand on Frank's shoulder, smiled, and said, "You know my name, Frank. You had me pegged back in 1974. You were a very fine detective."

"But what should I call you now?" Frank was respectful.

"Most people just call me Father, but you can call me, Friend."

"Of course, they do." Frank returned Winter's smile.

"It's snowing. Let me grab my robe." Frank scanned the room, looking for his favorite robe, the one Maddie brought him from his home.

"You're not going to need a robe where we're going," said Winter.

Frank looked at Old Man Winter and said, "Before we go, can I ask you a question?"

"You were right about that one too, Frank," smiled Winter, knowing what Frank was going to ask him. "Yes, Penny is indeed a saint. When she turned forty, the eights were aligned, and she would complete the circle of ten."

"So she was right about that?" smiled Frank, proud of his former partner.

"And you, the eights, Frank." Winter placed his fatherly hand on Frank's shoulder.

"But why take her then? She was still so young?" Frank didn't understand.

"That was her journey, Frank," Winter smiled. "It was her time."

"You see, Frank. You and Penny share a common journey. The two of you are intertwined. You always have been. You knew it in your heart the first day you met, long before she became your partner. The loss of Penny and Jeanie is what enabled you to fulfill your sainthood," explained God.

"Sainthood?" Frank said aloud, looking out the window at the snow, his eyes welling with tears.

"I didn't take Jeanie or Penny from you," God continued. "They were only a part of your journey, and their loss led you forward and helped shape your future. A future that would help to save lost souls," God said. "The times in your life when you felt lost were merely the moments in which you were finding yourself."

"But why?" Frank paused in his confusion.

"Why did you put me through the heartbreak of loss?"

"It was that very heartbreak of loss that fortified your soul. The power of your loss led you to a place of helping others cope with theirs," said God. "That was your destiny, Frank. Everything that ever happened to you along the way was simply a piece of your puzzle, a step in your journey."

"Why then did you make me believe you were evil when you were, in fact, divine?" Frank still didn't understand.

Winter smiled and placed his hand on Frank's shoulder again. "Frank, I never made you believe anything other than what you wanted to believe. People see the things they choose to see."

"You see, my son, you were angry with me because you thought I took Jeanie from you. You believed what was once good was now bad. When you saw me as the old man, the one that everyone told you was good, you only saw evil."

Frank looked at God, "But Penny saw it too."

God smiled and said, "Penny wanted nothing more than to see evil and conquer it when in fact, there was no evil there at all. She was consumed with righting wrongs and ridding the Earth of the evil that she saw everywhere around her, when in fact, it simply wasn't there. The old man in the solarium was me. There were no demons in the basement of FalconClaw. They lived only in her mind."

"And the elevator?" asked Frank.

"What you saw, Frank, was a reflection of yourself," said God. "You were telling yourself that you were trapped, that you were hurt. You were hurting for the person on the other side of the elevator doors. When in fact, it was you on both sides of those doors. The doors were a metaphor for the wall you built between you and the forgiveness you needed to bestow upon yourself. You blamed yourself for Jeanie's death, but you weren't responsible for it. That was simply Jeanie's journey. It was her story."

"Then why let it play out? Why not just show yourself?" Frank asked God.

"Frank, the devil you saw in the solarium, was only the demon that lived in your mind. You chose to see evil instead of the good standing before you. I needed to allow you to work out what was right, what was wrong, what was evil, and what was good. That process is what led you to save so many others from their wayward lives. It was your loss, Frank, that allowed you to save so many others from theirs. You did good, my son."

"Frank, in both Penny's case and yours, you needed to find your truth without me helping you," explained God. "I entered both of your lives at that moment to serve only as a guide, not to lead you down a path, but rather to light your way. I was your light, and you were Penny's."

The hopeful look of anticipation ran from Frank's eyes. "So, Penny is in Heaven, now?"

Winter smiled, and at that moment, the door to room thirty-eight began to open slowly. Frank, like a child, was nervous that he would be caught out of his bed by young Nurse O'Connell.

As the door open completely, though, Frank's eyes went wide and again were replete with sorrow-filled joy.

"Hey, Partner," said Penny.

Frank sobbed and fell to his knees.

God looked down at Frank and said, "I hope you don't mind, but Penny wanted to walk with us too."

"It's good to see you again, Frank." Penny smiled and helped her friend to his feet. "You lived a good life, and now it's time to go."

"But I'm no saint, Penny. Why me?"

God spoke up as Penny stood by smiling. "Frank, you always looked out for Penny and the children that were lost. You protected them and helped them find their way home. You did God's work. Your sins are all forgiven, my son," said God. "There's always room in Heaven for one more saint."

"Penny, did you see Jeanie up there?" Frank wore a hopeful look.

Penny smiled as her eyes turned toward the door. Frank's followed hers as Old Man Winter looked on. A woman walked through the door, one that Frank knew very well. It was his Jeanie. His best girl was standing before him. Frank hit his knees again and wept.

Jeanie stood over Frank as he cried, stroking his thick black hair. "I missed you, Frankie. I'm so proud of you. You're a saint."

"We're all proud of you, Frank," said God.

Jeanie rubbed Frank's back as Penny looked on.

Frank climbed back to his feet and held Jeanie, sobbing in her arms. "I'm so sorry, Jeanie! I was unfaithful." He still lived with the guilt of kissing another woman.

Jeanie smiled at her Frankie Boy. "You weren't unfaithful, Frankie." Jeanie knew the guilt that tormented her Frankie. "I love you, and you love me, and now we'll never be apart again. Ever."

Frank cried and smiled. He still couldn't understand why he was graced with the miracle that was the ending to his life until Penny, Winter, and Jeanie all looked at him and then over to the corner of the room. Frank's eyes followed theirs, and there, sitting on the chair in the corner, was a fourteen-year-old girl holding a red balloon. It was Margaret Ellen Fox. She released the balloon from her hand as she rose from the chair, then walked over to Frank as he knelt to greet her.

"Can I walk with you too, Detective Bruno?" Frank could not speak at that moment, but with tears, nodded yes.

Everyone smiled as Frank stood and took her hand. As Frank turned toward the window to enter Heaven, the others, including Margaret, all smiled and turned to look behind him. The curtain next to Frank's hospital bed began to sway, and a little boy's laugh could be heard coming from behind it.

"Okay, come on, Benjamin," said Margaret Fox. Just then, little Benjamin Watkins skipped to Frank's side. There, he placed his hand in Frank's and said, "Thank you for giving me a name, Detective Frank."

Frank's tears flowed. He cupped little Benjamin's head with his hand and pulled him close. As the boy looked up to Frank, Frank could see the scar beneath Benjamin's chin was no longer there. The miracle was now complete in Frank's heart, and he was ready for his walk.

"Can I walk with you guys, too?" asked little Benjamin.

"You bet you can, Ben!" said Frank. "You bet you can!"

Winter and the others looked at Frank as if to say, "It's time." And he acknowledged them without words.

"Come on, Frank, many others are looking forward to seeing you," said Penny.

And just like that, the room was empty, the curtains dancing in the winter breeze as the snowflakes joined them.

An hour later, a panicked Katie O'Connell ran from room thirty-eight, screaming for help. She ran back to her station, frantically pushing buttons on the phone.

When detectives from the 39th District finally arrived, they saw a shaken O'Connell being consoled by two other nurses while being questioned by two uniformed officers. Just down the hall, outside of room thirty-eight, a hospital security guard stood watch. His badge number? 888.

Two Philadelphia police detectives, one male and one female, entered the dark, freezing cold room, their frozen breath preceding them. Inside, they saw an empty bed and robe lying on the floor and the window hanging wide open. The snowflakes fell peacefully through the window and onto the floor, melting into a puddle that reflected the night sky and the purity of the falling snow. The heart rate monitor continued to pulse at a relaxed forty beats per minute as its cord dangled to the floor. In the corner of the room, now floating free, a red balloon hung in the air.

The female detective looked behind the curtain next to the bed and said, "Well, whatta we have here?" On the floor was an old empty bassinette box with faded red letters running down the side that read J.C. Penny's. At that moment, both detectives heard the sound of a little boy laughing just outside the window.

The male detective, who was standing closest to the window, looked out to investigate. Looking down at the snow, he said, "Hey, Penny, come take a look at this." Detective Penny Bristow walked over to where her partner, Frank Collazo, was standing. The two detectives looked out the window and down at the snow. Both could see six sets of footprints leading away from the hospital. It seemed that Old Man Winter had come calling. Again.

The End

National Center for Missing & Exploited Children

While this book includes fictional crimes born from my imagination, I wanted to shine a bright light on two cases in the book that are real. Their stories, while old, have impacted me greatly and need to be told again and again until justice is brought to all those involved in the death and disappearance of two beautiful children.

In addition to featuring two non-fictional criminal cases in the story of Old Man Winter – Heavenly Gates, I will donate a portion of the book's profits to National Center for Missing & Exploited Children.

As a father of four children, my heart breaks for the children featured in my story and all of the children who die violently at their killers' hands or go missing each year in the United States and the world. May none of them ever be forgotten.

America's Unknown Child – The Boy in the Box

Please allow me to introduce you to the Boy in the Box, who died in late February 1957 and is currently resting in Ivy Hill Cemetery in the Cedarbrook neighborhood of North Philadelphia. He was found in a box just off of Susquehanna Rd, Fox Chase, Philadelphia, PA, on February 25, 1957.

While my story includes a fictional ending to the criminal investigation, the case was never solved, and The Boy in the Box is only known as 'America's Unknown Child.' I hope one day his headstone can bear his actual name.

Here's a little bit of his story: Content courtesy of a Wikipedia page dedicated to the case and the child. Page link included below article.

In February 1957, the boy's body, wrapped in a plaid blanket, was found in the woods off Susquehanna Road in Fox Chase, Philadelphia. The naked body was inside a cardboard box which had once contained a bassinet of the kind sold by J. C. Penney. The boy's hair had been recently cropped, possibly after death, as clumps of hair clung to the body. There were signs of severe malnourishment, as well as surgical scars on the ankle and groin and an L-shaped scar under the chin.

The body was first discovered by John Stachowiak, a young man who was checking his muskrat traps. Fearing that the police would confiscate his traps, he did not report what he had found. A few days later, college student, Frank Guthrum spotted a rabbit running into the underbrush. Knowing that there were animal traps in the area, he stopped his car to investigate and discovered the body. Guthrum, like Stachowiak, was reluctant to have any contact with the police, but he did report what he had found the following day, after hearing of the disappearance of Mary Jane Barker.

The police received the report and opened an investigation on February 26, 1957. The dead boy's fingerprints were taken, and police at first were optimistic that he would soon be identified. However, no one ever came forward with any useful information.

The case attracted massive media attention in Philadelphia and the Delaware Valley. *The Philadelphia Inquirer* printed 400,000 flyers depicting the boy's likeness, which were sent out and posted across the area, and were included with every gas bill in Philadelphia. The crime scene was combed over and over again by 270 police academy recruits, who discovered a man's blue corduroy cap, a child's scarf, and a man's white handkerchief with the letter 'G' in the corner. All clues that led nowhere. The police also distributed a post-mortem photograph of the boy fully dressed and in a seated position, as he may have looked in life, in the hope, it might lead to a clue. Despite the publicity and sporadic interest throughout the years, the boy's identity is still unknown. The case remains unsolved to this day.

On March 21, 2016, the National Center for Missing & Exploited Children released a forensic facial reconstruction of the victim and added him into their database.

In August 2018, Barbara Rae-Venter, the genetic genealogist who helped to identify the Golden State Killer using a DNA profiling technique, said that she was using the same method to try to identify the Boy in the Box. Amateur groups that use online databases, such as the Doe Network and Websleuths, have also tried to solve his identity.

Please take the time to learn more about America's Unknown Child by reading the full article.

https://en.wikipedia.org/wiki/Boy_in_the_Box_(Philadelphia)

If you know anything about the case, please contact the Philadelphia Police Department.

Margaret Ellen Fox

Please allow me to introduce you to Margaret Ellen Fox, born February 4, 1960, Missing June 24, 1974 – Burlington, NJ. Last seen near Mill & Hight Streets in Mt. Holly, NJ.

While her story contains a fictional ending in my book, Margaret Ellen Fox is still missing and her abductor(s) still at large or deceased. I hope that this book can shed some light on her disappearance and also prevent the heart-breaking disappearances of children everywhere.

Here is some of her story, courtesy of The Charley Project. Weblink provided below story.

Margaret was last seen in Burlington, New Jersey, on June 24, 1974. She was planning to go to High and west Broad Streets in Mount Holly, New Jersey, to have an interview with a man who called himself John Marshall.

Margaret's younger brother, Joe, accompanied her to the bus stop and saw her get on. Witnesses reported seeing her near Mill and High Streets after she got off the bus in Mount Holly, but she has never been heard from again.

Margaret had advertised for a babysitting job, and 'Marshall' responded to the ad on June 19. He told her he needed a babysitter for the following weekend, but he postponed meeting her several times. Finally, he said he would meet her in a red Volkswagen. He gave Margaret a telephone number to reach him. The number was traced to a public phone booth at a supermarket in Lumberton, New Jersey.

In the hours after Margaret was reported missing, police started recording all phone calls placed to her residence. One was from a man who demanded $10,000 for Margaret's safe return. He stated, "$10,000 might be a lot of bread, but your daughter's life is the buttered topping." This caller has never been identified. You can listen to the call by visiting the FBI's website.

https://www.fbi.gov/contact-us/field-offices/newark/news/press-releases/reward-and-new-information-offered-on-the-anniversary-of-a-burlington-county-cold-case

Margaret has never been heard from again, and 'John Marshall' has never been identified. Several other parents in the area complained that someone had attempted to lure their daughters with fake job offers. A suspect's 1976 confession to involvement in her disappearance was widely publicized but turned out to be a hoax.

Margaret took piano lessons in 1974, and she liked to ride horses. She graduated from St. Paul's Grammar School in Burlington two weeks before she vanished. Her parents are now deceased, but her siblings are still alive, and some still live in the Burlington area. Her case remains unsolved.

If you have any information regarding Margaret's whereabouts, please contact the FBI immediately.

Please take the time to read more about Margaret's story by visiting The Charley Project at https://charleyproject.org/case/margaret-ellen-fox

Detective Penelope Brace – Real-life Philadelphia Police Detective

Penelope Brace, Born - March 1942 – Died 2019

In this work of fiction, Detective Penelope Bryce died in 1974. However, the real-life inspiration behind the character, Detective Penelope Brace, lived a long, fulfilling life and left behind a legacy that will endure for generations. Her story of standing up for herself and all women led to a permanent change in discriminatory hiring and promotion practices, not only in the City of Philadelphia but around the country. I am honored to shine a light on Penelope Brace's legend and legacy. I am equally proud to bring her story and legal case back into today's conversation about gender equality in the workplace.

Efforts to contact Mrs. Brace's extended family were unsuccessful, but I would like to thank them for carrying on her inspirational story and name. I hope to learn more one day about Penelope Brace through the memory of her family. Finally, thank you, Penny, for being my muse and inspiring me to write a story with such a strong female lead as my main character. You will never be forgotten!

Penelope Brace
Her challenge started it all

6-year fight
City and U.S. settle suits on sex bias against police

By Jane Eisner
Inquirer Staff Writer

The City of Philadelphia and the federal government announced an agreement yesterday in the six-year court battle over allegations that the Police Department discriminated against women in its hiring and promotion practices.

The agreement calls for the city to award a total of $700,000 in back pay to victims of sexual discrimination and commits the department to a 30 percent hiring goal for female police officers.

If approved by U.S. District Judge Charles R. Weiner, the proposed consent order could settle a series of discrimination suits brought against the department by the federal gov-

ernment and female police officers. The Fraternal Order of Police and several female officers, also named in a consolidated suit, have not yet signed the agreement.

The legal actions had their beginning in 1974 when Penelope Brace, a police officer, challenged the department's hiring and promotion practices.

The main provisions of the consent order call for the city to award $550,000 in back pay to 96 women who were victims of discrimination and to an unknown number of "rejected applicants," said John M. Gadzichowski, a senior trial attorney in the U.S. Department of Justice.

Some of the women will receive as

(See POLICE on 2-A)

The inspiration behind FalconClaw

Ravenscrag – Located in Montreal, Canada

Learn more:

https://en.wikipedia.org/wiki/Ravenscrag,_Montreal

Follow Me On Twitter

@BlackEarthHWGH

@AuthorMichaelC

@MichaelwCook

and on Goodreads

and on Medium

@AuthorMichaelCook

Old Man Winter is also available on:

www.OldManWinterNovel.com

Other titles by this author:

Black Earth – How We Got Here

What truths lie in the black void between the stars?

Back to Black Earth

What truths will be revealed?

www.BlackEarthNovel.com

Made in the USA
Monee, IL
27 October 2021